THE WORLD BIBLIOGRAPHICAL SERIES

This series, which is principally designed for the English speaker, will eventually cover every country in the world, each in a separate volume comprising annotated entries on works dealing with its history, geography, economy and politics; and with its people, their culture, customs, religion and social organization. Attention will also be paid to current living conditions – housing, education, newspapers, clothing, etc.– that are all too often ignored in standard bibliographies; and to those particular aspects relevant to individual countries. Each volume seeks to achieve, by use of careful selectivity and critical assessment of the literature, an expression of the country and an appreciation of its nature and national aspirations, to guide the reader towards an understanding of its importance. The keynote of the series is to provide, in a uniform format, an interpretation of each country that will express its culture, its place in the world, and the qualities and background that make it unique. The views expressed in individual volumes, however, are not necessarily those of the publisher.

VOLUMES IN THE SERIES

Wales

WORLD BIBLIOGRAPHICAL SERIES

General Editors:
Robert G. Neville (Executive Editor)
John J. Horton

Robert A. Myers   Ian Wallace
Hans H. Wellisch   Ralph Lee Woodward, Jr.

John J. Horton is Deputy Librarian of the University of Bradford and currently Chairman of its Academic Board of Studies in Social Sciences. He has maintained a longstanding interest in the discipline of area studies and its associated bibliographical problems, with special reference to European Studies. In particular he has published in the field of Icelandic and of Yugoslav studies, including the two relevant volumes in the World Bibliographical Series.

Robert A. Myers is Associate Professor of Anthropology in the Division of Social Sciences and Director of Study Abroad Programs at Alfred University, Alfred, New York. He has studied post-colonial island nations of the Caribbean and has spent two years in Nigeria on a Fulbright Lectureship. His interests include international public health, historical anthropology and developing societies. In addition to *Amerindians of the Lesser Antilles: a bibliography* (1981), *A Resource Guide to Dominica, 1493–1986* (1987) and numerous articles, he has compiled the World Bibliographical Series volumes on *Dominica* (1987) and *Nigeria* (1989).

Ian Wallace is Professor of Modern Languages at Loughborough University of Technology. A graduate of Oxford in French and German, he also studied in Tübingen, Heidelberg and Lausanne before taking teaching posts at universities in the USA, Scotland and England. He specializes in East German affairs, especially literature and culture, on which he has published numerous articles and books. In 1979 he founded the journal *GDR Monitor*, which he continues to edit.

Hans H. Wellisch is Professor emeritus at the College of Library and Information Services, University of Maryland. He was President of the American Society of Indexers and was a member of the International Federation for Documentation. He is the author of numerous articles and several books on indexing and abstracting, and has published *The Conversion of Scripts* and *Indexing and Abstracting: an International Bibliography*. He also contributes frequently to *Journal of the American Society for Information Science, The Indexer* and other professional journals.

Ralph Lee Woodward, Jr. is Chairman of the Department of History at Tulane University, New Orleans, where he has been Professor of History since 1970. He is the author of *Central America, a Nation Divided*, 2nd ed. (1985), as well as several monographs and more than sixty scholarly articles on modern Latin America. He has also compiled volumes in the World Bibliographical Series on *Belize* (1980), *Nicaragua* (1983), and *El Salvador* (1988). Dr. Woodward edited the Central American section of the *Research Guide to Central America and the Caribbean* (1985) and is currently editor of the Central American history section of the *Handbook of Latin American Studies*.

VOLUME 122

Wales

Gwilym Huws
D. Hywel E. Roberts
Compilers

CLIO PRESS

OXFORD, ENGLAND · SANTA BARBARA, CALIFORNIA
DENVER, COLORADO

British Library Cataloguing in Publication Data

Huws, G. (Gwilym) *1944–*
Wales. – (World bibliographical series, v. 122).
1. Wales – Bibliographies
I. Title   II. Roberts, D. Hywel E. (David Hywel Emlyn)
1946– III. Series

ISBN 1–85109–118–1

Clio Press Ltd.,
55 St. Thomas' Street,
Oxford OX1 1JG, England.

ABC-CLIO,
130 Cremona Drive,
Santa Barbara,
CA 93117, USA.

Designed by Bernard Crossland.
Typeset by Columns Design and Production Services, Reading, England.
Printed and bound in Great Britain by
Billing and Sons Ltd., Worcester.

Contents

Contents

Contents

Introduction

This selective, annotated bibliography is aimed at an audience ranging from the informed reader to the scholar who wishes to obtain background information on a particular subject, or subjects, in a field other than his or her own. The readership might also include people anticipating a long stay in Wales, or requiring a greater acquaintance with the country as a result of business, academic, research or professional interests. In addition we anticipate that this volume will be of value to librarians and information providers who wish to expand their collections of material so that they more adequately represent Wales, or so that they may have access to a readily available reference source in order that they may answer questions about Wales and the Welsh.

Wales, as one of the countries of the United Kingdom, is, like Scotland, a nation, but not a nation state. A glance at this bibliography will show that Wales has many of the trappings of nationhood, such as national institutions, and organisations, a degree of devolved government, as well as some unique national problems, characteristics and strengths. Closer scrutiny of the materials listed here should also indicate, we hope, that Wales has a distinct history, and culture, a literary tradition of some magnitude, and its own unique language. Moreover, it is to be hoped that this selection of materials covering a wide range of disciplines, will go some way to explaining what is meant by being Welsh, as opposed to being British.

Wales is the westerly facing peninsula of mainland Britain, with the English and the Irish being near-neighbours. The country occupies an area of some 8,000 square miles, and has a coastline of some 750 miles. It is probably true to say that Wales has a more contrasting physical and human landscape in proportion to its size than any other country in the world. The population of Wales is approximately 2.76 million people. However, how many of those claim, or wish to claim, that they are Welsh is a matter of debate, such is the heterogeneity of the population and such is the rapidity of demographic and social changes taking place at the present time. A very large proportion of the population (perhaps as many as seven out of every ten) live in, or close to, the South Wales industrial conurbation and the capital city, Cardiff. The remainder of the population lives in the relative rural isolation, or splendour, depending on your point of view, of the remainder of Wales, where agriculture is the dominant influence on life.

Traditionally, Wales has two contrasting characteristics – loyalty and a certain conservatism in terms of religion, customs, language, literature and social habits, where long traditions can be invoked. Nonetheless, politically, and in many other spheres of life, the Welsh can claim to be radical. What is certainly true is that Wales is currently undergoing the most important and large-scale sequence of changes in its history. Industrially, the old traditional employers such as coal, steel, heavy engineering, quarrying and mining, are being replaced by light industry, tourism and service industries. Socially the country is having to cope with the side-effects of tremendous economic and industrial change. Culturally, the nation is having to seek answers to the problems of emigration and in-migration, rural depopulation and Anglicisation. After all, the Welsh are living next door to a predominant culture and language of some magnitude which inevitably infiltrates Welsh daily life and culture via the radio, television, newspapers, books and inter-marriage. In addition, mention should also be made of perceived inequalities in wealth and economic power, and a feeling of political impotence felt by many because Wales is overwhelmingly radical socialist, and yet is governed from London by Conservatives.

Notwithstanding this, in the words of a Welsh folk-song, "rym ni yma o hyd' – despite everything and everybody, the Welsh are still here, and are likely to be around for a very long time such is their enterprising, optimistic, and yes persistent nature.

In our effort to convey an accurate picture of Wales, we encountered certain difficulties, not least of which were those arising out of the country's living Welsh language and its written and spoken culture. This bibliography includes bilingual material in parallel texts, but it was deemed inappropriate to list materials published in the Welsh language in a bibliography aimed at an international audience. We were therefore constantly having to remove scholarly, standard, or ideally representative texts from certain subject areas with the result that certain imbalances may have arisen. Indeed, we anticipate that many of our fellow countrymen (and women) may be critical of parts of our work on that count. We are aware of weaknesses in areas such as religion, for example, where sects, denominations and major studies of them are excluded because their medium is predominantly Welsh. Only in our listing of primary bibliographies in literature and language, and dictionaries have we listed materials in Welsh.

The second problem we encountered, was selecting from the growing number of publications relating to specific localities, regions and areas within Wales. Modern Welsh historians refer to this particular phenomenon as 'localism', a trend which is very discernible in the publishing field, with local history, reminiscences, and local industry studies growing apace. The most notable product of this trend is the growth in the number of highly successful amateur publishing ventures in the form of monthly local community Welsh-language newspapers. We have sought to include those publications which are essentially local in nature only if they were of a more general value or significance, or indeed when more general works dealing with the whole of Wales were not available, or were of an inconsequential nature.

The third problem we encountered was the unevenness of the advancement of Welsh studies in all subject areas. Thanks to the work of some of our major institutions, our museums, our libraries, our national university and its press, we were able, in some areas, to make a selection from a wide range of materials. However, we also found ourselves having to select from a very limited number of studies in other fields, such as finance and banking, because Wales is normally considered to form an inseparable part of the British financial and banking system. We would have encountered even greater problems had not the movement in pursuit of full nationhood and self-government resulted in the establishment of a Welsh Office in Cardiff, and other numerous national bodies to perform specific and increasingly numerous functions in relation to Wales, and Wales alone. In the areas of the economy, tourism, industry, statistics, administration, social conditions, transport and many others areas we were able to choose from, and cite, studies and publications generated by these organisations and bodies. Nevertheless, we had to consider carefully whether such publications met the other criteria we established for our selection of material – objectivity and accessibility. We can only hope that our selection has been successful. As sections of this work will show, the movement for greater political autonomy has been gathering momentum for several decades. Significant periodic advances in that process, and the discussion and the greater awareness of Wales that such advances have generated, have invariably been reflected in an increased output of published works about the country. Without these peaks in output our bibliography would have been very limited indeed. Consequently, we have been able to restrict our selection of materials to those works and studies published in more recent times (works published before the middle sixties are few in number) and predominantly to works published as monographs. We have, from time to time, deemed it necessary to cite selected journal articles to augment and supplement our choice of monographs. Similarly, periodical articles have also been included in those instances where the available monograph materials were inappropriate, or inadequate. We have not hesitated to cite what we, and others, regard as outstanding and standard studies even though they fall outside our normal date and format criteria.

We have adhered to the bibliographical conventions offered to us by the publisher only making minor modifications, when necessary, to accommodate the use of the Welsh language in titles.

Our annotations are also broadly in keeping with the style recommended for the series. The vast majority provide a purely objective summary, or description of the contents, but on occasion we draw the reader's attention to a particular characteristic, or aspect, of the work, especially if care is required when the item is consulted or used, or when we feel that an evaluative comment is appropriate.

We have arranged the materials into a classification scheme which reflects both the availability of suitable materials and the particular aspects of Wales that we wish to project to define its character or reflect its nature. However, our contents schema is not substantially different to that adopted by other volumes in the series. Works within individual chapters or sub-chapters are arranged alphabetically by the titles of the works.

It was never our intention to mislead the users of this bibliography by omitting works reflecting the problems, the inadequacies, the social issues and tensions, and the controversies and conflicts within Wales. We hope that our selection of materials in those areas is fair and representative.

We also hasten to add that the material listed here is our personal selection. There will be experts in certain fields and disciplines who will wish to question our choice and offer alternatives, and we realize that in some subject areas such views will be significant and probably valid. However, we offer this selection in the knowledge that we have at least considered the merits and characteristics of each in the context of our task and commission, after having viewed and consulted each document.

There are many people who have contributed substantially to the task of bringing this work to fruition. Our own colleagues in the Department of Information and Library Studies have offered advice and brought items to our notice, the Information and Library Studies Library and its staff have given us considerable assistance, – the

Welsh collection of that library being the nucleus of our work; the Librarian of the National Library of Wales and The Keeper of Printed Books gave us every facility and assistance, indeed all the staff of the Library were most helpful. Our colleagues in the University's central Hugh Owen Library, at the Welsh Office Library in Cardiff, and others whom we contacted for various items of information, all contributed in no small measure. As usual, Ann Hill executed the work of transferring scruffy hand-written text to the required format in her own inimitable and expert way. Without her, we would still be floundering or whatever bibliographers do when they panic at the sight of deadlines. In an indirect way the many students who have studied systematic bibliography in our respective classes have also contributed – we have learned from their experiences and from their labours. It has been a salutory experience – setting ourselves the kind of exercise we normally set others! We hope that we shall be better teachers in future as a result.

Our families had to put up with our prolonged periods of absence whilst we undertook this work, but without their support and patience, it would not have been possible at all, and for that reason and many others we dedicate this work to them.

Gwilym Huws
D. Hywel E. Roberts
Department of Information and Library Studies,
The University College of Wales,
Aberystwyth,
Wales.

August 1990

The Country and its People

1 **Anatomy of Wales.**
Edited by R. Brinley Jones.   Peterston-super-Ely, Wales: Gwerin, 1972.
253p. bibliog.
A collection of twelve essays on various facets of Welsh life written by subject specialists for the general reader. The essays deal with the following topics: geography; history; society; economy; industry; religion; politics; education; language and literature; and music and art.

2 **Background to Wales: a course of studies in modern Welsh life.**
Prys Morgan.   Llandybie, Wales: Christopher Davies, 1968. 91p. bibliog.
The articles which formed the basis of this work were originally written for sixth-form students pursuing an Advanced Level course in Welsh studies. However, this book is also suitable for a wider audience, including the general reader who wishes to understand more about the basic characteristics of Welsh society and its Welshness. The topics covered include art, sport, music, surnames and the relationship between the Welsh and the Celts. A useful contribution in that it discusses topics which are not normally included in most general works on Wales and the Welsh.

3 **A book of Wales: an anthology.**
Selected by Meic Stephens.   London: Dent, 1987. 322p.
This anthology of prose and poetry by Welsh and Anglo-Welsh writers from the sixth century to the present day provides a literary guide to a better understanding of Wales and the Welsh. The items have been carefully selected in order to represent a range of themes such as birth, childhood, marriage, friendship, community, solitude, love of country, war, peace and death. Although the compiler includes material from the entire history of literature in Wales, there is a deliberate bias towards twentieth-century material.

The Country and its People

4 Introducing Wales.
R. Brinley Jones. [London:] The British Council. 1978. 44p. illus. maps.
This book is designed to provide the visitor with a brief introduction to Wales and the Welsh but it is also an informative guide for anyone interested in the country and its people. The aspects which are covered include geography, economics, history, government, religion, education, language, literature, music and the visual arts. The author avoids the stereotype image of the Welsh people.

5 The land of the red dragon.
Compiled by Heather Kay. Cardiff: University of Wales Press, for the Girl Guides Association of Wales. 1979. 4th ed. 106p. illus.
This book was originally published in 1950 so that Welsh Girl Guides could learn something about the background of their own land. This enlarged and revised edition will provide the general reader with a brief introduction to Wales. The first section is a series of short essays by subject specialists on various facets of Wales, its people and culture. This is followed by a section which provides an account of David, the patron saint of Wales, as well as an explanation of the banner and emblems of Wales and the words of the National Anthem. The volume also includes a selection of Welsh legends and folk songs.

6 The land remembers: a view of Wales.
Gwyn Williams. London: Faber, 1977. 252p. bibliog.
A personal view of the condition of Wales based on the author's viewpoint as seen from rural west Wales. Williams hopes that the reader will receive an insight of Wales not only as a country of great scenic beauty but also one with its own distinct culture and traditions. The book deals with the crisis which confronts Welsh culture today and leaves the reader in no doubt that the author believes that language and nationhood are inseparable and that the death of one will inevitably lead to the death of the other.

7 The matter of Wales: epic view of a small country.
Jan Morris. Harmondsworth, England: Penguin, 1986. 442p. bibliog.
A perceptive personal tribute to Wales and the Welsh people inspired by the visionary hero, Owain Glyndwr, who led an unsuccessful insurrection during the fifteenth century to restore political independence for the Welsh. The author's love of the landscape and admiration of the people's struggle over the centuries to preserve their separate identity are the main themes of this well-written essay. Amongst the topics which are examined are landscape and natural history, religion, the character of the Welsh people, history, art, literature and music.

8 My Wales.
George Thomas, with photographs by Lord Snowdon. London: Century Hutchison, 1986. 160p. illus.
A personal portrait of Wales and the Welsh written by the former Speaker of the House of Commons and former Secretary of State for Wales. His views of Wales are based to a large extent on his upbringing in the Rhondda Valley during the early part of this century and the book includes references to the hardships and tragedies which the Welsh have suffered during this century. The essential features of Welsh life today have been captured in the splendid photographs produced by Lord Snowdon for this volume. In much the same way, the early photographs of the Rhondda Valley

reproduced here help to recapture life in the mining valleys of South Wales during the early part of this century.

9 The new Wales.

Edited by David Cole. Cardiff: University of Wales Press, 1990. 245p. illus.

A collection of essays which form a guide to an understanding of the Welsh and which aims to erase the popular stereotype view of the country and the people. Although most of the essays have been written by subject experts the book is designed for the general reader, particularly visitors to Wales and businesses which trade in Wales, or which are contemplating establishing themselves in the country. The book covers the following aspects of Welsh life: industry; agriculture; tourism; topography; land reclamation; architecture; art; drama; music; pop music; literature; sport; the media; education; religion and social conditions.

10 Wales.

Trevor Fishlock. London: Faber, 1979. 89p. illus. bibliog. (Discovering Britain Series).

A short booklet on Wales and the Welsh people. Although written originally for young people, it provides a balanced introduction for the general reader to the landscape, history, language and culture of Wales.

11 Wales: a new study.

Edited by David Thomas. Newton Abbott, England: David & Charles, 1977. 338p. illus. maps. bibliog.

A collection of essays on various aspects of the landscape and people of Wales produced at a time when the country was experiencing far-reaching industrial, demographic and linguistic changes. The essays have been written for the informed general reader and for students and as such they provide a useful introduction to a number of topics such as geography, history, agriculture, industry, communications, tourism and Welsh society. Care needs to be taken when consulting some of the statistics as they are now dated.

12 Wales and the Welsh.

Trevor Fishlock. London: Cassell, 1972. 196p. bibliog.

Trevor Fishlock was the Welsh Affairs correspondent of *The Times* during the late sixties and early seventies with a brief to provide informed comment on events in Wales and on the Welsh way of life. This volume attempts to describe and analyse the sixties which proved to be one of the most eventful decades in the history of Wales. The work was written chiefly for those who wish to know more about the Welsh people and the forces at work in Wales at the time. In addition to presenting a balanced view at a highly explosive period in the struggle for political and cultural identity, the writer also includes an insight into some of the lighter aspects of Welsh life.

The Country and its People

13 **Wales: the imagined nation. Studies in cultural and national identity.**
Edited by Tony Curtis. Bridgend, Wales: Poetry Wales Press, 1986.
306p. bibliog.

A valuable collection of essays which explore the problems which individuals living in Wales have in order to define their Welshness. Welsh national identity, which is the central theme of the volume, is explored in relation to various cultural activities such as literature, films, theatre and television, and the visual arts.

14 **Wales: the shaping of a nation.**
Prys Morgan, David Thomas. Newton Abbott, England: David & Charles, 1984. 272p. bibliog.

A general guide to Wales and the Welsh, written for the intelligent layman. The authors have selected ten themes which they believe are the most important to understand contemporary Wales. These themes are the landscape, history and language, public administration, the relationship between Wales and England, industrialisation, rural Wales, the radical tradition, the growth of national institutions, names, literature and music.

15 **Wales! Wales!**
Dai Smith. London: Allen & Unwin, 1984. 173p. illus.

This work was originally published as a companion to a series of six television programmes on the same theme. The six essays provide extended treatment of the same central issue, namely defining Welshness. The author claims that many professional Welsh historians are re-inventing the past to serve the political needs of the present. His perspective of Welsh history and of 'Welshness' is based on his upbringing in the industrialised and predominantly Anglicised valleys of South Wales. In this personal interpretation, Smith claims that the experience of population and industrial growth during the second half of the nineteenth century altered the essence of Wales. He also dismisses the claim of Wales as an exploited colony of the English and attempts to analyse the divide between Welsh-speaking and Anglicised Wales.

16 **A Welsh eye.**
Gwyn Thomas, with drawings by John Dd. Evans. London: Hutchinson, 1984. 176p. illus.

The first edition of this book was published in 1964. It provides a highly personal view of Wales and the Welsh people and their history and is written by a prolific Anglo-Welsh writer who captured the essence of life in the mining communities of the south Wales valleys during the first half of this century in his novels and short stories. The mixture of joy and sadness portrayed in a colourful style which characterised his fictional work is also to be found in this autobiographical guide. Although it is a highly idiosyncratic view of Wales, it is nevertheless highly entertaining and sheds some light on many characteristics of the land and its people.

17 **Wynford Vaughan-Thomas's Wales.**
Wynford Vaughan-Thomas, with photographs by Derry Brabbs.
London: Michael Joseph, 1989. 223p. illus. maps.

A portrait of Wales and the Welsh presented in the form of an autobiographical guide by this distinguished broadcaster and writer from Swansea who explored his native land in a variety of different ways. In addition to his perceptive analysis of Wales and the Welsh, this attractive volume also includes a selection of stories and anecdotes which capture the character of the people. The large collection of magnificent colour photographs found in the book portray the essence of the Welsh landscape. This work provides the general reader with an excellent introduction to the country and people of Wales.

Geography and Geology

Geology and geomorphology

18 **Bibliography and index of geology and allied sciences for Wales and the Welsh Borders 1897-1958.**
   D. A. Bassett.   Cardiff: National Museum of Wales, 1961. 376p.
This is the first in a series of works bringing together the scattered and diffuse literature relating to geology, geomorphology, soil science and related sciences. The volume lists materials published during the period 1897-1958. 'It covers the literature appertaining to Wales, including Monmouthshire, and the greater part of Cheshire, Shropshire and Herefordshire' and is arranged chronologically. The second volume in the series is item 19.

19 **Bibliography and index of geology and allied sciences for Wales and the Welsh Borders 1536-1896.**
   D. A. Bassett.   Cardiff: National Museum of Wales, 1963. 246p.
The second in a series of works bringing together the scattered and diffuse literature relating to geology, geomorphology, soil science and related sciences. This volume lists materials published during the period 1536 to 1896 – 'to help both amateur and professional geologists to trace the sources of geological facts on Wales and the Borders. Arranged chronologically'. The companion volume in the series is item 18.

20 **Classical areas of British geology: Capel Curig and Betws-y-coed.**
   M. F. Howells, E. H. Francis, B. E. Leveridge, C. D. R. Evans.
   London: HMSO, 1978. 73p. maps. bibliog.
A study and commentary of the 1:25000 Ordnance Survey sheet SH75 (Geological maps of England and Wales series) published on behalf of the Institute of Geological Sciences. The sheet includes Snowdonia, the most spectacular area of geological interest in Wales. The bibliography is particularly useful, and the work is illustrated.

21 Classical areas of British geology: geological excursions in the Harlech Dome.

P. M. Allen, Audrey A. Jackson.   London: HMSO, 1985. maps. bibliog.

Published on behalf of the British Geological Survey, this is intended as a guidebook and contains geological notes and large scale maps of selected excursions. It is aimed both at students of the subject and the interested layperson, as is clear from the major subdivisions of the work – 'geological excursions' and 'geological notes on popular walks'. The area delineated is in north west Wales, and the work includes illustrations.

22 Geological excursions in Dyfed, south-west Wales.

Edited by M. G. Bassett.   Cardiff: National Museum of Wales for the South Wales Group of the Geologists' Association, 1981. 327p. maps.

This work forms part of a valuable series suitable both for those with specialist interests and the interested layperson. Dyfed has varied features, including a coastline of outstanding natural beauty. The work consists of detailed descriptions of nineteen itineraries of interest and provides guidance and analysis, aiming to provide a 'fairly comprehensive stratigraphical and geographical coverage'. A companion volume is listed in item 23, and both are illustrated.

23 Geological excursions in South Wales and the Forest of Dean.

Edited by Douglas A. Bassett, Michael G. Bassett.   Cardiff: Geologists' Association, 1971. 267p.

Part of a valuable series, issued in response to an 'increasing demand for readily available literature for visitors interested in the subject and particularly those pursuing formal courses'. The work contains two excursions in the Forest of Dean, twelve in central south Wales, including the industrial valleys area, and seven in Dyfed, which are updated and expanded in the companion volume listed in item 22, both are illustrated.

24 Geology explained in North Wales.

John Challinor, Denis E. B. Bates.   Newton Abbot, England: David & Charles, 1973. 214p. maps. bibliog.

A work which has two objectives: to provide an introduction to the geology of the area, taking numerous examples; and to provide at the same time a guide to an understanding of the nature and evolution of the geology of the area. Ten regions are analysed and three additional sections are included which seek to provide: a summary description of the geology of North Wales; a summary of the principles of geology, and a brief study of geology; and man's influence on it in North Wales. The book is well illustrated.

25 Geology explained in South Wales.

T. R. Owen.   Newton Abbot, England: David & Charles, 1973. 211p. maps.

A broad description and analysis, divided into ten studies from Pembrokeshire in the west to industrial Glamorgan in the east, including the inland industrial valleys. This is a companion volume to that for North Wales listed in item 24. The book is well illustrated.

26 **The glaciation of Wales and adjoining regions.**
Edited by Colin A. Lewis.   London: Longman, 1970. 378p. illus. maps.
A series of essays, which provide an overview of the Pleistocene period in Wales as
well as area studies of north-west Wales, north-east Wales, the Cardigan Bay area (the
west coast), the Upper Wye and Usk valleys region, south-east and central-south
Wales and Pembrokeshire.

27 **The land of Wales.**
David Q. Bowen.   In: *Wales: a new study*. Edited by David Thomas.
Newton Abbot, England: David & Charles, 1977, p. 11-35.
An introductory survey of the nature of the geology and geomorphology of Wales,
with particular studies of coastal morphology and offshore geology, subjects largely
ignored in general works relating to Wales. The text is fully exemplified and illustrated
by maps and diagrams.

28 **A landscape classification of Wales.**
Welsh Office.   Cardiff: Welsh Office Planning Services, 1980. 106p.
maps. bibliog.
A consultative document, the objective of which is to attempt to provide a broad
classification of the physical anatomy of the landscape of Wales – it represents one of
the earliest attempts at creating such a classification in Britain. It is fully illustrated and
provides a very useful guide to the types of landscape and scenery encountered in
Wales and a good analysis of its evolution.

29 **North Wales: British regional geology.**
Bernard Smith, T. Neville George.   London: HMSO, 1961. 3rd. ed.
97p. maps. bibliog.
A work which outlines the salient geological features of North Wales, incorporating
contemporary advances in survey and research activity. It is arranged in a
chronological sequence by period and also offers an interesting historical study of
geological research of North Wales; the bibliography is extensive and particularly
useful. Companion volumes in the series are listed in item 31.

30 **The relief and drainage of Wales.**
E. H. Brown.   Cardiff: University of Wales Press, 1960. 186p. maps.
bibliog.
A study in what is defined as 'denudation chronology', providing what remains the
standard definition and history of Welsh scenery and landscape and the geomorphology
of Wales.

31 **Soils and their uses in Wales.**
C. C. Rudeforth, R. Hartnup, J. W. Lea, T. R. E. Thompson, P. S.
Wright.   Harpenden, England: Soil Survey of England and Wales,
1984. 336p. maps. bibliog. (Regional Bulletin, no. 11).
This study is the product of an ambitious project which commenced in 1969 to produce
soil maps of the whole of England and Wales and to describe soil distribution and
related land quality in appropriate detail. Wales was issued with its regional maps in

8

1983 and this bulletin in 1984. The bulletin has five sections: a description of the region (geology, relief, climate, land use); background to soils; a description of soil associations; land drainage; and agriculture and forestry interpretation. The survey was undertaken 'with the aim of providing a systematic inventory capable of being used or interpreted for a wide range of purposes including agricultural advisory work and many facets of land use planning and national resource use'.

32   **South Wales: British regional geology.**
T. Neville George.   London: HMSO, 1970. 3rd. ed. 152p. maps. bibliog.

A volume published under the auspices of the Institute of Geological Sciences of the Natural Environment Research Council. This edition reflects advances in survey work, research and elucidation of the stratigraphy and structure of the geology of South Wales, particularly in the area of the coalfield. The bibliography is extensive. Companion volumes in the series relating to Wales are listed in items 29 and 32.

33   **The waterfalls of Wales.**
John Llewelyn Jones.   London: Hall, 1986. 242p. maps.

This is essentially an illustrated, popular study. Nevertheless it is one which seeks to exemplify and relate the combination of climatic and geological factors and some of the resultant landforms, paying particular attention to the mingling of different rock formations and strata, drainage patterns and the influence of glaciation.

34   **The Welsh Borderland: British regional geology.**
F. W. Pocock, T. H. Whitehead.   London: HMSO, 1958. 2nd. ed. 82p. maps. bibliog.

This edition, with a new Foreword, was reprinted in 1964 and follows the pattern of the series – companion volumes relating to Wales are listed in items 29 and 31. The study is arranged chronologically, with a useful introduction to geological research activity in Wales and an extensive bibliography.

35   **Welsh landforms and scenery.**
G. Melvyn Howe, Peter Thomas.   London: Macmillan, 1963. 155p. bibliog.

A standard study, subdivided into an analysis and description of tectonic features, igneous features, gradational features (including fluvial and glacial influences) and coastal features. The work is copiously illustrated and exemplifed.

36   **The world's landscapes: Wales.**
F. V. Emery.   London: Longmans, 1969. 136p. maps. (World Landscapes Series).

This illustrated work provides an analysis in three parts; the primeval landscape (the earliest and natural landscape); the landscape before 1800 (medieval Wales and the effect of the clearing of woodlands); and the post-1800 landscape, with an analysis of man's influence and of the industrial landscape of Wales.

Climate and vegetation

37 **Climate and vegetation.**
Graham N. Sumner. In: *Wales: a new study*. Edited by David Thomas.
Newton Abbot, England: David & Charles, 1977, p. 36-69.
An introductory survey of Welsh weather, climate, water resources and hydrology, the influence of climate on the environment, and of vegetation and soil, fully exemplified by maps, diagrams and statistical tables.

38 **The climate of Great Britain: Wales; climatological memorandum 140.**
Bracknell, England: Meteorological Office, 1983. 20p. maps.
A comprehensive analysis of the climate of Wales 'in a form suitable for use in schools and by members of the general public'. The memorandum defines and describes the area, and analyses the temperature, humidity, sunshine, rainfall, snow, thunder and hail, clouds, visibility, wind and weather extremes, and compares the data with that for the rest of the United Kingdom. Much of the information is presented graphically in an easily understood and interpreted form.

General geography

39 **Cambria: a Welsh Geographical Review. Cylchgrawn Daearyddol Cymreig.**
Swansea: Department of Geography, University College, Swansea,
Wales: 1974-. annual, with occasional double issues.
A geographical periodical primarily serving Wales and Welsh geographers and intended to be a place for the publication of substantive geographical research in, and upon, Wales, and an outlet for research, comment and discussion of relevance to geographical teaching and research within Wales. In addition, it seeks to provide for a broader audience outside Wales and presents a view of current geographical research and thinking within and about Wales. The language of publication is predominantly English, issues are for the most part thematic, with reviews, notices, and other short items of information appended.

40 **Geography, culture and habitat: selected essays (1925-1975) of E. G. Bowen.**
Edited by Harold Carter, Wayne K. D. Davies. Llandysul, Wales:
Gomer Press, 1976. 275p. bibliog.
An anthology of essays and papers on aspects of the geography of Wales by the doyen of Welsh geographers. They include studies of heritage and development, settlement patterns, social and cultural geography, historical geography and regional studies, together with a tribute to the author and a complete bibliography of his works.

41 A modern geography of Wales.
Mary Price.   Llandybie, Wales: C. Davies, 1974. 202p. maps.

Although primarily intended as a school textbook for secondary school pupils, this illustrated work is an important study as it reflects recent changes in Wales and refers to contemporary issues and controversies in a convenient and readable way. Sections are devoted to the physical, climatological, soil and agricultural geography of Wales, as well as to forestry, mining and quarrying, energy, communications, tourism, water supply, population studies, ports, environmental issues and to industrial and social geography.

42 Towns and villages.
Wayne K. D. Davies.   In: *Wales: a new study.* Edited by David Thomas. Newton Abbot, England: David & Charles, 1977, p. 190-225.

A study which traces, and seeks to explain, the predominant place of urban settlement patterns in the distribution of population in Wales. It provides an analysis of the socio-economic character of Welsh settlements and a contrasting study of rural settlement. The study also alludes to contemporary issues, such as inner-city problems and planning.

43 The towns of Wales.
Harold Carter.   Cardiff: University of Wales Press, 1965. 362p. maps.

A major study in urban geography, divided into three sections: the phases of town growth; the functions of Welsh towns; and the morphology of Welsh towns. These developments are fully exemplified by illustrations.

44 Urban essays: studies in the geography of Wales.
H. Carter, W. K. D. Davies.   London: Longman, 1970. 289p. bibliog. (Geographies for Advanced Study series).

This illustrated work provides an insight into the analytical techniques employed in urban studies and the study of urban morphology, using Welsh examples throughout, including towns and villages in north, mid- and south Wales. The authors analyse housing patterns, suburbanization and urban problems.

45 Wales: a geographical profile.
F. V. Emery.   In: *Anatomy of Wales.* Edited by R. Brinley Jones. Peterston-super-Ely, Wales: Gwerin Publications, 1972, p. 1-16. maps.

A study which delineates the major geographical environments a visitor to Wales might encounter, and also provides an analysis of the major influences on the geography of Wales from the early nineteenth century to the present. The text is illustrated by a number of thematic maps.

46 Wales: a physical, historical and regional geography.
Edited by E. G. Bowen.   Cardiff: University of Wales Press, 1967. 171p. maps.

This is the standard study of the geography of Wales, and contains contributions by various specialists in the areas of weather, climate, soil, vegetation, historical geography, industrial development, population studies and culture, followed by ten regional studies.

47 **Wales: a study from the air.**
Michael Williams. London: Heinemann, 1974. 148p.

Presents the contemporary environment of Wales as viewed from the air, together with an accompanying commentary to explain and interpret the photography. As well as depicting the physical characteristics of Wales, the photographs are also selected to reflect the primary economic uses of the land – farming, forestry, water supply, quarrying and mining. The urban locations represent ports and industrial centres. Transport and communications are also represented.

Atlases and maps

48 **Antique maps of Wales.**
John Booth. Montacute (Somerset), England: Montacute Bookshop, 1977. 132p. bibliog.

A study based on the maps of Wales in the author's own collection, which is extensive and representational. The work reflects the mapping of Wales undertaken during the period 1573 (the date of the first known map of Wales) to 1865, concentrating on the work of the main cartographers of the period. It also includes a useful summary of map collecting techniques, a glossary of terms and a list of further readings and dealers.

49 **Atlas Cenedlaethol Cymru. National Atlas of Wales.**
Edited by Harold Carter. Cardiff: University of Wales Press, 1980. Loose leaves in case.

This publication consists of over 200 maps providing sections on the physical environment, political development, culture, economic history, land use and agriculture, industry, services and communications, population and settlement and urban and regional planning. Individual sheet maps consist of an opening of four pages, the centre two of which bear the maps. One principal map describes the topic with subsidiary thematic maps used to highlight different elements, or to develop the theme. A commentary in English and Welsh is given on the remaining sheets. This collection is the product of outstanding research, scholarship and cartographic representation.

50 **Estate maps of Wales, 1600-1836.**
Aberystwyth, Wales: National Library of Wales, 1982. 51p. bibliog.

An illustrated catalogue produced and issued to coincide with a major exhibition staged at the National Library of Wales. It includes a useful introductory chronological history of the mapping of Wales, together with notes on the development of surveying and mapping techniques during the period.

51 **Marine plans and charts of Wales.**
Olwen Caradoc Evans. London: Map Collector's Circle, 1969. 46p.
(Map Collectors' Series (sixth volume), no. 54).

A chronological listing, with annotations, of marine plans and charts from 1586 to 1886 which depict part or all of the coastline and seas around Wales, with a brief but useful historical introduction to navigation charts, their compilation and evolution.

52 **A source-book of geological, geomorphological and soil maps for Wales and the Welsh Borders (1800- 1966).**
Douglas A. Bassett. Cardiff: National Museum of Wales, 1967. 239p.

A study designed to assist in the work of locating geological, geomorphological and soil data, and to complement the bibliographical compilations by the same author (see items 18 and 19). It includes a chronological summary of primary advances in cartography as they relate to Wales, a comprehensive listing of maps for Wales and the Border counties and detailed indexes.

53 **Wales in maps.**
Margaret Davies. Cardiff: University of Wales Press, 1958. 2nd. ed. 111p.

This is the first attempt at producing a thematic atlas for Wales, and is intended for use in secondary schools and by undergraduate students. It remains a useful source book in those areas where it has not been superseded by the *National Atlas of Wales*. Major themes are illustrated, usually by one map: physical geography; historical geography; agriculture and settlement; commerce and industry; and population.

54 **Welsh Office map catalogue.**
Cardiff: Welsh Office, Cartographic Services Planning Services Division. 1967-. occasional.

The Welsh Office Planning Services Division is the most significant producer of thematic maps relating to Wales, and even though many are initially produced for internal use, or to accompany reports, surveys and other Welsh Office publications, most are made available for purchase. Extremely valuable maps are issued for sale in the following areas; local government administration (county, district and community boundaries), agriculture, climate, education, the environment, health, industry, parliamentary matters (constituencies), population, ancient monuments, topographical base maps, transport and communications, utilities and miscellaneous, and other areas such as housing, collieries, mineral workings, sports, employment, community boundaries reviews and consultative schemes.

Tourism and Travel

Early travellers' accounts

55   The Cambrian traveller's guide and pocket companion.
George Nicholson.   Stourport, England: the author, 1808. 719p.
An early attempt at producing an illustrated, comprehensive, one-volume guidebook for the tourist and traveller. It lists alphabetically the main settlements, mansions, gentry homes, churches, inns, mountains and other natural features, as well as ferries, bridges and passes. There is a considerable emphasis on places of antiquarian interest and historical significance, together with notes on natural history, botany and mineralogy. Further observations are included on trade, agriculture and the 'manners and customs of the inhabitants'. Very much a product of its period, many of its theories and interpretations are fallacious, whilst its spelling of proper names and places is very idiosyncratic. It includes references to towns in England having trade, or other links, with Wales.

56   A second walk through Wales.
Richard Warner.   Bath, England: R. Guttwell, 1800. 365p.
A companion volume to *A walk through Wales 1797* (item 59), this work describes further journeys undertaken in 1798, concentrating on the larger towns and villages. As was the case in the earlier work, Warner describes the journeys in a series of letters to friends and acquaintances. The style and observations are amusing but often idiosyncratic in their spelling of Welsh place names and on account of rather unfortunate and subjective comments on lifestyles.

57   Tours in Wales.
Thomas Pennant.   London: the author, 1810. 3 vols.
An illustrated account of the journeys of perhaps one of the more famous travellers to Wales. These tours relate to what the author refers to as 'the tamer parts of our country'. The title is slightly misleading in that the work predominantly describes mid- and north Wales: volume I, north-east Wales; volume II north-west Wales, including

14

Snowdonia; volume III Anglesey and the North Wales coastal area, concluding with a description of selected mid-Wales towns, especially those on the border with England. The approach is primarily historical, with considerable emphasis on antiquities, and historical events and personalities, but there are references to natural history and topography, and the work is particularly interesting for its comments and observations on the conditon of towns in Wales and on contemporary social and economic life.

58   **Two successive tours throughout the whole of Wales. . .**
     Henry Skrine.   London: Elmsley & Bremner, 1798. 280p.

This work describes tours in North and South Wales and is interesting in that the South Walian tour includes visits to the south western coastal areas (once Pembrokeshire, now Dyfed), often not included in similar works of the period, presumably an account of its relative inaccessibility. It includes visits to southern mid-Wales, again rarely included in itineraries of the period. The spellings employed are idiosyncratic, and the style is essentially factual, indeed many journeys are described by means of nothing more than passing references to towns, features and things observed, but some of the comments are nevertheless interesting summations of contemporary conditions, especially in the towns.

59   **A walk through Wales in August 1797.**
     Richard Warner.   Bath, England: R. Cruttwell, 1797. 238p.

This was a popular work in its day, and was frequently reprinted during the early years of the nineteenth century, a sequel was subsequently published (item 56). Warner describes in letters to friends and acquaintances a tour from South Wales through mid-Wales and its mountain terrain, to the coast of west Wales, then to North Wales, returning south via the border districts. The observations are often amusing, often idiosyncratic, sometimes unfortunate, offering erroneous interpretations of places and names and perpetuating the rather patronising views of the period towards Wales and its people.

60   **Wild Wales.**
     George Borrow.   Oswestry, England: Gallery Books, 1988. 733p.

A facsimilie version of a 1901 edition, which was itself a carefully edited version to replicate Borrow's first edition in terms of spelling and general organization. Borrow is perhaps the most famous traveller to Wales to record his observations. His account was first published in 1862 and relates to his journey through Wales in 1854. Compared with the many works of this genre issued for Wales, this is the most accurate and sympathetic account of life in Wales in the mid-19th century.

Contemporary tourism

61   **An evaluation of the tourism content of structure plans in Wales.**
     Judy White.   Cardiff: Wales Tourist Board, Strategic Planning and
     Research Unit, 1985. 133p. bibliog.

A study to ascertain the extent to which local planning authorities had utilised the structure plan process to develop their tourism policies. Sections are devoted to the impact of structure planning in Wales, to specific objectives and policies for tourism and to an assessment of the strengths and weaknesses of the approaches and attitudes to tourism as they are reflected in the plans.

62   **Annual report of the Wales Tourist Board.**
      Cardiff: Wales Tourist Board. 1969-.
Reports and reflects the activity, plans and problems of the tourist industry in Wales, its new initiatives, marketing strategies, controversies, and the condition and state of the various sectors within the industry. This publication also provides primary and secondary data and notes the activities of regional and other related tourist organisations and information centres throughout Wales.

63   **Harbour and marina study.**
      Wallace Evans & partners.   Cardiff: Wales Tourist Board, 1982. 130p.
      maps.
A report of a major study outlining the tourism potential of the Welsh coastline, its ports and its harbours. It has been the basis of many subsequent developments – and controversies, throughout the ensuing decade.

64   **Inland water in Wales: development opportunities for tourism, recreation and sport; a joint report.**
      [Cardiff]: Wales Tourist Board, Welsh Water Authority, Sports Council for Wales, Mid Wales Development, 1985. 30p. maps.
A discussion document summarizing the tourist and recreational uses of water, described as a key leisure resource, outlining the considerable potential for growth and development in Wales, and identifying specific possible projects.

65   **Leisure and pleasure for profit.**
      Gwynfor O. Davies.   In: *The new Wales*. Edited by David Cole.
      Cardiff: University of Wales Press, 1990, p. 33-48.
A general study of the growth of tourism and particular amenities during the seventies and eighties, and significant landmarks during that period.

66   **Manpower in tourism: the situation in Wales.**
      Brian Archer, Sheila Shea.   Cardiff: Wales Tourist Board, 1976. 100p.
A study undertaken by the Institute of Economic Research, University College of North Wales, Bangor, which provides full and detailed statistics of employment in tourism, and an evaluation of the direct and indirect benefits in terms of expenditure and costs. The approach is by sector and type of tourism.

67   **Study on the social, cultural and linguistic impact of tourism in and upon Wales.**
      Cardiff: Wales Tourist Board, 1988. 126p. maps.
The report of a study undertaken by the European Centre for Traditional and Regional Cultures, Llangollen, in 1986 and 1987, 'the purpose of which was to provide objective and independent policy guidance, drawing upon research evidence gathered in Wales and from experience elsewhere'. Sections of the study include a statement on

16

the general nature of the impact of tourism, the methodologies employed, results and conclusions (socio-cultural benefits and disadvantages), and a review of current policies in the light of research findings.

68   Tourism employment in Wales.
S. Medlik.   Cardiff: Wales Tourist Board, 1989. 84p. bibliog.

A study of the scale and structure of tourism employment in Wales which was carried out in 1989, with particular reference to the nature of employment, and the key sectoral characteristics, together with an assessment of trends in tourism and the labour market in Wales. This work contains a particularly useful bibliography and appendices.

69   Tourism in Wales.
Cardiff: Wales Tourist Board, 1969. 71p. bibliog.

This is one of the earliest modern studies of tourism in Wales, and as such, is an important source of information about early policies, recurring problems, particular sectors, marketing strategies and individual attractions. It is also one of the earliest policy statements issued by the Wales Tourist Board.

70   Tourism in Wales – a plan for the future.
Cardiff: Wales Tourist Board, 1976. 180p.

A consultative review of the development of tourism policies together with an assessment of demographic trends and their influence on tourism and of anticipated demand. The plan also provides an indication of accommodation resources, tourist amenities and products, financial assistance and incentives, in addition to policy proposals in relation to the functions and goals of the Board.

71   Tourism in Wales: developing the potential, a Wales Tourist Board strategy. Twristiaeth yng Nghymru.
Cardiff: Wales Tourist Board, 1987. 85p.

A policy statement and strategy for development during the period 1987-92. It presents an assessment of growth potential, of the competition, of promotional requirements, of the new attractions required, and of the impact of conservation and enhancement of tourism resources. This work also provides a summary of the major factors influencing the development of tourism in Wales, historically and at the present time.

72   Tourism Wales: Twristiaeth Cymru.
The official journal of the Wales Tourist Board. 1984-. 3 times per year.

Essentially directed at the needs of those engaged in, or employed within, the industry, it is nevertheless a very useful source of data, about the industry, its activities, its development, its problems, and its future planning. It contains regional sections, statistics, advice and news items.

73 **Tourist Wales.**
David Thomas. In: *Wales: a new study*. Newton Abbot, England:
David & Charles, 1977, p. 252-71.
An objective analysis of the growth of tourism (including its historical origins) and a
profile of the contemporary state of the industry, with copious statistics and
illustrations. Current tensions and issues are analysed, such as the impact of second
homes, environmental concerns and transport problems, and individual attractions are
also discussed.

Travel guides

General

74 **AA touring guide to Wales.**
Edited by Russell Beach. Basingstoke, England: Automobile
Association, 1975. 297p. maps.
A major guidebook which offers: eight introductory essays on various topics including
industry, crafts, land reclamation; a selection of forty-three 'day drives' from various
locations; a gazetteer of 800 towns; forty town plans with a special feature on castles; a
gazetteer of locations associated with sporting pursuits; a touring atlas of Wales (three
miles to one inch) which also augments the text of the remainder of the work; and a
touring atlas of Great Britain, showing locations of Welsh ancient monuments. An
authoritative and lavishly illustrated work of its type, even though its basic gazetteer is
very selective.

75 **AA Touring Wales: the complete touring guide.**
Basingstoke, England: Automobile Association, 1987. 137p. maps.
A work which is essentially a guide for the motorist, with strategic towns selected as a
base for driving tours in areas with contrasting attractions, activities, landscapes and
scenery. Various other sections include a study of the castles of Wales, a consideration
of the architecture of selected towns, town plans and a gazetteer of places and their
attractions.

76 **The complete Wales.**
Edited by Reginald J. W. Hammond. London: Ward Lock, 1976.
318p. maps. (Red Guide Series).
This guidebook provides information on, and descriptions of, all major tourist centres,
and supplies information on accommodation, the range of activities, entertainment,
sports and other pursuits in each, together with suggested tours and itineraries from
each. Its organisation reflects the principal travelling routes, with a basic north to south
arrangement together with a concluding section on mid-Wales and the borders. It is
copiously illustrated, and includes useful route and town maps.

77 **The Country Life picture book of Wales.**
Roger Thomas. London: Country Life Books, 1981. 128p.
A lavishly-illustrated guide to Wales, which covers landscape and scenery, flora and fauna, tourist attractions, aspects of rural, cultural and economic life as well as social conditions and settlement patterns.

78 **Exploring Wales.**
W. T. Barber. Newton Abbot, England: David & Charles, 1982. 208p. maps.
A work which provides a brief historical background together with fourteen chapters devoted to various locations, each preceded by a map of salient features and places to visit. Adequate instructions are provided to visitors, and the notes and commentaries are succinct but sufficient, giving references and facts of interest for each location.

79 **Exploring Wales.**
William Condry. London: Faber, 1970. 304p.
A work arranged by county (pre-1974 local government reorganisation) boundaries, and citing references to history, topography, natural history and folklore. The author offers guidance and instruction on routes whatever the mode of travel. A useful general work.

80 **More mysterious Wales.**
Chris Barber. Newton Abbot, England: David & Charles, 1986. 242p.
A companion volume to *Mysterious Wales* (item 81) with a particular emphasis on the more obscure locations often not included in other more general guidebooks. It lists a variety of ancient sites to visit, 'with an associated mixture of folklore and history.' The work is fully illustrated and includes a descriptive commentary on each location.

81 **Mysterious Wales.**
Chris Barber. Newton Abbot, England: David & Charles, 1982. 243p.
A fully-illustrated study of places to visit in Wales associated with the country's legends and folklore, with a short commentary and factual description on each location. Such locations include megalithic monuments, ancient stones, crosses, wells and water, lakes, caves, lost cities and lands, superstitions and saints, and information provided is not always contained in works of a more general nature. A sequel to this study was issued in 1986 (item 80).

82 **The Shell guide to Wales.**
Edited by Wynford Vaughan-Thomas, Alun Llewellyn. London:
Michael Joseph, 1969. 360p. maps. bibliog.
A gazetteer of places of interest and significance in Wales, with an introduction. This volume is lavishly and copiously illustrated and a reprint was issued in 1977.

Tourism and Travel. Travel guides

83 **Wales.**
Edited by Stuart Rossiter. London: Ernest Benn, 1969. 300p. maps.
(Blue Guide Series).
The introductory essays in this volume, once regarded as being authoritative, now seem rather dated. The work has three main sub-divisions: north, mid- and south Wales and it includes maps, town plans and ground plans for sites of significance. Its information is detailed and is based on recommended routes.

Mid-Wales

84 **Mid Wales: a tourist guide.**
Cardiff: Wales Tourist Board, 1984. 72p. maps.
A work in a regular series of regional guidebooks, having a standard format, and offering general background information, more specific information on activities and pursuits, maps, a gazetteer of towns and principal villages, and other travel information and guidance on routes.

85 **Mid Wales Companion.**
Moira K. Stone. Oswestry, England: Cynefin (a Welsh Conservation Foundation) and Anthony Nelson, 1989. 224p.
A work which seeks to offer a fuller introduction to an area often inadequately treated in other more well-established series which have a rather unhelpful north and south subdivision. It has a series of short essays on population and its distribution, industry, land use, transport, natural history, religion, rural life, geology and geography, and, in addition, provides some interesting perspectives on issues relating to the Welsh coastline.

86 **Ordnance Survey leisure guide: Brecon Beacons and Mid Wales.**
London: Automobile Association & Ordnance Survey, 1989. 120p. maps.
A lavishly-illustrated guidebook which is a combination of the more traditional sections (lists of accommodation, activities and attractions (with maps), lists of information centres and a gazetteer), together with more significant contributions in the form of essays on the landscape, the wildlife, early industry, spas, agriculture and rural occupations. Its companion volume is listed in item 91.

North Wales

87 **The companion guide to North Wales.**
Elizabeth Beazley, Peter Howell. London: Collins, 1975. 398p. maps.
(Companion Guide Series).
A well-researched and illustrated volume, based on respected sources and authorities. The work claims to have two objectives: to provide a guidebook for those seeking help to travel and explore the country in an informed way; and to provide a standard guide to topography and history.

88 **North Wales: a tourist guide.**
   Cardiff: Wales Tourist Board, 1979. 81p. maps.
A well-illustrated work in a regular series with a standard format, i.e., a brief introduction followed by sections devoted to holiday activities and pursuits, places of interest, a gazetteer of towns, information centres, and appropriate maps and plans.

89 **North Wales (Northern section).**
   Edited by Reginald J. W. Hammond.   London: Ward Lock, 1975.
   192p. maps. (Red Guide Series).
This work concentrates on the north Wales coastal belt and Snowdonia, and provides lists of general and specific information to tourists and visitors, together with a brief introduction to the use of the Welsh language and to Welsh place-names.

90 **North Wales (Southern section).**
   Edited by Reginald J. W. Hammond.   London: Ward Lock, 1971.
   159p. maps. (Red Guide Series).
This publication deals with the area south of Snowdon to Aberystwyth and the area to the east as far as the border with England. Its format is detailed, giving an abundance of information for tourists and general travellers in seven well-defined geographical sub-divisions.

91 **Ordnance Survey leisure guide: Snowdonia and North Wales.**
   London: Automobile Association and the Ordnance Survey, 1989. 120p.
   maps.
A lavishly-illustrated guidebook providing a gazetteer, a directory of activities and pursuits, an atlas illustrating tours and walks, together with essays on Welsh nationhood, Snowdonia, natural history, sheep farming, folklore, myths and legends, transport and industrial archaeology. Its companion volume is listed in item 86.

92 **Portrait of North Wales.**
   Michael Senior.   London: Robert Hale, 1973. 240p.
A guidebook to the counties of Gwynedd and Clwyd sub-divided into their major identifiable geographical areas, i.e. the coastal belt, Snowdonia, Anglesey, the Llŷn Peninsula and Ardudwy. Copiously illustrated, the text maintains a theme reflecting cultural and linguistic independence and current influences. Its companion volume is listed in item 94.

South Wales

93 **The companion guide to South Wales.**
   Elizabeth Beazley, Peter Howell.   London: Collins, 1977. 351p. maps.
   (Companion Guide Series).
A well-researched and fully-illustrated work, drawing on respected sources and authorities. It seeks to provide a guidebook to facilitate exploration of South Wales, and to provide a standard guide to the topography and history of the area.

94 **Portrait of South Wales.**

Michael Senior.   London: Robert Hale, 1974. 221p.

Divides South Wales into six areas, i.e., west Wales, Swansea Bay, the Brecon Beacons, the Valleys, the Capital city, and Gwent in the south east. Senior seeks throughout to define Welshness in the Anglicised areas and analyses the impact of external influences. This is both an authoritative work and a popular travel guide and the volume is copiously illustrated. Its companion volume is listed in item 92.

95 **South Wales.**

Edited by Kenneth Lowther.   London: Ward Lock, 1981. 160p. maps.

(Red Guide Series).

Provides detailed tourist information for the area which is defined as Dyfed, Glamorgan, Gwent and the Brecknock area of Powys. It seeks to correct popular misconceptions concerning the effect of industrialisation on South Wales and its potential as a tourist area.

96 **South Wales: a tourist guide.**

Cardiff: Wales Tourist Board, 1984. 72p. maps.

An illustrated work in a regular series, with a standard format consisting of a brief introductory summary, sections on tourist attractions and amenities, maps, a gazetteer, and general travel and tourist advice.

Flora and Fauna

General

97 **Edward Lhuyd FRS 1660-1709.**
Frank V. Emery. [Cardiff]: University of Wales Press, 1971. 93p. bibliog.

A short bi-lingual biography of one of the most eminent of early Welsh natural historians and scholars. The contemporary Welsh natural history society bears his name – The Edward Lhuyd Society.

98 **The natural history of Wales.**
William Condry. London: Collins, 1981. 287p. maps. bibliog.

A work which seeks to provide a general introduction to the subject but which is inevitably selective. In botany, it is restricted to flowering plants and ferns; in the animal kingdom it deals with mammals, birds, fish, reptiles and amphibians and a selected number of insects, mainly butterflies and moths. Invertebrates are largely omitted but there is a preliminary study of coastline natural history. The appendices are very useful, especially the list of reserves and places of particular interest. Also of value is the glossary of Welsh terms and the bibliography.

99 **The naturalist in Wales.**
R. M. Lockley. Newton Abbot, England: David & Charles, 1970. 231p. bibliog.

An introductory work which concentrates primarily on habitats and climatic influences, and man's influence. Chapters are devoted to wild mammals, birds, flowers, and various other forms of wildlife including amphibia, insects and moths, fish, snails and slugs, and lepidoptera. Listings of nature centres and sources of information are added, as is an index of Welsh birds.

100 **Nature guide to Wales.**
June E. Chatfield. London: Usborne, 1981. 128p. maps. bibliog.
An introductory guide, particularly useful for its analyses of habitats. It also provides a gazetteer and numerous maps of the most significant and popular sites of outstanding interest in Wales – reserves, zoos, museums and study centres. Glossaries of terms and lists of useful addresses are appended. Although aimed at those with a beginner's interest this is a well designed and presented work.

101 **Nature in Wales. A natural science journal for Wales and the Borderland.**
National Museum of Wales, 1955-. irregular.
Originally the house magazine of the West Wales Field Society, it became the magazine of the other numerous Field Societies in Wales, but has been published since 1982 as a new series by the National Museum of Wales. The periodical has a particularly good format and contains excellent photographs.

102 **Welsh wildlife in trust.**
Edited by William S. Lacey. Bangor, Wales: North Wales Naturalists' Trust, 1970. 184p. maps.
An anthology of twenty-two essays by various contributors. The treatments vary from the historical to a study of the role of various bodies and societies in Wales in the study of natural history, to conservation, and to specific studies of species, specific habitats and localities. The volume was published in European Conservation Year and contains useful appendices.

Area studies: exemplars

103 **Glamorgan County History. Volume I. Natural History.**
Edited by A. M. Tattersall. Cardiff: William Lewis (Printers) Ltd., 1936. 444p. maps.
A major study of the natural history of Glamorgan, a major part of south Wales, an industrial area with a variety of geology, geography and habitats. This volume provides a general survey followed by major studies of geology, climate and meteorology, soils, botany and zoology.

104 **The natural history of Bardsey.**
Peter Hope Jones. Cardiff: National Museum of Wales, 1988. 148p. bibliog.
An authoritative study of an area of outstanding significance, representative of modern methods and techniques and approaches to natural history in Wales. It includes sections, dealing, for example, with studies of geology and soils, hydrology, climate and weather, plant habitats, invertebrates, breeding birds, migrants, marine life, and human influence on wildlife.

105 **The nature of central Wales.**
Fred Slater. Buckingham, England: Barracuda Books, 1988. 176p.
maps. bibliog. (Nature of Britain Series).
Published under the auspices of the Wildlife Trusts of Powys and the University of
Wales Institute of Science and Technology, this is a lavishly-illustrated series of essays
on topics such as upland flora and fauna, mires and marshes, conservation, woodlands
and river and still water flora and fauna, subjects not always adequately developed in
more general studies.

106 **The nature of west Wales.**
Edited by David Saunders. Buckingham, England: Barracuda Books,
1986. 163p. maps. bibliog. (Nature of Britain Series).
This work was published under the auspices of the West Wales Trust for Nature
Conservation, west Wales being the county of Dyfed. It provides an interesting area
study, typical of many for Wales, but noteworthy as it is an anthology of essays on
various topics such as the uplands, the woodlands, mainland coast and islands and
nature conservancy, and also on account of its lavish illustrations. This book is both an
authoritative work and a popular study suitable for many audiences.

Flora

107 **The Flora of Monmouthshire.**
A. E. Wade. Cardiff: National Museum of Wales, 1970. 236p. maps.
A significant volume, one of the first modern studies of a single county, and one which
seeks to establish a pattern for subsequent publications. It offers a guide to the
distribution of plants within the area, providing a much greater depth of detail than is
possible in a volume seeking to encompass the whole of Wales.

108 **Flowering plants in Wales.**
R. Gwynn Ellis. Cardiff: National Museum of Wales, 1983. 338p.
maps. bibliog.
A scholarly and fully-illustrated guide to the occurrence and distribution of over 2,700
flowering plants that have been found growing wild in Wales. The catalogue of plants
includes both native and naturalized plants and all recorded casuals, introduced forest
trees, subspecies, hybrids and microspecies. The work also includes essays which
analyse the influence of geology and climate on Welsh flora and their distribution.

109 **Plant hunting in Wales.**
Gwynn Ellis. Cardiff: National Museum of Wales, [n.d.]. 46p. maps.
Three illustrated essays tracing the history and development of the recording of Welsh
flora from the Roman period, with an overview of historical sources – books, notes and
diaries. The work also includes an account of the work of prominent collectors such as
Edward Lhuyd (1660-1709), J. J. Dillenius (1684-1747), Samuel Brewer (1607-1742)
and others.

110   **Welsh ferns, clubmosses, quillworts and horsetails: a descriptive handbook.**
H. A. Hyde, A. E. Wade, S. G. Harrison.   Cardiff: National Museum of Wales, 1978. 178p. bibliog.

This illustrated work is the standard study on the subject and is currently (1990) in its sixth edition. The introduction includes references to the major collections of the National Museum of Wales, followed by a key to genera of native Welsh *Pteridophyta*, followed by the classification of the species.

111   **Welsh timber trees: native and introduced.**
H. A. Hyde.   Cardiff: National Museum of Wales, 1977. 4th. ed. 165p. maps.

A work originally compiled in 1930 at a time when systematic studies of trees throughout Britain were being undertaken, with the aim of making available 'to a wider public in Wales the results of these and similar studies and to encourage further observations'. Subsequent editions were expanded as new species were introduced into Wales – this editon gives particulars of 350 specimen trees or stands of trees. The introduction is particularly useful for it presents a chronological study of Welsh woodlands, both native and introduced, and an assessment of their current state and their future.

112   **Welsh wild flowers.**
A. R. Parry.   Cardiff: National Museum of Wales, 1973. [34p].

A study of fifty flowering wild plants, with a short introductory essay outlining the major influences on the flora of Wales, such as land clearing, afforestation, agriculture and conservation. The work also traces the origins of the Welsh names given to plants and flowers.

Fauna

113   **Birds of the Welsh coast.**
T. G. Walker.   Cardiff: University of Wales Press, 1956. 100p.

An introductory study by a pioneering ornithologist in Wales. Twenty-four species are described in this work (primarily issued for the young ornithologist) together with a list of 126 other birds which may be found on the Welsh coast.

114   **Cambrian bird report.**
[Bangor], Wales: Cambrian Ornithological Society, 1962-. annual.

Published until 1985, this annual report of bird sightings in various locations in Wales (primarily in the north) is to be resurrected in the near future as a Wales bird report. Data in the series notes species, numbers of sightings, climatic conditions, with short essays and notes on unusual, or rare, occurrences.

115 **A guide to the birds of Wales.**
David Saunders.   London: Constable, 1974. 341p. maps.
A brief introduction to Wales and to the history of Welsh ornithology, is followed by a
consideration of each county in Wales and its bird life and the societies, activities and
watching sites within each area. The check-list of birds at the end of each section is an
important source of information.

116 **A guide to Gower birds.**
Harold E. Grenfell, Derek K. Thomas.   Swansea, Wales: Gower
Ornithological Society and Glamorgan Naturalist Trust, 1982. 104p.
An introduction to a significant and popular bird-watching area, and a work which is
highly representative of many such publications issued for most regions of Wales. It
records a complete list of birds observed in the area up to 1981.

117 **RSPB guide to birdwatching in Clwyd.**
Valerie McFarland, edited by Roger Lovegrove.   Sandy (Beds.),
England: Royal Society for the Protection of Birds, 1989. 53p. maps.
An illustrated work encompassing an area of very varied habitats, coastal and inland,
lowland and upland, industrial and rural. It is particularly interesting for its listing of
uncommon species observed at various locations within the county which lies within
migration routes. The general introductory essays are also interesting.

118 **RSPB guide to birdwatching in Snowdonia.**
Roger Lovegrove, Darren Rees.   Sandy (Beds.), England: Royal
Society for the Protection of Birds, 1987. 74p. maps.
Lists the forty-nine best sites to which the public has access. This illustrated work has
sections devoted to summer woodland birds, riverside, lake and stream birds, hillside,
moorland and mountain birds, birds of prey, wildfowl and migrant birds.

119 **Welsh seashells.**
June E. Chatfield.   Cardiff: National Museum of Wales, 1977. 44p.
An illustrated survey, with preliminary essays outlining the variety of coastline habitats
and different types of shore in Wales and the shells found on them. Shells are grouped
according to the type of shore on which they are found.

120 **Where to watch birds in Wales.**
David Saunders.   London: Christopher Helm, 1987. 245p. maps.
A work whose treatment of the subject is by geographical areas and particular
locations within those areas, describing habitats, species, watching facilities, and
significant timings. The list of Welsh and scientific names is particularly useful.

Prehistory and Archaeology

General

121 **Archaeologia Cambrensis. Journal of the Cambrian Archaeological Association.**
Cardiff: Cambrian Archaeological Association, 1846-. annual.
A learned journal which normally consists of a small number of scholarly articles on archaeological studies and reviews of publications on Welsh archaeology and related subjects. For almost 150 years this journal has been the main vehicle for publishing reports on excavations in Wales. The periodical also publishes a report of the annual meeting of the Cambrian Archaeological Association together with a list of the officers and accounts of the association.

122 **Archaeology in Wales.**
Council for British Archaeology, Group 2: Aberystwyth, Wales. 1961-. annual.
A publication which is a valuable source of information for all those working in the field of archaeology in Wales. It includes descriptions of the work undertaken by the Wales group of the Council for British Archaeology as well as other national and local bodies, together with short accounts of recent excavations and discoveries of field monuments and artefacts dating from prehistoric times to the industrial era.

123 **Historic monuments of Wales: ways of making them more enjoyable, more enlightening, more profitable: a report.**
John Brown. Worcester, England: John Brown Tourism Marketing & Development Services, 1983. 470p. illus. bibliog.
The aim of this report was 'to examine and to make recommendations for improving the attractiveness, the standard of presentation, marketing and commercial performance of the ancient monuments in the care of the Secretary of State for Wales'. The first part of the report presents the general findings with a summary of recommendations,

whilst the second part consists of reports and recommendations on the large number of sites visited by the author in compiling this study.

124 **A hundred years of Welsh archaeology.**
Edited by V. E. Nash-Williams. Gloucester, England: Cambrian Archaeological Association, 1946. 160p.

This volume, written for the general reader and the professional archaeologists, was produced as part of the centenary celebrations of the Cambrian Archaeological Association in 1946. It presents a broad survey of archaeology in Wales from prehistoric times to the medieval period in the light of the findings of Welsh archaeologists between 1846 and 1946. In addition to an introductory essay on the history of the association, there are contributions on: prehistoric Wales; Roman Wales; settlement sites and other remains of the early Christian period; inscribed and sculptured stones of the early Christian period; medieval castles; and the great monastic houses of medieval times.

125 **Index to Archaeologia Cambrensis, 1901-1960.**
Compiled by T. Rowland Powel, with lists and notes by Donald Moore. Cardiff: Cambrian Archaeological Association, 1976. 313p. map.

A comprehensive index to 'persons, places, objects and topics mentioned in the annual volumes of *Archaeologia Cambrensis* from 1901 to 1960'. In view of the importance of the journal *Archaeologia Cambrensis* (see item 121) this is an indispensable bibliographic tool for scholars and researchers of Welsh archaeological studies.

126 **Prehistoric and early Wales.**
Edited by I. Ll. Foster, Glyn Daniel. London: Routledge & Kegan Paul, 1965. 244p. bibliog. (Studies in Ancient History and Archaeology).

A general study of prehistoric and early Wales based on a series of lectures delivered by a group of specialist scholars at the British Summer School of Archaeology held at Bangor in 1959. The volume is designed to present the general reader, as well as archaeologists and historians, with an introductory survey to the history of Wales from the first appearance of man up to the seventh century AD.

127 **Rescue archaeology in Wales.**
Henry Owen-John. Swansea, Wales: University College of Swansea, 1986. 58p. illus. (The Mainwaring-Hughes Award Series).

A short booklet which aims to present the reasoning behind rescue archaeology and to describe its current organisation and significance in Wales. To illustrate the work the author has selected case-studies from his involvement in rescue archaeology in south-east Wales which he considers to be broadly representative of work undertaken in other parts of the country.

128 **Welsh archaeological heritage.**
Edited by Donald Moore, David Austin. Lampeter, Wales: Cambrian Archaeological Association & Saint David's University College, 1986. 171p. illus. maps.
The proceedings of a conference organised by the Cambrian Archaeological Association which contains a range of papers on the management of Welsh archaeological heritage in the 1980s. The papers describe the rôle played by various organisations in Wales which are collectively responsible for preserving, recording and presenting archaeological remains.

Inventories and archaeological guides.

129 **Ancient monuments in Wales. Henebion Cymru.**
London: HMSO, 1975. 79p.
A list of approximately 2,300 ancient monuments in Wales prepared by the Department of the Environment on behalf of the Secretary of State for Wales, who is required to produce a list of ancient monuments which are considered to be of national importance and which are protected under the Ancient Monuments Act. The list has been arranged by the pre-1974 county units and further classified by the name of the parish and by type.

130 **Ancient monuments of Wales.**
London: HMSO, 1976. 136p. illus. bibliog. (An Illustrated Guide to the Ancient Monuments, no. 4).
An illustrated guide to ancient monuments in Wales which until recently were maintained by the Department of the Environment. The first part of the book, which is aimed at the non-specialist, consists of a survey of ancient monuments and historical buildings presented in the form of essays by established authorities in the field and which cover the following periods: prehistoric; Roman occupation; early Christianity and the emergence of Wales; the Middle Ages and the Industrial Revolution. The second part is an annotated gazetteer of archaeological monuments.

131 **The ancient stones of Wales.**
Christopher Barber, John Godfrey Williams. Abergavenny, Wales: Blorenge Books, 1989. 192p. illus. bibliog.
The main part of this book is a gazetteer of approximately 400 prehistoric stone monuments in Wales. This provides the non-specialist with a lucid survey of prehistoric remains found in Wales and a very practical guide for those who wish to pay a visit to some of them. The remainder of the work is a mixture of sound factual information about prehistoric stone monuments and rather dubious references to mysterious happenings linked to some of these stones.

132 **Early medieval settlements in Wales AD 400-1100: a critical assessment and gazetteer of the archaeological evidence for secular settlements in Wales.**
Edited by Nancy Edwards, Alan Lane. Bangor, Wales: Research Centre University College of North Wales; Cardiff: Department of Archaeology, University College Cardiff, 1988. 157p. illus. maps. bibliog.

This report presents a reassessment of previously held views on medieval settlements in Wales which has been prompted by the foundation of the Early Medieval Wales Archaeology Research Group. It is hoped that the report will stimulate further interest and research in this field. The sites which have been examined are classified into three groups, namely those which definitely belong to this period, possible medieval sites and and those which have been rejected.

133 **Guide catalogue of the Bronze Age collections.**
H. N. Savory. Cardiff: National Museum of Wales, 1980. 258p. illus. bibliog.

A standard guide to a section of the prehistoric collections housed in the National Museum of Wales. In part one the author presents a scholarly guide to the various Bronze Age periods. The catalogue, which forms part two of this book, records over 500 items from Wales in the collection. This guide is an invaluable reference book for both the amateur enthusiast and the professional archaeologist.

134 **Guide catalogue of the early Iron Age collections.**
H. N. Savory. Cardiff: National Museum of Wales, 1976. 119p. illus.

This volume provides a standard guide to part of the prehistoric collections housed in the National Museum of Wales. In part one the author, who is the Keeper of Archaeology at the National Museum of Wales, presents an interpretative guide to the collection of Iron Age objects. The catalogue which follows records all the items at the Museum which are believed to belong to the Iron Age period, or which are relevant to the establishment of Iron Age culture in Wales although Bronze Age in type. This study will be of value as a reference source for the professional archaeologist and the amateur enthusiast.

135 **Heritage in Wales: a guide to ancient and historic sites in the care of Cadw: Welsh Historic Monuments.**
David Robinson. London: Queen Anne Press, 1989. 208p. illus. bibliog.

An illustrated guide for the non-specialist to some 120 historic sites which are in the direct care of the Secretary of State for Wales and administered on his behalf by Cadw: Welsh Historic Monuments. The sites range from neoloithic chambered tombs dating back to 4,000 BC to a Victorian 'castle'. The book also contains a gazetteer to the sites giving basic information on the location. To assist the general reader to gain a better understanding of the subject the author has included a glossary of unfamiliar terms, biographical notes on key historical figures, and a chronological table of the monuments.

Prehistory and Archaeology. Inventories and archaeological guides.

136 **An inventory of the ancient monuments in Brecknock (Brycheiniog). The prehistoric and Roman monuments. Part ii; hill forts and Roman remains.**
Royal Commission on Ancient and Historical Monuments in Wales. London: HMSO, 1986. 196p. illus. maps. (Inventories of the Royal Commission on Ancient and Historical Monuments in Wales).

This is the standard reference book covering the prehistoric and Roman monuments found in the pre-1974 county of Brecon. It includes a detailed inventory of hill forts and other remains of the Roman occupation together with a report which lists those monuments which are worthy of preservation. The volume also includes a scholarly introductory essay on the significance of this period in the history of the county of Brecon.

137 **An inventory of the ancient monuments in Glamorgan vol. 1: pre-Norman.**
Royal Commission on Ancient and Historical Monuments in Wales. Cardiff: HMSO, 1976. 3 parts. (Inventories of the Royal Commission on Ancient and Historical Monuments in Wales).

A standard guide to the ancient monuments found in Glamorgan which date from pre-Norman times. As with other volumes in the series this is an indispensable volume for professional archaeologists, historians, and also the amateur enthusiast. Together the three volumes provide an inventory of approximately 1,000 ancient monuments which date back before the eleventh century. There is also a list of those monuments considered worthy of preservation because of their exceptional importance as well as scholarly essays providing the historical background. The contents are as follows: Part 1: The Stone and Bronze Age; Part 2: The Iron Age and the Roman occupation; and Part 3: the early Christian period.

138 **An inventory of the ancient monuments in Glamorgan, vol. III: medieval secular monuments, part ii: non-defensive.**
Royal Commission on Ancient and Historical Monuments in Wales. Cardiff: HMSO, 1982. 398p. + plates. illus. maps. bibliog. (Inventories of the Royal Commission on Ancient and Historical Monuments in Wales).

A comprehensive inventory of over 500 non-ecclesiastical and non-military monuments in the county of Glamorgan together with a general introduction to the history of medieval Glamorgan and to each type of monument.

139 **An inventory of the ancient monuments in Wales and Monmouthshire.**
The Royal Commission on the Ancient and Historical Monuments and Constructions in Wales and Monmouthshire. London: HMSO, 1911-37. 8 vols. (Inventories of the Royal Commission on the Ancient and Historical Monuments in Wales).

The original series of inventories of ancient and historical monuments and other smaller findings belonging to individual Welsh counties which illustrate the civilisation and living conditions of the people from earliest times onwards. The volumes also contain a list of recommendations as to which of these monuments should be preserved. The series covered the following eight of the thirteen pre-1974 counties: vol 1: County of Montgomery, 1911; vol 2: County of Flint, 1912; vol 3: County of Radnor, 1913; vol 4: County of Denbigh, 1914; vol. 5: County of Carmarthen, 1917; vol 6: County of Meirioneth, 1921; vol 7: County of Pembroke, 1925; and vol 8: Anglesey, 1937.

140   **An inventory of the ancient monuments of Caernarvonshire.**
Royal Commission on Ancient and Historical Monuments in Wales and Monmouthshire.   London: HMSO, 1956-64. 3 vols. (Inventories of the Royal Commission on Ancient and Historical Monuments in Wales).

The standard guide to the ancient monuments and archaeological sites of the pre-1974 county of Caernarfon up to the middle of the eighteenth century. This is an indispensable reference book for the professional historian and archaeologist. In line with other contributions to this series, the publication includes a comprehensive inventory of monuments, a list of those monuments which are considered worthy of preservation as well as scholarly introductory essays on the historical context. The contents are as follows: vol 1: East (The cantref of Arllechwedd and the commote of Creuddyn), (1956); vol 2: Central (The cantref of Arfon and the commote of Eifionydd), (1960); and vol 3: West (The cantref of Lleyn together with general survey of county), (1964).

141   **Schedules of ancient monuments of national importance = Cofrestr o henebion o bwysigrwydd cenedlaethol.**
Cadw. Welsh Historic Monuments.   Cardiff: Cadw. Welsh Historic Monuments, 1985-. Ongoing.

Cadw is responsible for recording, protecting and helping to conserve historic buildings and ancient monuments in Wales on behalf of the Secretary of State for Wales. This series of booklets publishes schedules of individual sites which are considered county-by-county. The reports provide basic information about the name, location and type of those monuments cited. To date volumes have been published on Powys, Glamorgan, Gwent, Gwynedd and Clwyd but eventually the whole of Wales will be represented.

142   **Wales: an archaeological guide: the prehistoric, Roman and early medieval field monuments.**
Christopher Houlder.   London: Faber, 1975. 197p. illus. maps. bibliog.

A concise guide to some 600 archaeological sites for the non-specialist. Generally speaking, priority has been given in the selection to the most accessible and best preserved monuments. The sites have been arranged into forty-five geographical areas that can be visited in a day or two's motoring. In addition to the guide, the book contains a short introductory essay on archaeology in Wales, again written with the non-specialist in mind. The author is a field officer with the Royal Commission on Ancient Monuments in Wales.

Medieval archaeology

143 **Castles in Wales.**
Roger Thomas. Basingstoke, England: Automobile Association;
Cardiff: Wales Tourist Board, 1982. 192p. illus. maps.

A gazetteer of over eighty Welsh castles together with a short introduction to their historical background. The entries for individual castles includes a description, and a colour photograph of the remains, together with a layout plan, or an artist's impression of the original building. The volume, which has been written with the general reader, particularly tourists, in mind, includes a full-colour atlas which helps to locate the castles.

144 **Castles in Wales and the Marches: essays in honour of D.J. Cathcart King.**
Edited by John R. Kenyon, Richard Avent. Cardiff: University of Wales Press, 1987. 248p. bibliog.

A collection of essays written by distinguished scholars to honour the contribution of David Cathcart King to the study of Welsh castles. The collection includes general studies of individual castles and essays on special features together with others on more general themes. This volume is intended for students, scholars and the serious enthusiast rather than for the general reader. A valuable feature of the book is that it includes a bibliography of studies on Welsh castles.

145 **The castles of the Welsh princes.**
Paul R. Davis. Swansea, Wales: Christopher Davies, 1988. 100p. illus. bibliog.

During the struggle for supremacy in Wales between the native leaders and the Normans in the twelfth and thirteenth centuries, a large number of castles were built throughout the length and breadth of the country. This book presents a guide to the native Welsh castles of that period, together with short historical and architectural introductions, a chronological table and short glossary. This book is suitable for the general reader.

146 **The early Christian monuments.**
V. E. Nash-Williams. Cardiff: University of Wales Press, 1950. 258p. + 71 plates. illus.

The inscribed and sculptured stone monuments of Wales built between the fifth and the twelfth century AD provide important evidence of the conversion of Wales to Christianity and of various racial and cultural movements which occurred during this period. The main part of this study is an inventory of over 400 monuments but it also includes a scholarly essay on the four groups of monuments (namely simple inscribed stones, cross-decorated stones, sculptured crosses and cross-slabs, and transitional Romanesque monuments) and a set of distribution maps which graphically illustrate the location of the different groups of monuments.

147 **Wales: castles and historic places.**
Wales Tourist Board. Cardiff: Wales Tourist Board, 1980. 3rd. ed.
92p. illus. maps.
A pocket guidebook to castles and other historic sites in Wales written for the non-specialist, particularly tourists. The main part of the booklet is a gazetteer which provides short descriptions of the sites and their location, together with a longer account of their historical significance and main features. The book also includes an outline history of Wales from prehistoric times to the fifteenth century.

Industrial archaeology

148 **The industrial archaeology of Wales.**
D. Morgan Rees. Newton Abbot, England: David & Charles, 1975.
302p. illus. bibliog. (The Industrial Archaeology of the British Isles).
This study, written by the first Keeper of Industry at the National Museum of Wales, Cardiff, presents the non-specialist reader with a general overview of the remains of over four hundred years of industrial activity in every corner of Wales. The main part of the volume describes a number of archaeological sites and also provides the technical and economical background to the changes which took place. Part two is a selective gazetteer of industrial sites in Wales.

149 **Mines, mills and furnaces: an introduction to industrial archaeology in Wales.**
D. Morgan Rees. London: HMSO, 1969. 117p. illus. maps. bibliog.
Wales has a long history of metal extraction which can be traced back to prehistoric times and the country can also boast that it made a significant contribution to the world supply of metals at certain stages during that history. This study is based on fieldwork undertaken by the author of gold, lead, zinc, and copper mines in Wales as well as activities such as iron-making, steel and tinplate works and forging and casting.

History and Genealogy

General

150 A bibliography of the history of Wales.
Philip Henry Jones.   Cardiff: University of Wales Press, 1989. 3rd. ed.
Microfiche.
This definitive bibliography of Welsh history from 400 AD to the present day has been greatly enlarged since the appearance of the second edition in 1962 and is an indispensable tool for the scholar and student of Welsh history. The work consists of 22,000 entries which have been arranged into broad chronological periods with an author/title and keyword-in-context index to the titles. The compiler has adopted a broad definition of Welsh history, so that the bibliography will be of value to those studying the history of such topics as architecture, Welsh literature, the Welsh language, education and religion, as well as more general historical studies.

151 An historical atlas of Wales from early to modern times.
William Rees.   London: Faber, 1967. 3rd. ed. 71p. + 70 plates.
This authoritative atlas offers both the student of Welsh history and the general reader with a useful outline and graphic presentation of the main developments in Wales from the Bronze Age to the industrialisation of the country during the eighteenth and nineteenth centuries.

152 Land of my fathers: 2000 years of Welsh history.
Gwynfor Evans.   Swansea, Wales: John Penry Press, 1974. 465p. illus.
This personal account of the history of Wales from earliest man to the present day, written by the former President of Plaid Cymru (the Welsh Nationalist Party), was originally published in the Welsh language. The original title, *Aros mae* (It endures), is a more accurate representation of the main theme which the author attempts to convey, i.e., the sense of unity and continuity in the history of Wales. Evans traces the struggle of the Welsh people to retain their unique civilisation in the face of military,

political and cultural imperialism by a series of invaders particularly the Romans, the Normans and the English and concludes that the fact that the Welsh language and identity have survived to this day is nothing short of a miracle. This is a highly readable and passionate account of the history of the Welsh nation.

153   A pocket guide: the history of Wales.
J. Graham Jones.   Cardiff: University of Wales Press, 1990. 177p. illus. bibliog.

Provides an introductory history of Wales and the Welsh people from the pre-Norman period to modern times. The book, which is aimed at the general reader, also includes short biographies of prominent figures in Welsh history and describes major historical sites.

154   Religion, language and nationality in Wales: historical essays.
Glanmor Williams.   Cardiff: University of Wales Press, 1979. 252p. illus. bibliog.

A collection of historical essays, by a distinguished Welsh historian, written for the non-specialist and the student of Welsh history. Most of the essays were originally delivered as public lectures and examines aspects of the interplay between religion, language and nationality. They cover a period which stretches from the departure of the Romans to the 1970s.

155   Short history of Wales: Welsh life and customs from prehistoric times to the present day.
A. H. Dodd.   London: Batsford, 1977. New ed. 173p. illus.

Despite invasion, conquest and eventual political assimilation with England, Wales has successfully managed to retain a distinct and vigorous culture and a strong national consciousness. This generously-illustrated volume, written as an introduction for the general reader by a distinguished Welsh historian, describes the social history of Wales from the earliest known inhabitants down to the political awakening of Wales during the nineteenth century.

156   Theses on Welsh history presented before 1970.
David Lewis Jones.   *Welsh History Review/Cylchgrawn Hanes Cymru,* vol. 5, no. 3 (June 1971), p. 261-304.

A comprehensive bibliography of theses on Welsh history presented at British and North American universities prior to the end of 1969. The items listed are arranged into eight chronological periods and further subdivided into specialised themes such as political and administrative, religious, social and economic, education and culture. Regular supplements to this bibliography have appeared in the *Welsh History Review* since 1971.

157   Wales.
Gwyn Jenkins.   London: Batsford, 1975. 96p. illus. bibliog. (Past Into Present Series).

A short illustrated history of Wales and the Welsh people from the cave-dwellers of pre-history to the present day, written as an introduction for the general reader. Although it covers the entire history of Wales, the main thrust of the work is the economic, political and social changes which occurred between the coming of industrialisation to Wales during the second half of the eighteenth century and the present day. The author shows that, despite both the contribution of Wales to the economy and politics of modern Britain and the industrialisation of the south-east, the Welsh people have retained a strong sense of national identity.

158   **Wales: a history.**

Wynford Vaughan-Thomas.   London: Michael Joseph, 1985. 269p. illus. maps.

An illustrated, general history of Wales written for the informed layman. This work was originally published as a companion volume to the highly acclaimed television series which was produced by HTV for Channel 4 and presented jointly by the Wynford Vaughan-Thomas and Professor Gwyn A. Williams. The story of the Welsh people from the first appearance of man in Wales some 15,000 years ago down to 1979 is presented in a lively and stimulating style which matches the aim of the author to 'stir the imagination of the man and woman who is coming to Welsh history for the first time'. The main thesis presented in the book is the ability of the Welsh people and their culture to survive despite the odds. Although written by a professional broadcaster rather than a professional historian this is a sound general history of Wales.

159   **The Welsh History Review. Cylchgrawn Hanes Cymru.**

Cardiff: University of Wales Press, 1960-. bi-annual.

A journal which publishes articles on the history of Wales for scholars, students and the interested layman. The publication also includes book reviews, obituaries and lists of periodical articles in the field of Welsh history. This journal has played an important rôle in the development of Welsh historical studies during the past thirty years.

160   **Welsh nation builders.**

Gwynfor Evans.   Llandysul, Wales: Gomer Press, 1988. 356p. illus.

Presents short essays on sixty-five important figures in the history of Wales from the Roman occupation to the second half of the twentieth century. The essays are arranged chronologically thus giving the reader an outline of the main developments in Welsh history. The author admits that he is a committed Welsh nationalist and that this fact colours his selection. The aim of the volume is to present the history of the country to young people and the general reader in a stimulating way by describing the contribution of leading individuals to Welsh history.

161   **Welsh society and nationhood: historical essays presented to Glanmor Williams.**

Edited by R. R. Davies, Ralph A. Griffiths, Ieuan Gwynedd Jones, Kenneth O. Morgan.   Cardiff: University of Wales Press, 1984. 270p. illus. bibliog.

When Glanmor Williams retired from the Chair of History at University College Swansea in 1982, this volume of essays was produced as a tribute to his enormous contribution to the study of Welsh history. The essays explore a number of themes relating to religion, social change and the concept of nationhood in Wales from the early medieval period down to the present day. As a further tribute, the work includes a bibliography of the works produced by Williams up to 1982.

162   **Wales through the ages.**
Edited by A. J. Roderick.   2 vols. Llandybie, Wales: Christopher
Davies, 1965. illus. bibliog.

These two volumes are based on a series of radio talks broadcast on the Welsh Home
Service during the winters of 1958-59 and 1959-60. The aim of the series was to present
to the informed layman the main developments in the history of Wales from the
earliest times to the twentieth century. Taken together the two volumes provide a
stimulating and readable introduction to Welsh history for the general reader and the
student.

163   **When was Wales? A history of the Welsh.**
Gwyn A. Williams.   Harmondsworth, England: Penguin; London:
Black Raven, 1985. 327p. bibliog.

Although the volume is meant to be a general history of Wales, little attention is paid
to prehistoric and Roman Wales because the author firmly believes that the history of
the Welsh people begins with Magnus Maximus in AD 383. The main theme of this
highly original examination of Welsh history is that the Welsh have always existed in a
state of emergency and their miraculous survival has been achieved 'by making and remaking themselves and their Wales over and over again'. The lively and thought-
provoking analysis of the history of the Welsh people provided in this work should
stimulate the student of Welsh history and the informed layman.

164   **The yearbook of Wales dates.**
Compiled by John May. Tongwynlais, Wales: Castle Publications, 1989.
75p.

A reference work which lists the dates of significant events in the history of Wales and
the Welsh people arranged by the calendar year.

From the Roman occupation to the Norman Conquest ca.50 AD – 1282

165   **Arthur's Britain: history and archaeology AD 367-634.**
Leslie Alcock.   London: Allen Lane; Harmondsworth, England:
Penguin, 1971. 415p. illus. maps. bibliog.

This study is an important contribution to an understanding of the history of the British
Isles during the two and a half centuries after the Romans departed. By the end of this
period, the Anglo-Saxons had become the most powerful ethnic group and the British
people had been forced to occupy the more westerly and northerly parts of the island.
The author discusses the documentary and archaeological evidence available to the
historian and also traces the main political and military events of the period. The book
includes an important chapter on the culture of the Britons.

History and Genealogy. From the Roman occupation to the Norman Conquest ca.50 AD – 1282

166   **Celtic Britain.**
Nora K. Chadwick.   London: Thames & Hudson, 1963. 238p. illus. bibliog. (Ancient People and Places, no. 34).
Provides a general introduction to the history and cultures of Celtic Britain during the period between the departure of the Romans at the beginning of the fifth century and the foundation of the Saxon kingdoms in the sixth and seventh centuries. This is a suitable introduction for students and the general reader alike.

167   **Celtic Britain.**
Charles Thomas.   London: Thames & Hudson, 1986. 200p. illus. maps. bibliog.
An examination of the history of Britain from the departure of the Romans around 400 AD to the establishment of English kingdoms in the latter part of the seventh century. This illustrated volume provides the general reader with a short introduction to this period.

168   **Conquest, coexistence and change: Wales 1063-1415.**
R. R. Davies.   Oxford: Clarendon Press; Cardiff: University of Wales Press, 1987. 530p. illus. maps. bibliog. (History of Wales, 2).
A general history of the Welsh people during the critical centuries of their struggle to retain their political independence in the face of the Anglo-Norman invasion and the eventual territorial conquest of Wales in 1282. As well as providing a detailed examination of this defeat, this study describes the resilience and resourcefulness of the Welsh people in retaining their identity during the following two centuries, culminating in Owain Glyndwr's insurrection of 1400-15. This comprehensive study is indispensable for those teaching and studying Welsh history, but it is also aimed at the informed general reader. In addition to its treatment of the military and political situation, it also describes the social and economic transformation of Wales during this period.

169   **Economy, society and warfare among the Britons and Saxons.**
Leslie Alcock.   Cardiff: University of Wales Press, 1987. 343p. illus.
A scholarly study of the archaeology and history of Wales and south-west England from the fifth to the eighth centuries. The volume includes the findings and interpretations of Alcock's excavations of an early Welsh prince's stronghold at Dinas Powys in the county of Glamorgan together with archaeological and other evidence on further fortifications in Wales and south-west England. The author also provides a synthesis of the economic and social life of the Britons and the Saxons as well as the contact and conflict between them from the fifth to the eighth centuries.

170   **Edward I and Wales.**
Edited by Trevor Herbert, Gareth Elwyn Jones.   Cardiff: University of Wales Press, 1988. 158p. (Welsh History and its Sources).
This volume forms part of a series funded by the Welsh Office Research Development Grant and produced at the Open University in Wales to provide an insight into vital periods in Welsh history and to demonstrate how professional historians interpret primary sources. This study deals with five major themes of thirteenth-century Welsh history, Welsh society and native power; the Edwardian conquest and its military consolidation, church and monasticism, crown and communities, collaboration and conflict. Each section contains a general essay and a collection of sources on which the

interpretation in the essay is based. The book has been written for those engaged in the formal, or informal, study of Welsh history and/or historical methodology.

171 A history of Wales.
J. E. Lloyd.   2 vols. [Vol. 1]: Carmarthen, Wales: Golden Grove, 1989. new ed. [Vol. 2]: London: Longman, Green and Co., 1948. 3rd. ed.

This work was originally published in 1911 and was acclaimed at the time as an outstanding contribution to the study of Welsh history, not only because of the determination of the author to provide an accurate interpretation of the facts, but also because of the masterly fashion in which the story of the Welsh nation is presented. Despite the fact that much new evidence about the early period of Welsh history has been discovered since the first edition was published, Lloyd's contribution is still recognised as one of the standard readings on Welsh history. Volume one covers the history of Wales from earliest man to the end of the first-half of the eleventh century and the second volume deals with the two-hundred-year struggle between the Welsh and the Normans, culminating in the fall of the last independent prince of Wales in 1282.

172 The Norman conquest.
David Walker.   Swansea, Wales: Christopher Davies, 1977. 109p. bibliog. (A New History of Wales).

This study forms part of a series providing sixth-form and higher education students as well as the general reader with a brief résumé of some of the major themes in Welsh history. In this volume, the author examines the impact of the Normans on Wales by attempting to answer such questions as who were the Normans, what brought them to Wales and how did their military campaigns and settlement patterns affect Wales during the Middle Ages?

173 The Roman frontier in Wales.
V. E. Nash-Williams.   Cardiff: University of Wales Press, 1969. 2nd. ed. 206p. bibliog.

This is the standard work on the Roman military conquest and occupation of Wales. Originally published in 1954, this new and revised edition was prepared by Michael G. Jarrett and takes into account the discovery of new sites and the findings of more recent excavations. The main section is a descriptive survey of legionary fortresses and other military sites found in Wales. Further chapters provide background information on the Roman invasion, the garrison and the siting and planning of different types of buildings.

174 Studies in early British history.
Edited by Nora K. Chadwick.   Cambridge: Cambridge University Press, 1954. 282p.

A collection of essays by a group of distinguished Cambridge scholars specialising in aspects of the history and culture of Britain during the fifth century AD i.e., immediately after the withdrawal of the Romans from Britain and before the establishment of the Saxon kingdoms. The essays cover themes in the history, language, literature and ecclesiastical practices of the period. Although not comprehensive in its coverage, it provides useful material for students of early history and literature.

175 Wales in the early Middle Ages.

Wendy Davies. Leicester, England: Leicester University Press, 1982. 263p. bibliog. (Studies in the Early History of Britain).

A comprehensive and scholarly synthesis of the settlement and history of Wales between the fifth and eleventh centuries. In addition to providing a well-illustrated and crtitical introduction to the history of the early medieval period, the author discusses developments in Wales within the wider European context. Davies demonstrates that the period saw the growth of a distinct cultural identity, particularly in the areas of language, literature and law, despite the political divisions between the four main kingdoms of Wales. The book covers themes such as landscape, economy, politics, law and order, the church and social structures, and provides a suitable analysis of the period for the informed layman and students.

From conquest to the Act of Union, 1282-1536

176 A history of Wales: 1485-1660.

Hugh Thomas. Cardiff: University of Wales Press, 1972. 246p. illus. maps. (Welsh History Textbooks).

Although originally designed as part of a series of textbooks on the history of modern Wales for sixth formers and higher education students, this book also provides the general reader with a lucid survey of the major political, economic, religious and social changes which occurred in Wales between 1485 and 1660. The author demonstrates that Wales was a more peaceful and secure society than was the case before the accession of Henry Tudor to the English throne and, moreover, that those with power and initiative gained material benefits from the greater freedom they experienced.

177 Owen Glendower.

Glanmor Williams. Oxford: Oxford University Press, 1966. 63p. illus. map. bibliog. (The Clarendon Biographies).

A brief study for the general reader of one of the major figures in Welsh history who led the Welsh people in a revolt against the English at the beginning of the fifteenth century. Although his national rising was eventually crushed, his campaign for Welsh political freedom remains an inspiration for all those who believe in self-government for Wales. The book not only describes the military campaigns but also the social and political background to the conflict between the English and Welsh at this time. In addition, Williams provides an assessment of what was achieved through the rebellion.

178 Recovery, reconstruction and Reformation: Wales c. 1415-1642.

Glanmor Williams. Oxford: Clarendon Press; Cardiff: University of Wales Press, 1987. 528p. bibliog. (History of Wales, no. 3).

This is the standard general history of Wales for the two centuries following the national uprising at the beginning of the fifteenth century led by Owain Glyndŵr. It is indispensable for those studying and teaching Welsh history of this period, but it should also meet the needs of the general reader who is interested in the history of Wales. Although this volume is comprehensive in scope, the main themes running through the study are the social and economic recovery following the Glyndŵr uprising, the political and legal reorientation of Welsh life and the far-reaching religious, cultural and linguistic outlook of the Welsh people following the Reformation.

Modern Welsh history I: from the Act of Union to the beginning of industrialisation, 1536-1780

179 **Class, community and culture in Tudor Wales.**
Edited by J. Gwynfor Jones. Cardiff: University of Wales Press, 1989. 300p.

A collection of eight essays by distinguished scholars which discuss the major aspects of the social and economic structures of Wales during the sixteenth century. Most of the contributions are extended versions of papers presented at a colloqium organised by the Department of Welsh History, University College, Cardiff, and held at the Gregynog Hall, Powys. The essays will be of interest to the general reader who wishes to understand more about the social history of Wales as well as Welsh history undergraduates for whom the volume is principally designed. Amongst the themes covered by the contributors are education, domestic architecture, social and economic structures in towns and the living conditions of the lower classes.

180 **The eighteenth century renaissance.**
Prys Morgan. Llandybie, Wales: Christopher Davies, 1981. 174p. (A New History of Wales).

This book forms part of a series providing sixth-formers, higher education students and the general reader with short, readable introductions to some of the major themes of Welsh history. Welsh historians have long recognised that the eighteenth century was a century of revival in agriculture, education, religion and industry. In this study the author argues that the most distinctively Welsh revival of the eighteenth century was the cultural revival or renaissance. The reasons for this revival and its development are discussed in some detail.

181 **The foundations of modern Wales: Wales 1642-1780.**
Geraint H. Jenkins. Oxford: Clarendon Press; Cardiff: University of Wales Press, 1987. 490p. bibliog. (History of Wales, no. 4).

This is the standard general history of Wales during the period immediately preceding the beginnings of the Industrial Revolution in Wales. Written by a distinguished Welsh scholar, it is an indispensable tool for those teaching and studying this period of Welsh history, but the work is also aimed at the informed and interested general reader. The central theme of the study is the development of strong social forces which transformed Welsh life even before the major social, economic and political changes which occurred after 1780.

History and Genealogy. Modern Welsh history I: from the Act of Union to the beginning of industrialisation, 1536-1780

182   **A history of modern Wales.**
David Williams.   London: John Murray, 1965. 308p. bibliog.
Originally published in 1950, this work was recognised for many years as the standard introductory volume to the history of Wales from 1485 to the twentieth century. The author outlines the main developments in the political, religious, economic and social history of Wales during this eventful period. His balanced treatment of various events, changes and movements means that the book is still a sound introduction to modern Welsh history for the student and the general reader.

183   **A history of Wales 1660-1815.**
E. D. Evans.   Cardiff: University of Wales Press, 1976. 267p. (Welsh History Textbooks, no. 2).
This book was originally designed as a textbook for schools and colleges but nevetheless it provides the layman with a broad survey of the major political, religious, economic and social changes which occurred in Wales between 1660 and 1815. The main areas of change described in this volume are the industrial growth, the Methodist revival, political awakening, educational movements and agricultural improvements.

184   **The remaking of Wales in the eighteenth century.**
Edited by Trevor Herbert, Gareth Elwyn Jones.   Cardiff: University of Wales Press, 1988. 192p. (Welsh History and its Sources).
This volume forms part of a series which demonstrates how professional historians interpret their sources and it is illustrated by themes from Welsh history. It contains five sections each dealing with a theme from the eighteenth century. Each section consists of an essay, a collection of original sources on which the essay is based, and a discussion on the strengths and weaknesses of the documentary material. The themes are politics, religion, education, the impact of industrial activities and the emergence of a new Welsh identity. The volume is designed for those engaged in the formal and informal study of Welsh history.

185   **Studies in Stuart Wales.**
A. H. Dodd.   Cardiff: University of Wales Press, 1971. 2nd ed. 251p. bibliog.
The history of Wales during the seventeenth century has generally been overshadowed by the more dramatic events which preceded and followed it. The author claims in this volume that, despite this, the century played a key role in the evolution of the Welsh people. This claim is supported in the author's analysis of six areas of activity, namely: social order; the role of Ludlow as an administrative capital for Wales; the relationship between Wales and Ireland; the operation of the county committee system in Wales; the evolution of party politics; and Wales and the 'Glorious Revolution'.

186   **Tudor Wales.**
Edited by Trevor Herbert, Gareth Elwyn Jones.   Cardiff: University of Wales Press, 1988. 177p. (Welsh History and its Sources).
This textbook, which is part of a series designed for higher education students, provides an insight into a period of Welsh history and into the interpretation of primary historical sources. It investigates the following themes from the Tudor period: the gentry, the lower orders, agrarian change and urban fortunes, religion and belief,

and government and politics. Each section has been prepared by a professional historian and consists of an essay, a collection of sources on which the essay is based and finally a discussion of the strengths and weaknesses of the documentary evidence.

187 **Wales in the eighteenth century.**
Editor: Donald Moore. Swansea, Wales: Christopher Davies, 1976. 181p. illus. maps.

A collection of nine articles which explore a wide range of themes and some of the less familiar aspects of eighteenth-century Wales. The topics covered include government and politics, influential families, domestic and industrial architecture, landscape, and road and bridge building. This book, with its generous selection of illustrations, is aimed at the general reader.

Modern Welsh history II: 1780-1900

188 **Acts of Parliament concerning Wales 1714-1901.**
Compiled and edited by T. I. Jeffreys Jones. Cardiff: University of Wales Press, 1959. 343p. (Board of Celtic Studies, University of Wales History and Law Series, no. 17).

A comprehensive list of the long titles of private and public Acts of Parliament either dealing exclusively with, or giving special regard to, places and persons in Wales produced over a period of almost two hundred years. The entries have been arranged under approximately twenty-five topics such as bridges, ferries, gas, electricity, the Welsh language and minerals. This volume is a valuable reference source for the student and the Welsh history scholar, as well as those concerned with Welsh legal issues and public administration in Wales.

189 **And they blessed Rebecca: an account of the Welsh toll-gate riots 1839-1844.**
Pat Molloy. Llandysul, Wales: Gomer Press, 1983. 352p.

The Rebecca Riots, which took place in west Wales against the injustices of the toll roads, are generally accepted as one of the major events in the social history of Wales during the nineteenth century. Indeed, much has been written by professional historians about the sociological and historical background of the disturbances. The author of this volume, an ex-Chief Detective Superintendant, approaches the theme from a different point of view and also provides a detailed and lively account of the 250 or so incidents which constitute the history of the riots. This study will appeal to the general reader who is interested in the social history of Wales, but it also contains much of interest to the more serious student of history.

190 **A breviate of parliamentary papers relating to Wales, 1868-1964.**
Jane Morgan. Cardiff: University of Wales Board of Celtic Studies, 1975. 202p.

A guide to the main parliamentary papers relating to Wales which were published between 1868 and 1964. The volume is intended as a reference source for research students and scholars of modern Welsh political and social history. The items which have been selected for inclusion have been arranged into the following subject categories: machinery of government; agriculture and food supplies; labour; coal, fuel, power and water; transport; trade and industry; broadcasting and publishing; ecclesiatical; housing and town planning; health; legal administration; police and law; education; social security; historic buildings.

191 **Communities: essays in the social history of Victorian Wales.**
Ieuan Gwynedd Jones. Llandysul, Wales: Gomer Press, 1987. 370p.

A collection of essays which originally appeared in learned journals, or were delivered as public lectures, which examine both the nature of Welsh communities in mid-nineteenth century Wales and the major forces responsible for creating them. The first group of essays illustrate the importance of the Anglican revival to Welsh social and religious history. The following group look at the nature of society in different South Wales valleys and the final group includes esssays on aspects of Welsh politics during the second half of the nineteenth century. Although most of these essays were originally produced for students and scholars of Welsh history, they should also provide the general reader with an insight into aspects of the social history of Wales during the nineteenth century.

192 **Exploration and explanations: essays in the social history of Victorian Wales.**
Ieuan Gwynedd Jones. Llandysul, Wales: Gwasg Gomer, 1981. 338p. bibliog.

The central theme of this collection of eight essays by a distinguished Welsh scholar is the nature of social change in Wales between 1850 and 1870. The two areas which are examined are aspects of the religious and political activities of the period. The final three chapters offer an assessment and explanation as to how Nonconformity grew into such a force in national politics and why it was to have such an influence on the aspirations and achievements of Wales until the end of the nineteenth century.

193 **A history of Wales 1815-1906.**
D. Gareth Evans. Cardiff: University of Wales Press, 1989. 331p. maps. bibliog. (Welsh History Textbooks, no. 3).

This book, which was originally designed as a textbook for schools and colleges, provides the general reader with a synthesis of the industrial, social, political and cultural developments which took place in Wales during the nineteenth century.

194 **A people and a proletariat: essays in the history of Wales 1780-1980.**
Edited by David Smith. London: Pluto Press, 1980. 239p.

A collection of essays by a group of historians belonging to the Welsh Labour History Society which examine issues from the last two hundred years during which Wales has experienced a period of rapid industrial and urban growth and decline, as well as a decline in its native language, culture and community life. The contributors attempt to reappraise certain themes and issues and also attempt to challenge various assumptions about the history of Wales.

195 **People and protest, Wales 1815-1880.**
Edited by Trevor Herbert, Gareth Elwyn Jones.   Cardiff: University
of Wales Press, 1988. 215p. bibliog. (Welsh History and its Sources).
This volume has the same objectives as others in this series (see, for example, items
184 and 186). It consists of six sections containing an essay, a collection of sources on
which the essay is based and a discussion of the strengths and weaknesses of the
documentary evidence cited. The major issues covered in these sections are:
parliament and people in mid-nineteenth century Wales; nonconformist response; the
Rebecca Riots; rural and industrial protest in North Wales; the Scotch Cattle and
Chartism.

196 **Politics and society in Wales, 1840-1922: essays in honour of Ieuan
Gwynedd Jones.**
Edited by Geraint H. Jenkins, J. Beverley Smith.   Cardiff: University
of Wales Press, 1988. 201p.
A collection of essays by leading Welsh historians on the occasion of Ieuan Gwynedd
Jones' retirement from the Sir John Williams chair of Welsh history at the University
College of Wales, Aberystwyth. The essays deal with social and political themes in
Wales during the second half of the nineteenth century and first quarter of the
twentieth. The topics covered include: Victorian Wales; an aspect of Irish immigration
to Wales in the 1840s; the Welsh language in an industrial society; social problems in
south-west Wales; a comparison of Tom Ellis and Lloyd George; amateur and
professional culture in Wales; the Cardiff strike of 1911; the rise of the Labour Party in
Llanelli; and a study of the ministry of J. D. Jenkins, Vicar of Aberdare. Another
valuable feature of this volume is that it includes a bibliography of the writings of
Ieuan Gwynedd Jones.

197 **Rebecca's children: a study of rural society, crime and protest.**
David J. V. Jones.   Oxford: Oxford University Press, 1989. 423p.
A scholarly examination of the Rebecca Movement to mark the 150th year since the
destruction of the first tollgate at Efailwen on the Carmarthenshire–Pembrokeshire
border in 1839. In the light of new information, the author provides a detailed
reappraisal of the riots and demonstrates, with supporting material, that the
disturbances in west Wales during the late 1830s and early 1840s were on a much wider
scale, and much less respectable in nature, than portrayed by historians. The
movement is evaluated in the context of rising crime rates and violent protests in rural
Wales during the latter part of the eighteenth century and the first half of the
nineteenth.

198 **The Rebecca Riots: a study in agrarian discontent.**
David Williams.   Cardiff: University of Wales Press, 1986. 377p.
bibliog.
This book, originally published in 1955, presents an account of the violent uprising of
Welsh farmers and labourers in west Wales against the injustices, and the burden, of
the toll-road charges during the 1830s and 1840s. Although the study includes a fairly
detailed description of the events during those years, the main thrust is to examine the
deep-seated causes of the disturbances, namely the breakdown in the social structure
of rural Wales, the antiquated system of government and administration, and a
backward economy.

199 **A select list of parliamentary papers relating to Wales, 1801-1850.**
Jane Morgan.   Cardiff: University of Wales Board of Celtic Studies,
1974. 232p.

A systematic list of parliamentary papers which include references to Wales. This work should prove to be an invaluable source of reference for research students and scholars working on aspects of local and national Welsh history during the first half of the nineteenth century. The items have been arranged under thirty-nine subject headings.

200 **Wales 1880-1914.**
Edited by Trevor Herbert, Gareth Elwyn Jones.   Cardiff: University
of Wales Press, 1988. 193p. bibliog. (Welsh History and its Sources).

This volume in this well-established series, (see items 184 and 186, for example) examines the following themes from the period 1880-1914: rural depopulation; Wales at work; language, religion and culture; popular protests; and David Lloyd George and Wales. Each section has been prepared by a specialist historian and includes an essay, a collection of source material on which the essay is based and finally an evaluation of the strengths and weaknesses of the documentary evidence cited.

Twentieth century

201 **Rebirth of a nation: Wales 1880-1980.**
Kenneth O. Morgan.   Oxford: Clarendon Press, 1981; Cardiff:
University of Wales Press, 1981. 463p. bibliog. (History of Wales,
no. 6).

A standard general history of Wales from 1880 to the present day which provides a synthesis of the political, constitutional, economic, social, religious, cultural and other activities of this period. This is an indispensable tool for those teaching and studying modern Welsh history, but the book is equally accessible to the informed general reader. The author has divided the period into three parts. Part 1 (1880-1914): a period dominated by the Liberal ascendancy in the political arena but also a period that saw industrial growth, social conflict and a cultural and national awakening. Part 2 (1914-45): a period dominated by World War I and its impact on Welsh life and the economic depression of the 1920s and 1930s; while politically it was a period which saw the emergence of the Labour Party as the major political force in Wales. Part 3 (1945-80): amongst the main themes of this era was the economic restructuring after World War II, the decline of the Welsh language and the rise of political nationalism.

202 **Wales between the wars.**
Edited by Trevor Herbert, Garerth Elwyn Jones.   Cardiff: University
of Wales Press, 1988. 296p. illus. bibliog. (Welsh History and its
Sources).

Another volume in this well-established series (see items 184 and 186, for example). In this volume the following themes are examined from the period 1919-39: economic decline; social reactions to economic change; politics; women between the wars; films;

and literature. Each section consists of an essay, a collection of primary and secondary sources on which the essay is based and a critical assessment of the sources used.

Genealogy

203 **Cofrestri plwyf Cymru. Parish registers of Wales.**
Compiled by C. J. Williams, J. Watts-Williams. Aberystwyth, Wales: National Library of Wales & Welsh County Archivists Group, 1986. 217p. illus. maps. (National Index of Parish Registers, no. 13).

A comprehensive and scholarly index of over 1,000 parish registers and bishops' transcripts of such registers held in repositories in Wales and the border counties. The index is not confined to listing the original version of such registers held, but also lists reproductions in microfilm and other forms. Most Welsh Parish Registers are deposited either in the National Library of Wales, or in one of the County Record Offices, and this survey was made possible through the collaboration of the staff of these institutions. This is an indispensable reference source for family historians and genealogists.

204 **The dictionary of Welsh biography down to 1940.**
Editors: John Edward Lloyd, R. T. Jenkins. London: Honourable Society of Cymmrodorion, 1959. 1,157p.

A major biographical dictionary of Welsh history. The editors originally planned this work to be a standard reference book on the history of Wales for both the scholar and general reader, and as a result, it includes entries also on non-Welsh persons by blood or birthplace, who lived and worked in Wales and had an impact on its history. Those Welsh men and women who made a substantial contribution in some form of activity outside Wales have also been included. In total, the volume consists of approximately 3,500 articles concerning major figures in such areas as politics and administration, law and industry, culture and scholarship.

205 **Enwau Cymraeg i blant. Welsh names for children.**
Heini Gruffudd. Talybont, Wales: Y Lolfa, 1980. 94p. illus. bibliog.

A selection of over 1,000 Welsh Christian names together with an explanation of their meaning and derivation and a reference, where appropriate, to a historical figure who bore the name. Although the book has been compiled primarily to encourage parents to adopt Welsh names for their offspring, the booklet also serves as a valuable reference source.

206 **In search of Welsh ancestry.**
Gerald Hamilton-Edwards. Chichester, England: Phillimore, 1986. 95p. illus. bibliog.

A practical guide for local and family historians and others working on some aspect of Welsh ancestry. The volume presents a short introduction to Welsh history and a chapter on Welsh Christian names and surnames. Other chapters provide information about family history records kept in the National Library of Wales, the County Record

Offices and elsewhere. The author also discusses other sources of information such as parish registers, wills and administrations and military records.

207 **Welsh genealogies AD 300-1400.**
Compiled by Peter Clement Bartrum. Cardiff: University of Wales Press on behalf of the Board of Celtic Studies, 1974. 8 vols. and supplements.

A comprehensive collection of Welsh pedigree tables with detailed indexes from the Dark Ages up to the generation born in ca. 1400 AD based chiefly on the content of medieval manuscripts held in the National Library of Wales and elsewhere. The purpose of this work is to make the contents of these manuscripts accessible in a more convenient form for scholars and others. Although the author is not able to claim total accuracy regarding the information obtained from the manuscripts consulted, this publication remains the major contribution to this field of study.

208 **Welsh genealogies A.D. 1400-1500.**
Peter Clement Bartrum. Aberystwyth, Wales: National Library of Wales, 1983. 18 vols.

This eighteen volume reference source continues the guide to Welsh genealogies described in no. 207 by including tables to the generation born up to ca. 1500. In this series, it is possible to trace the pedigrees of new families including some English and Norman-French ones as well as those which featured in the earlier series. Once again, the main sources used are the manuscript collections in the National Library of Wales. In addition to the tables, there are comprehensive indexes to place-names and personal names.

209 **Welsh surnames.**
T. J. Morgan, Prys Morgan. Cardiff: University of Wales Press, 1985. 211p.

A detailed and scholarly study of the development and changes in surname patterns in Wales and the border counties from the Middle Ages to the present day. The main section of this reference book is a dictionary of these surnames showing their origin and variants. This is an indispensable tool for students of Welsh family history and genealogy but it will also be of interest to a wider audience.

Military history

210 **A history of the Royal Regiment of Wales (24th/41st Foot) and its predecessors: 1689-1989.**
J. M. Brereton. Cardiff: Royal Regiment of Wales, 1989. 512p. illus. maps.

The Royal Regiment of Wales was formed in 1969 by the amalgamation of the South Wales Borderers (founded in 1689) and The Welch Regiment (founded in 1719). The book therefore spans three hundred years of military history involving these two regiments and provides accounts of individual battles and campaigns in all parts of the world. This well researched study is aimed at the military historian, members of the Regiment and the general reader.

211   **That astonishing infantry: three hundred years of the history of the Royal Welch Fusiliers (23rd Regiment of Foot) 1689-1989.**
Michael Glover.   London: Leo Cooper, 1989. 356p. illus. maps.
bibliog.
The official history of the regiment published on the occasion of its 300th anniversary and written by a distinguished military historian. The Royal Welch Fusiliers has a distinguished record in battles and campaigns from the days of Marlborough onwards and has accumulated 145 Battle Honours. The achievements of the regiment are described and evaluated here in the context of the development of the British Army as a whole. The book is aimed at military historians and the general reader and also includes a chronological summary of the regiment's history, a list of recipients of the Victoria Cross and of Battle Honours.

212   **The Welsh Guards.**
John Retallack.   London: Frederick Warne, 1981. 176p. illus.
A short account of the Welsh Guards which covers the period from its foundation in 1915 to the end of the 1970s. During the first thirty years of its existence the Guards were involved in the two World Wars. This history, written by a former member, is a tribute to the contribution of the Guards during those two confrontations and their rôle in lesser skirmishes since 1945. The author stresses that, despite its short history, a strong regimental tradition and spirit exists.

Population

General

213 Genetic and population studies in Wales.
Edited by Peter S. Harper, Eric Sunderland.   Cardiff: University of
Wales Press, 1986. 433p. maps. bibliog.

A study of the heterogeneity of Wales divided into three parts: historical and cultural
essays (in-migration [i.e., population movements into Wales from other parts of the
United Kingdom as opposed to traditional immigration from overseas and Common-
wealth countries], linguistic influences, archaeology, physical evidence of man in
Wales); anthropological essays (including genetic studies for Wales, or specific areas
within Wales); and medical practice, health, illnesses and diseases of particular
significance in Wales and cytogenetic studies. A collection of essays by prominent
experts, which is rather complex for the uninformed in parts, but which seeks to bring
together seminal studies hitherto distributed in many sources.

Migration and rural problems

214 Depopulation in mid Wales.
London: HMSO, 1964. 88p. maps.

A study to ascertain the extent and the nature of the problems caused in Wales by
rurality, remoteness and de-population with respect to the economy, culture, wealth,
family life and transport and education. The volume includes an assessment of the
necessary remedial action as well as a number of appendices which are useful as they
present a factual, statistical survey of the demography of mid-Wales.

215 **Migration into, out of and within Wales in the 1966-71 period. Mudo i Gymru, o Gymru ac oddi mewn i Gymru yn ystod y cyfnod 1966-71.** Cardiff: HMSO, 1979. 23p. maps. (Welsh Office Occasional Paper, no. 4).

This publication is based on the Department of the Environment Migration Research Report which provided more data on the migration process than had been previously available in the various Census surveys and publications. In three parts, the study initially examines the characteristics of migrants who come to Wales and their origins, then it examines the particular flows within counties and finally the movement of people into, and out of, individual districts. A document which generated considerable discussion at the time it was published.

216 **'A million on the move'?: population change and rural Wales.** Graham Day. *Contemporary Wales*, vol. 3, (1989), p. 137-59.

A study of rural depopulation since 1970, the nature and composition of population movements, the economic transformation and the labour market. It also contains a very significant assessment of both the consequences of migration, and the efforts made to halt depopulation and to attract a new population.

217 **Rural Wales: population changes and current attitudes.** Cardiff: Institute of Welsh Affairs, 1988. 71p.

An analysis of published data, primarily of population in rural Wales, together with specially commissioned surveys of the circumstances and attitudes of the population of rural Wales and major sub-groups within that population – youth, retired people, farming families and in-migrants. Sections are devoted to analyses of demographic trends, migration, wealth and incomes, housing and the state of the Welsh language.

Census, 1981

218 **Census 1981. County reports.** Office of Population Censuses and Surveys.   London: HMSO, 1982. 2 vols.

A report for each county in Wales with statistical tables as follows: *Tables* 1–3 General; 4–11 Demographic characteristics; 12–16 Economic characteristics; 17–33 Housing and amenities; 34–41 Household composition; and 42 The Welsh language. Volume 2, (tables 43–50) contains selected ten per cent sample tables.

219 **Census 1981. Economic activity: Wales.** Office of Population Censuses and Surveys. London: HMSO, 1984. Microfiche.

A report for each county in Wales, with each set of data tabulated at county and district level. The following Tables are presented: *Table 1* Usually resident (economic activity) population: economic position and employment status by area of usual

Population. Projections

residence and area of workplace by sex (and married women). *Table 2* Usually resident (economic activity) population economically active: occupation orders (1970 classification) and occupation groups by area of usual residence and area of workplace (population in employment) by sex (and married women). *Table 3* Usually resident (economic activity) population in employment: industry classes by area of workplace by sex (and married women). *Table 4* Usually resident (economic activity) population economically active: socio-economic group by area of usual residence by sex (and married women).

220   **Census 1981. Regional migration, Wales.**
Office of Population Censuses and Surveys. London: HMSO, 1984.
86p.
The data is tabulated as follows: *Table 1* (for Wales and for individual counties). Migrants within one year preceding census aged sixteen and over resident in the region: area of former usual residence, by socio-economic group of economically active persons and economic positions of economically inactive persons by sex (and married women). *Table 2* (for England and Scotland). Migrants within one year preceding census aged sixteen and over formerly resident in the region: area of former usual residence by area of usual residence at census by socio-economic group of economically active persons and economic position of economically inactive persons by sex (and married women). *Table 3* (for Wales only). Migrants within one year preceding census aged sixteen and over: type of move by economic position and employment status by sex. *Table 4* (for Wales only). Migrants within one year preceding census aged sixteen and over and economically active: type of move by occupation orders by sex. *Table 5* (for Wales only). Migrants within one year preceding census aged sixteen and over in employment: type of move by industry divisions by sex.

221   **Census 1981. Report for Wales.**
Office of Population Censuses and Surveys. London: HMSO, 1983.
151p. maps.
The data is ennumerated as follows:
Tables 1–3 General; 4–11 Demographic characteristics; 12–16 Economic characteristics; 17–33 Housing and amenities; 34–41 Household composition; 42 The Welsh language; 43–50 Selected ten per cent sample tables; and 51–52 Further population and household data: by country of birth by sex.

Projections

222   **1987 Based household projections for counties of Wales.**
Amcaniadau teuluoedd ar gyfer siroedd Cymru: sail 1987.
Cardiff: Welsh Office, 1983-. biannual.
These statistics draw on the Welsh Office population projections for the counties of Wales, the basis of which are the mid-year estimates of population produced by the Office of Population Censuses and Surveys. The data is presented in a Wales summary, followed by county summaries, followed by comparisons within Wales.

54

223 **1987 Based population projections for the counties of Wales.**
Amcaniadau poblogaeth ar gyfer siroedd Cymru: sail 1987.
Cardiff: Welsh Office, 1989. 21p. maps.

This publication, which is part of a biennial population projection booklet series presents the most recent population projections for the counties and district health authorities of Wales. The data enumerated includes summary projections for Wales, fertility assumptions, mortality ratios, birth and death rates, migration statistics and comparisons over two-year periods, for Wales as a whole, with county projections.

Welsh Overseas

224 **Americans from Wales.**
Edward George Hartmann.   New York: Octagon Books, 1978. 291p.
bibliog.

This book, which was originally published by Christopher Publishing House, Boston, in 1967, presents an outline history of the Welsh people in America and a survey of contemporary Welsh-American activities. The author traces the story of the Welsh people who emigrated, their trials and tribulations and finally their contribution to the life of their adopted country. The work includes chapters on: Welsh-American journalism and publishing; eisteddfodau and hymn-singing festivals; and Welsh-American societies and clubs. The appendices provide informative data on Welsh-American religious establishments and short biographies of distinguished Welsh-Americans. Another valuable feature of the volume is that it includes an extensive bibliography of the history of Welsh emigration to America.

225 **Australians from Wales.**
Lewis Lloyd.   Caernarfon, Wales: Gwynedd Archive & Museum
Service, 1988. 282p.

This volume, based partly on the wealth of original source material housed in the archives of Gwynedd, traces the history of the Welsh people, and people of Welsh descent, in the history of Australia with special reference to the strong maritime links which were developed in the second-half of the nineteenth century. During the two-hundred years of European settlement in Australia, Welsh men and women contributed to each stage of its development 'as convicts, and early "free settlers", as diggers, prospectors, swagmen, farmers, stockmen, drovers, publicans, shop assistants'. In writing about their experiences Lloyd provides the reader with a microcosm of several waves of Welsh emigration to Australia. One chapter is devoted to famous Australians who were Welsh, or from Welsh descent.

226 **Crisis in Chubut: a chapter in the history of the Welsh colony in Patagonia.**
Geraint Dyfnallt Owen. Swansea, Wales: Christopher Davies, 1977. 161p.

An account of the circumstances which led many of the Welsh in Patagonia at the turn of the twentieth century to consider establishing a Welsh colony under the British flag as a part of the British Empire. The author traces the story of the 200 Welsh settlers who left Patagonia for Canada in 1902 and also discusses others who considered a similar move to South Africa.

227 **Cymru ac America. Wales and America.**
David Williams. Cardiff: University of Wales Press, 1975. 2nd. ed. 89p. illus.

Although this short bilingual booklet was written originally for secondary school children, its account of the contribution made by Welsh people to the growth and development of the United States and of the motives which led thousands of Welshmen to leave Wales, also offers a sound introduction to the subject for the general reader.

228 **The desert and the dream: a study of Welsh colonization in Chubut, 1865-1915.**
Glyn Williams. Cardiff: University of Wales Press, 1975. 230p. illus. maps.

A detailed study of the early history of the Welsh efforts to establish a Welsh colony in the lower Chubut valley in Patagonia, South America. The account examines: the motives which lay behind the establishment of such a colony; the social conditions of Wales which forced people to contemplate emigration during the nineteenth century; why Patagonia was selected for this adventure; and the experiences and struggles of the settlers during the first fifty years. Finally, the author assesses how successful the Welsh settlers were in their goal of preserving the Welsh language and culture.

229 **A geographic study of the Welsh colonization in Chubut, Patagonia.**
David Hall Rhys. PhD thesis, University of California, Los Angeles, 1976. (Available from University Microfilms International, Ann Arbor, Michigan, order no. 76-28079).

The main part of this study is an examination of the impact of the environment on Welsh settlers in the lower Chubut valley between 1865 and 1915. Rhys also investigates the position of the descendants of the Welsh people in this part of Patagonia today in order to evaluate the interaction between the Welsh and Latin cultures during the past 110 years.

230 **Madoc: the making of a myth.**
Gwyn A. Williams. Oxford: Oxford University Press, 1987. 226p. illus. bibliog.

During the sixteenth century a myth was created that North America had been discovered by Madog ab Owain Gwynedd during the twelfth century, some three hundred years before Columbus had sailed west in search of new territories. This legend was adopted by the English state in an attempt to justify its imperial ambitions.

In this scholarly and stimulating study, the author analyses the origins of the myth and provides an explanation for its development. The work also includes a detailed account of the adventures of John Evans during the eighteenth century in his search for the Welsh-speaking 'Indians' of North America who were supposedly the descendants of the Welsh people who sailed with Madog.

231 **In search of the red dragon: the Welsh in Canada.**
Carol Bennett.   Renfrew, Canada: Juniper Books, 1985. 244p.

An outline history of Welsh emigration to Canada together with a description of the contribution made by Welsh people, and those of Welsh extraction, to the religious, social, political and cultural life of Canada. The volume also includes a useful list of present-day Welsh societies in Canada.

232 **The search for Beulah land: the Welsh and the Atlantic revolution.**
Gwyn A. Williams.   New York: Holmes & Meier, 1980. 190p.

An imaginative recreation of the emergence of radicalism in Wales during the 1790s with special attention to the influence of the American Revolution and the Madog myth on the relationship between Wales and North America. It includes a detailed examination of the career of Morgan John Rhys [a nonconformist minister and leading supporter in Wales of the French Revolution who later encouraged Welsh people to emigrate to North America to enjoy greater political and religious freedom] and also offers an explanation as to why whole families emigrated to North America during the 1790s.

233 **A shared history: change and continuity in a Welsh-Argentine Andean ethnic community.**
Jane Spencer Edwards.   PhD thesis, University of Pennsylvania, 1978. (Available from University Microfilms International, Ann Arbor, Michigan, order no. 7816297).

An ethnographic study based on fieldwork undertaken by the author in Chubut. It focuses on the sense of continuity and its nature amongst Welsh-Argentines, despite the cultural shifts which have taken place from one generation to the next. The methodology adopted was to collect data by participant observation and by recording the narratives of local tradition.

234 **Welsh convict women: a study of women transported from Wales to Australia, 1787-1852.**
Deirdre Beddoe.   Barry, Wales: Stewart Williams, 1979. 166p. illus. bibliog.

Traces the story of some 300 Welsh women from all parts of Wales who were convicted for a range of crimes and transported to Australia. Through the records kept of the victims the author is able both to provide some information about their origins, appearance and occupation, the crimes they had committed as well as to present a picture of conditions during their voyage to Australia and their fate in the new country. This study will be of interest not only to those who wish to learn more about Welsh-Australians but also students and the general reader interested in the social history of Wales and women's history.

235 **Welsh fever: Welsh activities in the United States and Canada today.**
David Greenslade. Cowbridge, Wales: D. Brown & Son, 1986. 303p.
illus.

A descriptive account of the spectrum of Welsh activities regularly organised by over 100 Welsh and Celtic organisations in the United States and Canada. The book includes detailed descriptions of the principal Welsh organisations in North America such as the National Gymanfa Ganu Association as well as a directory of Welsh contacts in North America arranged by state (United States) and province (Canada). The data for this study was collected as a result of a 23,000-mile journey undertaken by the author between 1982 and 1983. The book is aimed at Welsh people living in North America and the people of Wales and elsewhere who wish to gain a better understanding of the ethnic activities of Welsh Americans.

236 **The Welsh in America: letters from the immigrants.**
Edited by Alan Conway. Minneapolis, Minnesota: University of Minnesota Press, 1981. 341p. bibliog.

No accurate figures exist regarding the number of Welsh people who emigrated to the United States during the nineteenth century but it is believed to be well in excess of 100,000. The collection of letters reproduced here shows the influence of America on Welsh immigrants. Most of the letters were published in Welsh-language weeklies and monthlies but have been translated for this volume; passages which have no bearing on the United States have been removed. The appearance of these letters (in which the writers share their anxieties and hopes, their despair and happiness) in the newspapers and periodicals read by their compatriots had a considerable influence upon emigration from Wales to the United States during the nineteenth century. The editor has organised the letters by themes such as the voyage, farming and coal mining.

237 **The Welsh in the United States.**
Elwyn T. Ashton. Hove, England: Caldra House, 1984. 182p. illus. maps.

Although the number of Welsh people who emigrated from Wales to America bears no resemblance to the large exodus from Ireland and Scotland, nevertheless the number of Welsh societies in the United States today testifies that their numbers were quite significant. This book traces various groups of Welsh emigrants to North America from the seventeenth century onwards. It also includes a section of short biographies on Welsh-Americans who have contributed towards the development of the American nation.

Languages and Dialects

General

238 **A list of books, articles etc. concerning various aspects of the Celtic languages received at the National Library of Wales. . .**
Gareth O. Watts. *Studia Celtica*, vol. 10/11 (1975/76), p. 419-25; vol. 12/13 (1977/78), p. 416-29; vol. 14/15 (1979/80), p. 392-404; vol. 16/17 (1981/82), p. 324-35; vol. 18/19 (1983/84), p. 330-47; vol. 20/21 (1985/86), p. 232-51; and vol. 22/23 (1987/88), p. 214-26.

A checklist of books, periodical articles etc. discussing linguistic and socio-linguistic studies of the Celtic languages. The list includes materials written in Welsh and other Celtic languages, as well as in English.

239 **Llyfryddiaeth yr iaith Gymraeg.** (Bibliography of the Welsh language). Compiled by Marian Beech Hughes, and edited by J. E. Caerwyn Williams. Cardiff: University of Wales Press, 1988. 238p.

A Welsh-language publication which represents the standard bibliography of Welsh-language studies. Commissioned by the Language and Literature Committee of the Board of Celtic Studies, it is intended for students and scholars of the Welsh language. The bibliography consists of over 3,500 entries including books, periodical articles and dissertations. Although the majority of the items were written in Welsh, other Celtic languages or English, it also includes materials written in French, German and other European languages. The volume also includes items on the Indo-European and Celtic origins of the Welsh language as well as short sections on the Irish, Gaelic, Manx, British, Cornish, and Breton languages.

240 **Papurau Gwaith Ieithyddol Cymraeg Caerdydd. Cardiff Working Papers in Welsh Linguistics.**
Cardiff: National Museum of Wales (Welsh Folk Museum), 1981-. annual.

This learned journal, produced jointly by the Welsh Language Research Unit at the University College Cardiff and the Department of Dialects at the Welsh Folk Museum, Cardiff, provides a forum for recent research into Welsh linguistic. It covers aspects such as phonetics, phonology, syntax, sociolinguistics and dialectology. The publication is aimed at students and scholars of Welsh linguistic studies and includes articles in English and Welsh.

241 **Studia Celtica.**
Cardiff: University of Wales Press on behalf of the Board of Celtic Studies of the University of Wales, 1966-. biennial.

A learned journal devoted mainly to philological and linguistic studies of the Celtic languages. English is the main language of the contributions, although the journal's editorial policy is to accept materials in any of the Celtic languages, as well as French and German. In addition to articles, this periodical also publishes book reviews, book lists, obituaries and news items.

242 **Welsh and English in contemporary Wales: sociolinguistic issues.**
Nikolas Coupland, Martin J. Ball. *Contemporary Wales*, vol. 3 (1989), p. 7-40.

A review of recent studies on socio-linguistics studies of the Welsh and English languages in Wales. A major features of the work is that it includes a substantial bibliography of recent publications in the field.

History and present position of the Welsh language

243 **A cauldron of rebirth: population and the Welsh language in the nineteenth century.**
Brinley Thomas. *Welsh History Review. Cylchgrawn Hanes Cymru*, vol. 13, no. 4 (1987), p. 418-37.

This article is a revised version of the 1985-86 O'Donnell lecture, delivered at several constituent colleges of the University of Wales during the academic year, in which the author disputes the orthodox view of historians that industrialisation was a powerful Anglicising force in nineteenth-century Wales. Thomas shows that there was a thriving cultural life conducted through the Welsh language in the new industrial communities of Wales during the second half of the nineteenth century and that industrialisation played a crucial part in making the language a dynamic force in the land during the final decades of the nineteenth century. The main thesis of Thomas's study is that the main turning points in the fortunes of the language came during the first two decades of the twentieth century, when a flood of over 100,000 people moved into the industrial areas from outside Wales, and then the Welsh economy collapsed after the end of World War I.

244 Culture in crisis: the future of the Welsh language.
Clive Betts. Upton, (Wirral) England: Ffynnon Press, 1976. 243p. illus. maps.

This book is the result of a journalist's investigation into the state of the Welsh language in the mid-1970s and much of the findings appeared originally in a series of ten articles in the *Western Mail* during April 1975. Betts describes the use of the Welsh language in various fields such as broadcasting and the press and also discusses its chances of survival. In the final section, the author draws up a set of policies in the fields of education, industry and commerce and local government which should be adopted by the various linguistic zones in Wales. Although written for the non-specialist and somewhat superficial in its analysis, the list of proposals for language survival provides stimulating material for those concerned with the fate of the language.

245 Culture, language and territory.
Harold Carter. London: British Broadcasting Corporation, 1988. 38p.

This paper was originally delivered as the BBC Wales Annual Radio Lecture and provides an important overview of the history and geography of the Welsh language. In the first part, the author considers the general relationship between culture, language and territory and then proceeds to discuss the importance of the Welsh language in maintaining a distinct Welsh identity. The significance of different historical periods on the status and fate of the language is dealt with and the author also assesses the different reactions of Welsh people to the decline of the language.

246 The decline of the Celtic languages: a study of linguistic and cultural conflict in Scotland, Wales and Ireland from the Reformation to the twentieth century.
Victor Edward Durkacz. Edinburgh: John Donald, 1983. 258p. maps. bibliog.

A comparative study of the history of Scottish Gaelic, Irish and Welsh from the sixteenth century onwards, with special reference to the position of these languages in the fields of education, religion and literature. This is a thematic, rather than a chronological, survey and so the author is able to compare the reasons for the decline of the three languages during the period covered.

247 The dragon's tongue: the fortunes of the Welsh language.
Gerald Morgan. Cardiff: Triskel Press, 1966. 144p. illus.

A popular introduction for non-specialists to the history of the Welsh language with special reference to its legal status and its place in education, together with details of the struggle to improve conditions for the language during the 1960s. Much has happened during the twenty-five years since this book was published, particularly the continuation and intensification of the direct action campaigns by the Welsh Language Society and the establishment of other organisations and institutions to foster the language. Nevertheless, this book does provide the general reader with a readable introduction to the history of the language up to the mid-1960s.

Languages and Dialects. History and present position of the Welsh language

248 **Dyfodol i'r iaith Gymraeg. A future for the Welsh language.**
Council for the Welsh Language.   Cardiff: HMSO, 1978. 78p.
In view of the concern expressed by many people in Wales regarding the future of the Welsh language, as well as criticism about the failure of the Government to respond adequately to this crisis, the Secretary of State for Wales established the Council for the Welsh Language during the 1970s to investigate what action should be taken to foster the language in various fields. This bilingual report lists recommendations to the Secretary of State which would form the basis of a policy to foster the Welsh language. The view of the report was that the Government should give a lead and not follow public opinion on the issue. The report includes the results of an investigation which showed that there was widespread support for the language amongst the Welsh population. The members of the Council urged that the following areas should be given priority to ensure the language's survival; education, broadcasting, publishing, the environment and planning.

249 **Language and history in early Britain: a chronological survey of the Brittonic languages from the first to the twelfth century A.D.**
Kenneth Jackson.   Edinburgh: Edinburgh University Press, 1953.
752p. (Edinburgh University Publications. Language and Literature: no. 4).
This is the standard analysis of the sound-system of the British language and its descendants, Welsh, Cornish and Breton, from the early period of the Roman occupation of Britain to the end of the eleventh century. It is an indispensable volume for scholars and students studying the phonology of the British language and the history and development of early Welsh.

250 **Language areas and changes, c.1750-1981.**
W.T.R. Pryce.   In: *Glamorgan county history vol. VI: Glamorgan society 1780-1980*. Edited by Prys Morgan. Cardiff: Glamorgan History Trust, 1988, p. 265-313.
A detailed examination of the linguistic geography of Glamorgan from pre-industrial times to the present day. This is an important contribution to an understanding of the history of the long-term changes concerning the language in the context of the size of the county and the spread of industrialisation to much of Glamorgan from the second half of the eighteenth century onwards. The article also includes a large number of maps which provide graphic representations of the linguistic changes taking place.

251 **Language contact and language change in Wales, 1901-1971: a study in historical geolinguistics.**
Colin H. Williams.   *Welsh History Review. Cylchgrawn Hanes Cymru*, vol. 10, no. 2 (1980), p. 207-38.
The total number and the percentage of Welsh speakers living in Wales declined dramatically during the first seventy years of the twentieth century. Although much has been written about the decline, this article is the first one which provides a scholarly examination of the main stages in language change through a geolinguistic analysis of the language censuses held between 1901 and 1971. The main focus of the study is the nature of the demographic and spatial changes within the Welsh-speaking population rather than the causes of the decline.

Languages and Dialects. History and present position of the Welsh language

252 **Language, ethnicity, and education in Wales.**
Bud B. Khleif.   The Hague: Mouton, 1980. 331p. bibliog.
(Contributions to the Sociology of Language, no. 23).
Presents the findings of an investigation into the core position of language in ethnicity and national identity, using Wales and the Welsh language as a case study. Although the study looks at the whole field of Welsh cultural resurgence, the main theme is the rôle that schools can play as an agency in cultural regeneration, with particular reference to the position in Wales.

253 **New domains of the Welsh language: education, planning and the law.**
Colin H. Williams.   *Contemporary Wales*, vol. 3 (1989), p. 41-76.
Attempts to analyse the structural changes taking place in the Welsh-speaking population and evaluates the impact that education, planning and the law are having in extending the use of the language into previously under-developed domains. Asserts that, in order to avoid marginalising the language during the near future, it will be imperative for it to expand from its present domains to become a fully institutionalised language in Welsh society.

254 **Non-violence and the development of the Welsh Language Society, c.1962-c.1974.**
Colin H. Williams.   *Welsh History Review. Cylchgrawn Hanes Cymru*, vol. 8, no. 4 (1977), p. 426-55.
The Welsh Language Society was established in 1962 as a pressure group to safeguard the Welsh language because of the dissatisfaction of a number of Welsh people regarding the effectiveness of conventional political campaigns to save the language. The author assesses the achievements and the problems of the Society between 1962 and 1974 following its decision to adopt non-violent direct action tactics to promote the cause of the language. Williams concludes that the Society has been largely responsible for making the language a 'key political factor' in Welsh politics.

255 **The old British tongue: the vernacular in Wales 1540-1640.**
R. Brinley Jones.   Cardiff: Avalon Books, 1970. 127p. bibliog.
An essay on the semantic problems facing the Welsh language during the second half of the sixteenth century and how these problems were resolved during the following one hundred years by a group of distinguished Welsh scholars. It also describes relevant aspects of the vernacular movement elsewhere, in order to provide the reader with a more complete understanding of the developments which took place in Wales.

256 **The sociology of Welsh.**
Edited by Glyn Williams.   *International Journal of the Sociology of Language*. vol. 66 (1987). 127p.
A special issue of the this journal which contains a collection of scholarly articles on the socio-linguistics of the Welsh language.

257 **The survival of the Welsh language after the Union of England and Wales: the first phase, 1536-1642.**
W. Ogwen Williams. *Welsh History Review. Cylchgrawn Hanes Cymru*, vol. 2, no. 1 (1964), p. 67-93.

Despite the geographic proximity of Wales to England, and the fact that the country was incorporated with England through the Act of Union of 1536, the Welsh language remains the mother tongue for many of the Welsh people. In this article, which was originally delivered as a lecture at the Congress of Celtic Studies held in Cardiff in 1963, the author outlines the main factors and circumstances which secured the survival of the language during the first 100 years after the passing of the Act of Union. Williams offers four reasons for its survival: the economy of Wales was chiefly agrarian and the country was relatively remote and isolated; Wales did not pose any military or political threat to its neighbour; state support for Protestanism permitted a Welsh translation of the Bible; and finally the status bestowed on the language by distinguished Welsh Renaissance scholars.

258 **The use of Welsh: a contribution to sociolinguistics.**
Edited by Martin J. Ball. Clevedon, Philadelphia: Multilingual Matters, 1988. 341p. bibliog. (Multilingual Matters, no. 36).

A collection of essays by specialists which explores the variations in the pattern of the use of the Welsh language today as determined by regional, social and stylistic factors. The book is arranged into six parts, namely: linguistic variations in Welsh; different levels of language; dialect studies; non-geographical varieties of Welsh; an examination of the use made of the Welsh language by children, and finally a discussion of the implications of integrating varying patterns of language use into grammatical descriptions. The collection will be of interest to the interested layman as well as socio-linguists and Celtic scholars.

259 **Welsh and English in Wales, 1750-1971: a spatial analysis based on the linguistic affiliation of parochial communities.**
W. T. R. Pryce. *Bulletin of the Board of Celtic Studies*, vol. 28, no. 1 (Nov. 1978), p. 1-36.

A detailed survey of geo-linguistics in Wales from 1750 to 1971 based chiefly on records of the language of worship in parish churches kept by Welsh dioceses during the eighteenth and nineteenth centuries. On the basis of such records, the author concludes that Wales was overwhelmingly Welsh in speech at least until the end of the mid-nineteenth century. The article itself and the accompanying maps illustrate the distinctive language areas and zones of Wales in the mid-eighteenth and nineteenth centuries.

260 **The Welsh language: a strategy for the future.**
Welsh Language Board. Cardiff: Welsh Language Board, 1989. 12p.

The Welsh Language Board was established by the Central Government in 1988 to advise the Secretary of State for Wales on matters relating to the Welsh language. This report presents the strategy recommended by members of the Board for the period 1989 to 1994 with details of aims, objectives and targets proposed by the Board.

Languages and Dialects. History and present position of the Welsh language

261 **Welsh language and Wales.**
Office of Population Censuses and Surveys. Census 1981.
London: HMSO, 1983. 50p.
Presents statistics which analyse the number of people living in Wales and over the age of three who were able to speak and read Welsh at the time of the 1981 official census. The statistical tables offer details of Welsh-speakers and Welsh readers by counties, districts and wards, by age and by sex. The volume also provides comparative tables of the proportion of Welsh-speakers for each census between 1921 and 1981.

262 **The Welsh language in the policy process.**
Peter Madgwick, Phillip Rawkins. In: *The territorial dimension in United Kingdom politics.* Edited by Peter Madgwick, Richard Rose. London: Macmillan, 1982, p. 67-99.
An examination of the response of pressure groups to the decline of the Welsh language and how they have tried to influence central government's policies and attitudes towards the language issue. The study considers the issue as seen from London as well as by those who are determined to safeguard the interests of the Welsh language.

263 **The Welsh language movement.**
Dafydd Glyn Jones. In: *The Welsh language today.* Edited by Meic Stephens. Llandysul, Wales: Gomer Press, 1979, p. 287-357.
A comprehensive survey of the aims and activities of public and private bodies established to safeguard and promote the Welsh language from the sixteenth century to the mid-1970s, with particular emphasis on the 1960s and 1970s.

264 **The Welsh language today.**
Edited by Meic Stephens. Llandysul, Wales: Gomer Press, 1979. new ed. 369p. bibliog.
The collection of essays in this volume provide information written by subject specialists about the position of the Welsh language within many facets of Welsh life for example, education, religion, journalism, broadcasting, law, publishing and government. Although the essays were intended to describe the position of the Welsh language during the 1970s, many also include an insight into the historical background. Since this revised edition was published, a number of major changes to the position of the language have taken place vis-à-vis activities such as broadcasting and education and therefore the work should be consulted with care. Nevertheless, it remains the best overview of the position of the language in Welsh life today.

265 **The Welsh language 1961-1981: an interpretative atlas.**
J. W. Aitchison, Harold Carter. Cardiff: University of Wales Press, 1985. 47p. maps.
This study, which is based on an analysis of the census returns, provides an interpretation of the changes which have taken place in the geography of the Welsh language in the twenty years between 1961 and 1981, together with an overview of the historical development of the language and its distribution pattern. A major feature of the publication is the series of maps which provide a graphic display of the linguistic changes analysed in the main text. This study provides a valuable contribution to an

understanding of the present condition of the language. It also evaluates the impact of the action taken in recent years to promote the use of Welsh in various fields, such as education and broadcasting, in the context of the distribution of Welsh-speakers.

Dictionaries

266 **Y geiriadur Cymraeg cyfoes. The dictionary of modern Welsh.**
H. Meurig Evans. Llandybie, Wales: Hughes a'i Fab, 1981. 611p.
A bi-lingual Welsh-English, English-Welsh dictionary of Welsh words in modern usage including technical terms recently coined by panels of the Welsh Joint Education Committee and of the University of Wales. The volume also includes lists of personal names, place-names, names of animals, birds, fish, plants and fruit as well as English translations of the most common Welsh proverbs. This dictionary is a useful tool for translating from one language to the other.

267 **Y geiriadur mawr. The complete Welsh-English, English-Welsh dictionary.**
H. Meurig Williams, W. O. Thomas. Llandybie, Wales: Christopher Davies, & Gwasg Gomer, 1989. 15th. ed. 367p.
This volume is generally recognised to be the standard bi-lingual Welsh-English dictionary and it is used extensively in schools, colleges, offices, libraries and the home. In addition to the main sections, the volume also includes Welsh-English and English-Welsh glossaries of personal names, place-names, animals, birds, fish, plants, flowers and fruits. An indispensable reference tool for those who wish to understand the meaning of a Welsh word, or who need to translate from Welsh to English, or vice versa.

268 **Geiriadur Prifysgol Cymru. A dictionary of the Welsh language.**
Cardiff: University of Wales Press, 1950-. In progress. Already published in separate parts:- Pts. 1-40, A- NAF. Also published in hardback form:- Vol. 1: A-Ffysur (parts 1-21 of the initial publication); Vol. 2: G-Llys. (parts 22-36 of the initial publication).
This standard dictionary of the vocabulary of the Welsh language from earliest times to the present day is published on behalf of the University of Wales Board of Celtic Studies. The dictionary provides various forms and meanings together with the English equivalent and etymology of 'all words in literary and colloquial use, a selection of the technical terms of the arts and sciences, and those obsolete or archaic words in the development of the language'. Apart from a brief introductory note on the coverage of the dictionary and the content and arrangement of individual entries, which are provided in both Welsh and English, the language of the dictionary is entirely Welsh except for English-language equivalents which are given in the body of the entries.

269 **Geiriadur termau. Dictionary of terms.**
 Editor: Jac L. Williams.   Cardiff: University of Wales Press, 1987.
 544p.

This work was originally published on behalf of the Technical Terms Committee of the Board of Celtic Studies in 1973. During the past few decades there has been an increase in the use of the Welsh language as a medium of instruction in secondary schools as well as for business and administrative purposes. Consequently, there has been a growing demand for standard forms of technical terms in various disciplines. This English-Welsh, Welsh-English dictionary of technical terms is an important contribution to the use of the language in these spheres of activity. The dictionary also includes a short description of how the problem of developing an adequate collection of technical terms was tackled in Wales.

Grammars

270 **A Welsh grammar.**
 Stephen J. Williams.   Cardiff: University of Wales Press, 1980. 184p.

This book, produced by a distinguished Welsh linguistic scholar, provides the student with a grammar of the standard literary Welsh of today with particular emphasis on accidence and syntax. It has been written for the non-Welsh speaking student who wishes to study the Welsh language.

271 **A grammar of middle Welsh.**
 D. Simon Evans.   Dublin: Dublin Institute for Advanced Studies,
 1976. 268p.

A general grammar of the Welsh language from the twelfth to the fourteenth centuries, written for scholars and students of medieval Welsh language and literature. In addition to the description of the phonology, morphology and syntax of the language, the author has prepared an introductory essay on the present state of medieval Welsh scholarship.

Dialects

272 **A bibliography of research on Welsh dialects since 1934.**
 G. M. Awbery.   In: *Papurau gwaith ieithyddol Cymraeg Caerdydd.*
 Cardiff Working Papers in Welsh Linguistics, no. 2 (1982), p. 103-19.

A bibliography of 171 items on research into Welsh dialects conducted since 1934. The work includes lists of published materials such as books and articles, and unpublished materials such as theses and reports. The items are arranged alphabetically by author with a subect index.

273 **The linguistic geography of Wales: a contribution to Welsh dialectology.**
Alan R. Thomas. Cardiff: University of Wales Press for the Board of
Celtic Studies, 1973. 558p. maps. bibliog.

A general survey of the dialects of the Welsh language which is based on an
investigation into the geographical distribution of a large number of words. The
researchers involved in the survey interviewed inhabitants at various points throughout
Wales which still retain some indigenous spoken Welsh. The data collected is
illustrated by means of a series of distribution maps with annotations. The information
collected and analysed is used to illustrate the major speech areas which emerge from
the survey.

Teaching Welsh

274 **Cwrs Cymraeg llafar. Conversational Welsh course.**
Dan L. James. Llandybie, Wales: Christopher Davies, 1970-72.
2 vols. (Welsh Learners Series).

An oral course, consisting of sixty-one units, for learning and practising Welsh at home
and in class. Each unit is made up of the following components: a short dialogue in
Welsh and parallel English version; pattern practice; vocabulary; relevant grammar;
self-corrective exercises; and creative use of the patterns and the vocabulary
introduced in the unit. The book also includes a guide to Welsh pronunciation and a
table of the mutation rules. Two sound records are also available to assist learners with
pronunciation.

275 **Living Welsh.**
T. J. Rhys Jones. London: Hodder & Stoughton, 1977. 445p. (Teach
Yourself Books).

A practical manual designed to enable a non-Welsh speaker to understand the
language, and which places an emphasis on learning spoken Welsh. The main section
of the book consists of twenty-one lessons with each lesson divided into five sections:
sentence structure; pattern practices; vocabulary; conversations; and questions. The
book also includes a short guide to pronunciation and mutations. The appendices
consist of a note on regional differences, on gender and on the mutation system as well
as a Welsh-English, English-Welsh word list.

276 **Llyfryddiaeth dysgu'r Gymraeg yn ail iaith 1961-1981.**
Helen Prosser. Aberystwyth, Wales: Centre for Research into Welsh
for Adults, University College of Wales, Aberystwyth (A bibliography
of learning Welsh as a second language 1961-81.)

An annotated bibliography in Welsh of over 1,000 entries – books, periodical articles,
pamphlets, work cards and other items – on aspects of teaching Welsh as a second
language published between 1961 and 1981. The aim of the publication is to assist
teachers, researchers, language advisers and others interested in the field of teaching
Welsh as a second language. Most of the items are either written in the Welsh language
or in English.

Place-names

277 A gazetteer of Welsh place-names. Rhestr o enwau lleoedd.
Edited by Elwyn Davies.   Cardiff: University of Wales Press, 1975.
3rd. ed. 119p.

This standard guide to Welsh place-names was prepared by the Language and Literature Committee of the Board of Celtic Studies. In the preface to the book, the editor explains that 'the main aim of the publication is to serve as a guide to the orthography of Welsh place-names with its function as a gazetteer only a secondary matter'. The book attempts to include the Welsh names of all towns and parishes and the chief villages, railway stations, post offices and natural features. The names of farm houses are only given if they have some historical or literary interest. It also includes a glossary of the chief elements in Welsh place-names to assist non-Welsh speakers to gain a better understanding of the meaning of place-names in Wales.

278 Non-Celtic place-names in Wales.
B. G. Charles.   London: London Medieval Studies, University College of London, 1938. 326p.

A scholarly survey of place-names found in Wales of English, French, Flemish and Scandinavian origin. The arrangement of the entries follows that of the English Place-names Society. The volume also includes an introductory essay which explains the historical background that brought these foreign elements into Welsh place-names.

279 Place-names.
Gwynedd Pierce.   In: *Settlement and society in Wales*. Edited by D. Huw Owen.   Cardiff: University of Wales Press, 1989, p. 73-94.

A scholarly contribution which demonstrates the value of place-name evidence to the historian, together with an account of the techniques and methodology used for their interpretation. The examples employed to illustrate their value are taken from Welsh place-names.

280 The place-names of Dinas Powys hundred.
Gwynedd O. Pierce.   Cardiff: University of Wales Press on behalf of the Board of Celtic Studies, University of Wales, 1978. 359p. map.

Only a handful of detailed regional studies of Welsh place-names have been published to date. This study of the place and field names of a compact and linguistically mixed area in the county of Glamorgan is the best example of those that have been published.

281 Place-names on maps of Scotland and Wales.
Southampton, England: Ordnance Survey, 1973. 23p.

Part III of this slim booklet is a glossary of the most common Welsh-language elements used on the maps of Wales. The list was compiled with the assistance of the Language and Literature Committee of the Board of Celtic Studies. The booklet also provides information for non-Welsh speakers on pronunciation, and the accent and consonant changes which occur in the Welsh language.

282 **Welsh administrative and territorial units: medieval and modern.**
Melville Richards. Cardiff: University of Wales Press, 1969. 324p.
maps.

The main purpose of this reference book is to aid scholars and others, to locate and
identify large and small territorial units dating from medieval and modern times and
also to provide a 'standardised form of spelling for Welsh names'. To assist the reader
to locate the place-names listed in the text, the book also contains over 100 maps.

The English language in Wales

283 **English in Wales: diversity, conflict and change.**
Edited by Nikolas Coupland in association with Alan R. Thomas.
Clevedon (Philadelphia), Pennsylvania: Multilingual Matters, 1990.
295p. illus. bibliog. (Multilingual Matters, no. 52).

An important collection of community dialect surveys of the English language in
Wales. It includes analysis of the English spoken in Port Talbot, Cardiff, Abercrave,
Glamorgan, north-Carmarthenshire and south-Pembrokeshire as well as more general
treatments on the social meaning of Welsh-English and standard Welsh-English.

284 **Welsh English.**
Alan R. Thomas. In: *Language in the British Isles*. Edited by P.
Trudgill. Cambridge: Cambridge University Press, 1984, p. 178-94.

This essay begins with a general overview of the two main English dialect models
found in Wales – the South Wales model and the North Wales model – with an
explanation of their main features and what factors have influenced their particular
structures. This is followed by an examination of South Wales English since this is the
variety spoken by the majority of the population. The English spoken by the
inhabitants of the upper Swansea Valley is used as the example for detailed analysis.

285 **Welsh language and the English language.**
Roland Mathias. In: *The Welsh language today*. Edited by Meic
Stephens. Llandysul, Wales: Gomer Press, 1973, p. 32-63.

An essay which outlines the history of the English language and the Welsh language in
Wales from medieval times to the present day, and traces the retreat of the Welsh
language in certain areas. The author then claims that much more has to be done to
assess the requirements of the English-speaking majority in a bilingual Wales.

Religion

Historical

286 **Ann Griffiths.**
A. M. Allchin. Cardiff: University of Wales Press for the Welsh Arts Council, 1976. 72p. bibliog. (Writers of Wales Series).
A study of the work of Ann Griffiths (1776-1805), one of Wales' foremost hymn writers, and an assessment of her place in the Welsh religious literary tradition.

287 **A bibliography of Welsh hymnology to 1960.**
H. Turner Evans. [Caernarfon], Wales: Welsh Library Association, 1977. 206p. bibliog.
This list of Welsh hymn writers up to 1960, together with their works, the first lines of some of their most famous, or popular, hymns is followed by references to relevant books, periodicals and manuscripts. Each hymn writer is introduced by means of a short biographical note and all of the entries are arranged alphabetically. Useful listings of bardic names and pseudonyms are included and the preliminary bibliography is a particularly useful listing of materials relating to this significant genre in Wales.

288 **Chapels in the Valley: a study in the sociology of Welsh nonconformity.**
D. Ben Rees. Upton (Merseyside), England: The Ffynnon Press, 1975. 222p.
A study of religion in the post-Industrial Revolution period in the industrial valleys of South Wales, concentrating on the chapels, their structure, rôle, functions and activities. Further consideration is given to the predominant influences on religious and cultural life and to some of the outstanding personalities of the period. The study is also significant for its treatment of the decline of Welsh nonconformity in industrial areas.

289 **Daniel Rowland and the great evangelical awakening in Wales.**
Eifion Evans.   Edinburgh: Banner of Truth Trust, 1985. 391p.
Presents a major study of religion in eighteenth-century Wales, a period noted for its
evangelical missions and revivals, through an analysis of one of the dominating
influences, Daniel Rowland (1711-90).

290 **Disestablishment in Ireland and Wales.**
P. M. H. Bell.   London: SPCK, 1969. 392p. maps. bibliog.
A study which seeks to explain the background to the controversy surrounding the
disestablishment of the Anglican church in Wales, an issue which dominated Welsh
religious life for decades prior to, and subsequent to, the formal disestablishment in
1914. Chapters 7-9 relate specifically to Wales and indicate how bitter controversies
permeated Welsh political, cultural, social and religious life.

291 **The fire in the thatch.**
Pennar Davies.   In: *Anatomy of Wales*. Edited by R. Brinley Jones.
Peterston-super-Ely, Wales: Gwerin Publications, 1972, p. 105-16.
An essay tracing the predominant periods and issues in the history of religion in Wales,
from its Celtic origins to the present day. The work includes an assessment of
contemporary trends, noting the significant influences and personalities. Davies
provides an introductory framework and context which would be particularly useful for
readers having little, or no, awareness of Welsh religious life and its literature.

292 **The great awakening in Wales.**
Derec Llwyd Morgan.   London: Epworth Press, 1988. 323p.
An English translation by Dyfnallt Morgan of *Y Diwygiad Mawr*, 'a composite study of
the beginnings, the psychology, the theology, the spiritual and social aspirations, and
the literary imagination of the eighteenth century Methodist Revival in Wales'. This is
a study in two parts 'history and development', a chronological study, and 'thought and
imagination' which relates to literary output, the hymn writers, such as Ann Griffiths
and William Williams as well as other literary figures and their work and influence.

293 **A history of the Church in Wales.**
Edited by David Walker.   Penarth, Wales: Church in Wales
Publications, 1976. 221p. bibliog.
A collection of essays by prominent church historians and religious scholars, tracing
the history of the Church. It is arranged chronologically and covers the age of the
saints, the medieval period and the Middle Ages, the Reformation, the period 1670-
1730 (when its relations with dissenting movements were particularly significant), the
eighteenth century, the Industrial Revolution, the nineteenth century, and the years up
to the period of disestablishment. This is a most useful work, providing an introduction
and an insight into significant events and issues.

294 **A history of the Church in Wales in the twentieth century.**
D. T. W. Price.   Penarth, Wales: Church in Wales Publications, 1990.
75p.
A short history in the form of a chronology with commentary, which also incorporates
a brief account of the disestablishment campaign. Useful appendices include: a

description of the organization of the Church in Wales; a list of dioceses in Wales; and a list of the Archbishops of Wales since 1920.

295 Literature, religion, and society in Wales 1660-1730.
Geraint H. Jenkins.   Cardiff: University of Wales Press, 1978. 351p. bibliog.

An important study of the religious and spiritual life of Wales in the period from the Restoration to the Methodist era. It is based on a detailed study of the religious literature of the period, and of authors and authorship, printing and the publishing trade, subscribers and book owners.

296 The monastic order in South Wales 1066- 1349.
F. G. Cowley.   Cardiff: University of Wales Press, 1986. 317p.

First published in 1977, this major work traces a period of great religious reform and intellectual ferment in Wales associated with the monastic orders. It includes a study of the activities of the monks, and it offers an assessment of their contribution to the development of agriculture and the economy of Wales, and their influence on cultural, intellectual and religious life.

297 Morgan Llwyd.
M. Wynn Thomas.   Cardiff: University of Wales Press on behalf of the Welsh Arts Council, 1984. 85p. bibliog. (Writers of Wales Series).

A study of an eminent religious and literary figure of the seventeenth century who exercised a predominant influence on Welsh Puritanism and religion in this period.

298 Religion and society in the nineteenth century.
E. T. Davies.   Llandybie, Wales: Christopher Davies, 1981. 102p. bibliog. (A New History of Wales Series).

A study of the growth of nonconformity and nonconformist denominations, the conflict with the established church, and the predominant influences of the period.

299 Religion in the Industrial Revolution in South Wales.
E. T. Davies.   Cardiff: University of Wales Press, 1962. 202p.

Examines the growth of nonconformity in the industrial areas of South Wales from the second half of the eighteenth century to the end of World War I, a period of rapid economic, social and cultural change. The study also traces the polarisation of society into social groups, economic groups and cultural groups, and the way in which religious life also reflected the major divisions within society.

300 The religious census of 1851: a calendar of the returns relating to Wales, Vol I: South Wales.
Edited by Ieuan Gwynedd Jones, David Williams.   Cardiff: University of Wales Press, 1976. 698p.

A transcription, with an introduction to place the census in its historical context, of the returns of the 1851 census – 'the only occasion in modern times when there was an official and comprehensive count of the accommodation, available for, and the actual attendance at religious worship'. A source of primary importance to historians of religion, society and education in Wales.

301 **The religious census of 1851: a calendar of the returns relating to Wales, Vol II: North Wales.**
Edited by Ieuan Gwynedd Jones, David Williams.   Cardiff: University of Wales Press, 1981. 438p.
A companion volume, on the same pattern, to that for South Wales published in 1976.

302 **The settlements of the Celtic saints in Wales.**
E. G. Bowen.   Cardiff: University of Wales Press, 1956. 175p. maps. bibliog.
A study of the beginnings of Christianity in Wales which is based upon studies of the prehistoric period and on cultural anthropology. Particularly interesting and significant are the investigations of detailed sitings of early Christian Churches and the resultant human settlements that grew around them.

303 **'They thought for themselves': a brief look at the story of Unitarianism and the liberal tradition in Wales and beyond its borders.**
D. Elwyn Davies.   Llandysul, Wales: Gwasg Gomer, 1982. 185p. maps.
A concise history of Unitarianism in Wales. Unitarianism was a small but significant nonconformist movement in the religious life of the country, and this is the first history of the movement in Wales written in English. Sections are devoted to the origins of Unitarianism in Wales, to studies of individual causes and chapels, to wider missionary activity, and to an assessment of the lives and work of prominent personalities within the movement.

304 **Traditions of the Welsh saints.**
Elissa R. Henken.   Cambridge: D. S. Brewer, 1987. 368p.
A systematic study of fifty Welsh saints and the major traditions associated with them, with references to sources – mainly recorded narrative. The patron saint of Wales, St. David, is among those who are studied in this original and interesting work.

305 **The Welsh Baptists.**
T. M. Bassett.   Swansea, Wales: Ilston House, 1977. 414p. bibliog.
This is the standard history of the Baptist nonconformist denomination in Wales. It is an English translation of a work originally published in Welsh and is the only modern standard history of any of the Welsh denominations published in English. Works for other denominations are only available in Welsh as are the vast majority of studies of individual causes and chapels. This volume is a comprehensive study from the early seventeenth-century beginnings of the movement which lay in Puritanism up to 1930. Major emphasis is placed on tracing chronologically the expansion in the work of the Baptists in Wales during the nineteenth century.

306 **The Welsh church from Conquest to Reformation.**
Glanmor Williams.   Cardiff: University of Wales Press, 1962. 602p. bibliog.
An outstanding historical study of religion in Wales during the period between 1283 and 1536, with a short introduction outlining the significant events from 1070 to 1282.

Religion. Historical

The work is divided into two main parts – a study of the period 1283 to the Glyndwr rebellion of 1400, and an examination of the pre-Reformation period in Wales. This volume is rather more than simply a religious history since it also has seminal studies devoted to literature, art, architecture, the economy of Wales and to social history.

307 **The Welsh Elizabethan Catholic martyrs.**
Edited by D. Aneurin Thomas. Cardiff: University of Wales Press, 1971. 331p.

A study, quoting extensively from contemporary evidence and documents, of significant episodes and events in the religious life of Wales during the reign of Elizabeth I. This was a period of great strife between Protestants and Catholics, and a period of controversy, violence and persecution. The study pays particular attention to the lives of Richard Gwyn and William Davies, both Roman Catholics, and both put to death for their beliefs.

308 **Welsh Reformation essays.**
Glanmor Williams. Cardiff: University of Wales Press, 1967. 212p.

Presents nine important essays on various subjects relating to the Reformation in Wales – including area studies, studies of prominent religious and literary figures, and the impact of the Reformation on the monastic economy.

309 **The Welsh revival of 1904.**
Eifion Evans. Bridgend, Wales: Evangelical Press of Wales, 1969. 213p. maps.

Welsh religious nonconformist history is characterized by revivalist episodes, and this study describes and analyses the most recent such episode, and the only one in the twentieth century. It was undoubtedly the most turbulent period in modern Welsh religious life, and this study gives particular attention to the rôle of Evan Roberts, the principal revivalist and evangelist, and the subject of considerable controversy.

310 **The Welsh saints 1640-1660.**
Geoffrey F. Nuttall. Cardiff: University of Wales Press, 1957. 93p.

Provides four studies of Puritanism in Wales, which examine its background and growth, three of its primary personalities (Walter Cradock, Vavasor Powell and Morgan Llwyd), and its impact on Welsh religious, social and political life.

311 **Williams Pantycelyn.**
Glyn Tegai Hughes. Cardiff: University of Wales Press on behalf of the Welsh Arts Council, 1983. 139p. (Writers of Wales Series).

A short study of Wales' foremost hymn writer who was also the most prolific prose writer of the eighteenth century and a major influence on the growth of Methodism.

312 **Yesterday in village church and churchyard.**
Donald Gregory. Llandysul, Wales: Gomer [n.d.]. 104p. bibliog.

A pictorial study of the history of churches and churchyards with detailed commentary, illustrating the many religious and social functions that they have performed. The vast majority of the illustrations are from Wales. The work is divided into short sections on early burial grounds, tithes, porches, yew trees, sanctuary, games, crosses, feasts, plays, markets and fairs, burials, festivals and social customs.

Contemporary

313 **Y Beibl yng Nghymru. The Bible in Wales.**
Aberystwyth, Wales: National Library of Wales, 1988. 93p.
A bilingual catalogue issued to accompany a major exhibition held at the National Library of Wales in 1988 to celebrate the 400th anniversary of the translation of the complete Bible into Welsh by Bishop William Morgan in 1588. A significant illustrated and annotated work outlining the contribution of translators, publishers and scholars.

314 **A Bible for Wales.**
Prys Morgan. Aberystwyth, Wales: Celebration National Committee, Gwasg Cambria, 1988. 65p.
A concise illustrated history of the translation of the Scriptures into Welsh, which includes a study of the motivation of the translators and an assessment of their contribution to the religious, literary and cultural life of Wales. The work was published as part of the celebrations held in Wales in 1988 to commemorate the first complete translation of the Bible into Welsh in 1588.

315 **Cardiff Province Directory and Year Book: Dioceses of Cardiff, Menevia and Wrexham.**
Cardiff: Cardiff Province, 1916-. annual.
The directory of the Roman Catholic Church in Wales, with five major sub-sections including Cardiff Province, its societies and institutions, the Archdiocese of Cardiff, the diocese of Menevia, the diocese of Wrexham, the Prayer of the Church and the Order for Mass. Each section with the exception of the last, is an alphabetical listing of churches, clergy, organisations, institutions and events, together with a list of significant dates and celebrations.

316 **The Church in Wales diocesan handbooks.**
[Cardiff]: Diocesan Offices. annual.
Each of the six diocese in Wales Bangor 1965-, Llandaff 1957-, Monmouth 1961-, St. Asaph 1863-, St. Davids 1929-, and Swansea and Brecon 1923- issue an annual handbook. They have a standard format and list similar information: names and addresses of officers and organisations; committees and bodies; establishments and representatives; as well as financial and other details relating to the management of the dioceses and individual churches.

317 **'Home again to Wales' the reflections of a visitor on the religion and culture of Wales, 1986-87.**
Gwyn Walters. Aberystwyth, Wales: Gwasg Cambria, 1987. 126p.
A controversial study of aspects of contemporary religion in Wales, written from an evangelical standpoint by a Welshman now resident in the United States. Walters records his research, as well as his impressions and observations following a period of study in Wales. He reflects upon contemporary preaching, the activity that takes place alongside preaching, presents observations on selected churches and reveals his conclusions on the state of religion, preachers, congregations, and church leaders. In addition, he assesses the contribution of the media and makes suggestions for achieving a religious renewal.

Religion. Contemporary

318 **The Methodist Church Handbook and Directory: the Cymru district.**
The Methodist Synod, 1852-. annual.
A list of committees, officers, representatives, sections, ministries and circuit stewards together with financial statements and membership statistics. Ministers, local preachers and chapels are also listed as well as other denominations, related organisations and bodies in Wales and outside. Originally published as *Dyddiadur* (Diary).

319 **The parish churches and nonconformist chapels of Wales: their records and where to find them. Volume one: Cardigan–Carmarthen–Pembroke.**
Bert J. Rawlins.   Salt Lake City, Utah: Celtic Heritage Trust, 1987. 648p.
The first volume in a proposed series of illustrated directories for Wales, primarily designed to assist Welsh genealogical research. It offers a source list of all parish churches and nonconformist chapels in each parish arranged alphabetically, and provides information about the history, location, denomination and availability of relevant records, published histories and documents for each.

320 **Prospects for Wales: from a census of the churches in 1982.**
Peter Brierley, Byron Evans.   London: Bible Society and MARC Europe, 1983. 64p.
Presents the tabulated results of a census held in 1982 (tabulated for each of the Welsh counties and for Wales as a whole) together with observations and commentary by representatives of each of the churches and denominations. Projections for 1985 are offered, and the results are accompanied by essays on the research methodology employed, the geography of religion in Wales, trends reflected in the data, and broad variations by age and sex.

321 **A time of paradoxes among the faiths.**
D. P. Davies.   In: *The new Wales*. Edited by David Cole. Cardiff: University of Wales Press, 1990, p. 205-18.
An interesting study contrasting the traditional and new religions of Wales, Christian and others, and an assessment of the reasons for the decline of some sects, denominations and movements and the growth in others.

322 **The Year Book. Y Blwyddiadur.**
The Presbyterian Church in Wales. Eglwys Bresbyteraidd Cymru. Caernarfon, Wales: Gwasg Pantycelyn for the General Assembly, 1897-. annual.
Contains details on the work and functions of the General Assembly, the Associations and the Presbyteries and provides the names and addresses of ministries and missionaries. It also covers the movement of ministers during the year, obituaries, establishments, and includes directions to churches as well as a list of names and addresses of other religious and related organisations.

Social Conditions

General

323 **Changing social conditions.**
C. C. Harris. In: *The new Wales*. Edited by David Cole. Cardiff: University of Wales Press, 1990, p. 218-32.
An assessment of the image of Wales created by its social conditons, in the context of certain indicators, i.e. employment, economic activity, household expenditure, incomes, the second home problem, language, culture and educational success and public entertainment. Harris asserts that contemporary social conditions in Wales are often paradoxical.

324 **Consumer issues in Wales.**
Cardiff: Welsh Consumer Council, 1987. 25p.
A report on the suggestions received by the Council for work and activities to be undertaken in subsequent years. Among the issues highlighted were: monitoring and coordinating legal services; the price and availability of foods; housing; money advice services; consumer committees for social services; health care facilities; consumer education; and schools in the community. Taken individually these suggestions and issues provide 'a snapshot' of concerns in Wales.

325 **Crisis of economy and ideology: essays on Welsh society, 1840-1980.**
Edited by Glyn Williams. Bangor, Wales: British Sociological Association, Sociology of Wales Study Group, 1983. 277p.
A collection of essays by prominent sociologists on a wide range of subjects relating to Wales and Welsh society. There are discussions of the relationship between Wales and the British state, migration and population movements, class relations, modernization and the tensions created, culture, language, education and studies of the growth of Welsh nationalism.

326 **Social and cultural changes in contemporary Wales.**
Edited by Glyn Williams. London: Routledge & Kegan Paul, 1978. 282p.

A volume of essays on social issues which is probably the first such collected work to be issued in recent times for the literature on the subject is normally dispersed in various periodicals, none of which has a continuing and thematic commitment to the sociology of Wales. The essays deal with a wide range of subjects, notably social deprivation, rurality, education, ethnic awareness and national identity, language and culture, religion, social ranking and social processes.

327 **Society in Wales.**
Iorwerth C. Peate. In: *Anatomy of Wales.* Edited by R. Brinley Jones. Peterston-super-Ely, Wales: Gwerin Publications, 1982, p. 43-53.

A concise but important essay which seeks to explain the structure of Welsh society from a historical perspective, taking as its starting point the codification of structure implicit in the laws of Hywel Dda in the tenth century. It also takes into account some of the subsequent influences on that structure, including immigration and political change, and analyses the gradual evolution of Welsh society.

328 **The Welsh and their country: selected readings in the social sciences.**
Edited by Ian Hume, W. T. R. Pryce. Llandysul, Wales: Gomer in association with the Open University, 1986. 365p. maps.

A collection of essays on a wide range of subjects, which is essentially concerned with the territories of Wales, and their distinctive culture regions. It is also a work which concentrates on presenting a portrait of contemporary Wales. The essays appear in four groups: spatial identity (language areas, culture regions, geography as a background to Welsh history); the traditional society (community studies, the sociology of Wales, trends in that sociology, and a study of 'gwerin' (folk)); ideologies (culture and policies, ethnicity, minority and linguistic rights, Welsh heartlands); and the context of political identity (separate administration, mass media and society, organisations, and political movements and their backgrounds).

329 **Welsh social trends. Tueddiadau cymdeithasol.**
Cardiff: Welsh Office and HMS0, 1977-. biennial.

A valuable publication, which describes its policy of issuing simplified graphic presentations of statistical data. It is this element of the work which renders it very useful to a wide range of users. The series has expanded significantly since 1977 as more statistics are gathered and issued on Welsh matters and on new subjects. The most recent editions include data on: population; vital statistics (births, deaths, mortality ratios); social characteristics (social habits, households, immigration); economic characteristics (earnings, unemployment, employment); social security; health and personal social services; education; housing; justice and crime; and finance (central and local government).

Housing

330 Attitudes and second homes in Wales.
Chris Bollom.   Cardiff: University of Wales Press, 1978. 126p.
(University of Wales Board of Celtic Studies, Social Science
Monographs, no. 3).

A study of what has become a very controversial issue, using Gwynedd as the case
study. Particular reference is made to the degree of hostility displayed by native Welsh
residents towards second home ownership by those they regard as outsiders.

331 Housing and homelessness in Wales: questions for the churches and society.
Penarth, Wales: Church in Wales Publications, 1985. 78p.

A collection of papers delivered at a forum in 1985, which took as its theme the social
and housing problems inherited from the country's industrial past and those arising
from current economic and industrial problems. There are chapters dealing with the
issues of homeless families, the under-privileged and housing for single, young people.

332 Housing in Wales.
Cardiff: Welsh Council, 1974. 86p.

The report presented to the Secretary of State for Wales by the Council on a range of
housing issues. It includes an analysis and assessment of: the housing stock; the
availability of land; finance for building; the second homes issue (the first time the
problem was raised and described in an official document); and housing for special
needs.

333 Second home ownership: a case study.
Richard de Vane.   Cardiff: University of Wales Press, 1975. 108p.
(Bangor Occasional Papers in Economics).

The report of a detailed study undertaken in North Wales in 1974 into the extent of
ownership of second homes, the characteristics of owners, their economic impact and
their influence on house prices. The tables of survey data are particularly revealing and
constitute a source of primary data.

334 Welsh house condition survey, 1973.
Cardiff: HMSO, 1975. 111p.

A document of primary significance since it highlights the hitherto diffuse nature of
data on housing in Wales and offers comments on previous studies and the sampling
methods they employed. Fifteen tabulations are given: condition by sub-region;
availability of amenities by sub-region; repair costs by sub-region; condition by tenure
of dwelling; condition by age of dwelling; condition by type of dwelling; condition by
size of dwelling; condition by gross value of dwelling; condition by availability of
amenities; condition by repair costs; condition by repair cost and age; repair costs by
age of dwelling; repair costs by tenure of dwelling; condition: changes 1968 to 1973;
and availability of amenities: changes 1968 to 1973.

335 **1986 Welsh house condition survey. Arolwg cyflwr tai Cymru.**
Cardiff: Welsh Office, 1988. 51p. maps.
The most recent survey data available, previous studies having been undertaken in 1968, 1973, 1976 and 1981. The survey method is described and a summary of the results is provided in both an all-Wales analysis and a district analysis. Twenty tables are given for districts and a further fourteen for Wales as a whole.

336 **Welsh Housing Associations Council. Cyngor Cymdeithasau Tai Cymru.**
Annual Report. 1988-. annual.
The growth and development of local community housing associations is a noteworthy characteristic of the Welsh housing scene in recent years. Each association produces an annual report of its expenditure and activities, but the Associations Council summarizes those reports by groups and offers a useful overview of activities.

337 **Welsh Housing Statistics. Ystadegau tai Cymru.**
Cardiff: Welsh Office. 1981-. annual.
Prepared by the Welsh Office from a range of sources, this publication provides detailed statistics and summaries of all aspects of housing in Wales, including: dwelling stock; new house building; clearances; rehabilitation of dwellings; sales; lettings and vacancies of public sector dwellings; the housing corporation; homelessness; private sector housing; local authority finance and rents; rates and rating; and a list of priority programmes and grants.

Pollution

338 **Community action versus pollution: a study of a residents' group in a Welsh urban area.**
Irene M. Hall. Cardiff: University of Wales Press, 1976. 130p. maps. (University of Wales, Board of Celtic Studies, Social Science Monographs, no. 2).
A fascinating study of the response of a community to industrial pollution, their work as an action group to effect the removal of the offending factory, the rôle of local and central government departments, and an analysis of the complexities of responsibility and legislation. Perceptions of blame and liability, of the nature of the pollution, the nature of the community and its mode of mobilisation are analysed, as are the results of the protest.

Poverty

339 Poverty and social inequality in Wales.
Edited by Gareth Rees, Teresa L. Rees. London: Croom Helm, 1980. 279p.

A collection of interdisciplinary essays, organized in two groups: dimensions of social inequality (income, wealth, housing, education, health, urban problems); and explanatory frameworks for the amelioration of inequality, Keynesian and Marxist theories, dual labour markets and dependency.

Rurality and deprivation

340 Mid-Wales: deprivation or development: a study of patterns of employment in selected communities.
G. Clare Wenger. Cardiff: University of Wales Press, 1980. 202p. (University of Wales, Board of Celtic Studies, Social Science Monographs, no. 5).

A study of particular problems in rural mid-Wales, notably employment and the availability of services and amenities. Attention is paid to the effect of these problems on communities, within the context of central government policies designed to stem depopulation, and an assessment is made of the relationships between demography, migration, culture, attitudes and the development and maintenance of employment.

341 State institutions and rural policy in Wales.
Jon Murdoch. *Contemporary Wales*, vol 2, (1988), p. 29-45.

A study of the rôle and functions of government organisations and agencies in developing an integrated policy for rural Wales, and the extent to which the various agencies (the Welsh Office, the Countryside Commission, the Nature Conservancy Council, the Forestry Commission, and the Development Agencies), fail in this respect at present. The list of references appended to the essay is a particularly valuable source of documents reflecting the work and policies of the various organisations and agencies.

Unemployment

342 Colliery closure and social change: a study of a South Wales mining valley.
John Sewell.   Cardiff: University of Wales Press, 1975. 81p. maps. (University of Wales, Board of Celtic Studies, Social Science Monograph).

A work which examines and describes the impact of industrial change as it affects the people of a mining village. Sewell considers the results of the severe contraction of the local coal industry, and pays particular attention to the miner, the families involved, employment alternatives, and the impact on local culture and society. Responses and attitudes to change are also analysed.

343 Out of school – out of work: a case study of youth employment in rural Wales.
Kathleen Claire McDermott.   Ann Arbor, Michigan: University Microfilms International, 1985. 189p.

An examination of a youth employment programme in Cardiganshire which was designed to alleviate problems of youth unemployment. The characteristics of the school leavers, their employment histories, and the nature of local labour markets are discussed, and the programme itself is also described and assessed in terms of its value and effectiveness.

344 Redundancy and recession in south Wales.
C. C. Harris.   Swansea, Wales: School of Social Studies, University College, Swansea; Oxford: Blackwell, 1987. 257p.

A study of the outcome of major redundancies during the contraction of one of the traditional large employers in South Wales, the steel industry. It analyses the reasons for the contraction of the British Steel Corporation's Port Talbot works i.e., the advent of new working methods and a change in the nature of labour requirements. Harris also assesses the change in the social characteristics and domestic circumstances of those who were made redundant. This is a major study of the human effects of industrial restructuring and of recession.

345 Unemployment in Wales: a study.
Cardiff: Welsh Council, 1973. 32p.

A study of the structure of unemployment, based on three selected representative areas: Anglesey, a rural area; Swansea, in the South Walian industrial belt; and Wrexham in industrial north-east Wales. The report analyses structural changes, hard-core unemployment, turnover, voluntary unemployment, vacancies, skills, youth opportunities, and presents a number of findings and conclusions.

Women

346 **Annual report: Welsh Women's Aid. Cymorth i Fenywod: Adroddiad blynyddol.**

Cardiff, 1987-. annual.

The bi-lingual report of this national women's organisation. The work of the organization includes establishing support groups and refuges for women and children who have suffered domestic violence, educating the public and authorities about the issue of domestic violence, and working for changes in the law, social policy and social attitudes.

347 **Women and work in contemporary Wales.**

Victoria Winckler. *Contemporary Wales*, vol. I (1987), p. 53-71.

This is essentially a general overview of the position of women within contemporary Welsh society. Winckler quotes evidence which suggests that, although there has been some change, in many respects the position of women remains unchanged and that inequality perpetuates, even in the new spheres of activity and industries where it is argued women remain marginalized. The study concentrates on three areas, employment, domestic work and trade unionism, since, it is argued they are central to the future improvement of the position of women in society. A very useful list of further readings is appended.

348 **Women in Wales: a documentary of our recent history. Volume I.**

Edited by Luana Dee, Katell Keineg. Cardiff: Womenwrite Press, 1987. 126p.

A study of aspects of the women's movement in Wales – in the areas of welfare and legislating for change, writing, publishing, printing and film, women and work, striking women, and training schemes and opportunities. The work includes additional names and the addresses of contacts, organisations and movements.

Social Services, Health and Welfare

349 **Activities of social services departments: Year ended 31/3/89.**
**Gweithgareddau adrannau Gwasanaethau Cymdeithasol: Blwyddyn yn
diweddu 31/3/89.**
Cardiff: Welsh Office, 1975-. annual.
This is the most recent in an annual series of statistical data summarizing the returns
made annually to the Welsh Office by local authority social services departments.
Tables of statistics relate to: residential accommodation for the elderly and younger
physically handicapped, as well as for the mentally ill and mentally handicapped;
residential accommodation for children; day services for the mentally handicapped and
day care centres; home help services; meal services; cases receiving certain kinds of
assistance; the register of handicapped persons; children's day care facilities; children
cared for by voluntary organisations; persons on mental handicap registers; and
activities relating to children.

350 **Health and personal social services statistics for Wales. Ystadegau
iechyd a gwasanaethau cymdeithasol personol: Cymru.**
Cardiff: Welsh Office, 1974-. annual.
Presents the tabulated returns from health authorities, local authorities, and various
other bodies concerned with health and closely related to social services, together with
those statistics collected by government departments. The main tables of statistics
include: demography (life expectation, deaths and causes of mortality, infant
mortality); finance expended on health and social services (revenue and capital);
manpower (hospitals, general practice, social service departments); specific hospital
data; general practice data; services offered in the community and home personal
social services (homes for the elderly, children in care, meals service); mental illness
and mental handicap (including hospitals and units); preventive medicine; morbidity
(various illnesses and conditions); abortions; and miscellaneous data (transfusions,
artificial limbs, drugs etc.). The statistical bases vary, as do period spans. This is a
wide-ranging publicaton of primary significance.

351 **Key statistical indicators for National Health Service management in Wales. Dangosyddion ystadegol allweddol i reolaeth y Gwasanaeth Iechyd Gwladol yng Nghymru.**

Cardiff: Welsh Office, 1981-. annual.

This publication is a major source of primary data on health care services in Wales. The tables relate to: hospital units of work; hospital costs; community health service costs; ambulance services; staff; nursing and midwifery staff; mental illness services; mental handicap services; hospitalisation rates; bed utilization in selected specialities; hospital waiting lists and times; estate management services; catering; health promotion and preventive medicine; community services; and family practitioner committee services.

352 **Local authority social services planning statements for Wales. Summary. Datganiadau cynllunio gwasanaethau cymdeithasol awdurdodau lleol Cymru.**

Cardiff: Welsh Office, 1976-. annual.

The most recent issue was published in 1988 (no. 9 in the series) for the period 1985-86 to 1987-88, and provides an all-Wales summary of the provision of personal social services, with an account of achievements and intentions for various client groups and priority activities. Statistical tables are provided relating to overall strategies, capital expenditure, services for the elderly, for children and young people, for the mentally and physically handicapped, and the mentally ill, offering county comparisons, and comparisons with assessments of need.

353 **Mental health statistics for Wales. Ystadegau iechyd meddwl Cymru.**

Cardiff: Welsh Office, 1980-. annual.

Details are given for the previous year together with some trend information from previous years. The tables provided include those relating to national hospital trends, hospital statistics for both mental illness and mental handicap, legal status, non-hospital services to the ill and handicapped, and censuses of patients.

354 **Staff of social services departments: year ended 30 September 1989. Staff adrannau Gwasanaethau Cymdeithasol: Blwyddyn yn diweddu 30 Medi 1989.**

Cardiff: Welsh Office, 1975-. annual.

Derived from returns made annually to the Welsh Office by local authorities, this publication offers data in tabulated form on staffing levels, the growth in staffing levels, the distribution of staff, percentage distribution and qualifications. It is organized on a Wales basis, followed by detailed analyses by county.

355 **Wales and medicine: an historical survey.**

Edited by John Cule. [Cardiff]: The British Society for the History of Medicine, 1975. 249p.

A collection of twenty-three papers given at the ninth British Congress on the History of Medicine. The subjects covered vary from an assessment of major medical personalities, to particular diseases and their incidence in Wales, the development of medical education in Wales, ancient medical practice, historical studies and literary studies. The work was conceived as the story of medicine in Wales, but the influence of politics on health services is also to be perceived in the studies. The work is illustrated.

356 **Wales and medicine: a source-list for printed books and papers showing the history of medicine in relation to Wales and Welshmen.**
John Cule. Aberystwyth, Wales: National Library of Wales, 1980. 229p.

Intended as a guide for medical historians, the work encompasses printed materials relating to medicine in Wales, as well as medical books written in, or translated into, Welsh. The work seeks to be comprehensive up to 1948 but is more selective thereafter.

357 **Welsh herbal medicine.**
David Hoffman. Abercastle, Wales: Abercastle Publications, 1979. 80p.

An illustrated work which provides a background for, and an insight into, the lives of ordinary Welshmen of the Middle Ages and the wisdom and practices of physicians of the period. Much of this popular work is devoted to a study of the most commonly used plants in Wales, giving a description of the plant, its modern medical uses and the uses made of it by physicians in the past as well as the folklore relating to it.

Politics

General and historical

358 **Aneurin Bevan: a biography.**
Michael Foot. 2 vols. Vol. 1: 1897-1945: London: Granada, 1982;
Vol. 2: 1945-1960: London: Davis Poynter, 1973.
A biography of one of the finest political figures to emerge in Wales during the twentieth century. Aneurin Bevan, a native of Tredegar in Gwent, was the youngest member of the British Government following the landslide Labour Party victory in 1945. In the ministerial posts he held in the aftermath of World War II he was the architect of a number of radical socialist reforms particularly in the areas of health and housing. This political biography, which traces Bevan's life and career from his childhood in a mining valley in South Wales through his various political battles during the 1930s and 1940s, is written by another distinguished political figure who succeeded Bevan as the Member of Parliament for the Ebbw Vale constituency. Bevan's background played an important part in moulding his political values, and the allegiances of a substantial proportion of the Welsh people in the general elections during his political career indicate that they shared his socialist views.

359 **A bibliography of United Kingdom politics: Scotland, Wales and Northern Ireland.**
Laurence Pollock, Ian McAllister. Glasgow: Centre for the Study of Public Policy, University of Strathclyde, 1980. 126p. (Studies In Public Policy, no. 3).
This bibliography is the product of the activities of the Political Studies Association Work Group on United Kingdom Politics founded in 1975. All the items selected for inclusion in the bibliography deal with the Scottish, Welsh and Irish dimension of British politics with a particular emphasis on the devolution debate. One section is devoted entirely to materials which discuss the position in Wales.

360 **David Lloyd George: a political life: The architect of change, 1863-1912.**
Bentley Brinkerhoff Gilbert. London: Batsford, 1987. 546p. illus.
bibliog.

A scholarly biography of one of the most distinguished British statesmen of the twentieth century written by a Professor of History at the University of Illinois. Gilbert traces Lloyd George's rise to power from his early upbringing in rural Wales, up to 1912 when he became Chancellor of the Exchequer. This appraisal of his political career examines in some detail the Welsh dimension of his political ideology and activities in the period before he became the Prime Minister of the United Kingdom and a major figure on the international stage during World War I.

361 **Etholiadau seneddol yng Nghymru 1900-1975 = Parliamentary elections in Wales 1900-1975.**
Beti Jones. Talybont, Dyfed, Wales: Y Lolfa, 1977. 191p.

A bilingual reference book which lists the results of general elections and by-elections for the British Parliament held in all Welsh constituencies during the first seventy-five years of this century. The book also includes short biographical notes on all those people who have represented Welsh constituencies in Parliament during this century, as well as a brief description of all the political parties represented in these elections. A useful source of information for those interested in the Welsh political scene.

362 **The forerunner: the dilemma of Tom Ellis 1859-1899.**
Neville Mastermann. Llandybie, Wales: Christopher Davies, 1972.
299p. bibliog.

The subject of this biography was one of the leading political figures in Welsh and British politics during the 1880s and 1890s before his early death in 1899. Ellis belonged to the group of radical nonconformists who were elected as Liberal Members of Parliament for a number of Welsh constituencies following electoral reforms in the latter part of the nineteenth century. During the early part of his career, he was the main advocate of some form of home rule for Wales. Some commentators claim that this goal was not achieved by the Liberal Government because Ellis sacrificed his early ideals in favour of his own personal ambition. This political biography provides a detached assessment of his career and achievements.

363 **Glamorgan politics, 1918-1985.**
J. Graham Jones. In: *Glamorgan County History Vol. VI: Glamorgan Society 1780-1980.* Edited by Prys Morgan. Cardiff: Glamorgan History Trust, 1988, p. 71-87.

A general survey of the support given to various political parties in the constituencies in Glamorgan between 1918 and 1980. The essay shows the emergence of the Labour Party in the industrial valleys and elsewhere in the county and shows, through an analysis of general and by-election results, that there has been little change in party allegiances since 1945.

364 **Merthyr politics: the making of a working class tradition.**
Edited by Glanmor Williams.   Cardiff: University of Wales Press,
1966. 109p.

A collection of four essays originally delivered to the Merthyr branch of the Workers'
Education Association. Merthyr was the first large industrial town in Wales and it was
also the crucible of Welsh working class politics during the nineteenth century and the
first decades of the twentieth. These four essays examine the four most significant
phases in the town's political awareness, namely the working-class rising of 1831, the
Liberal ascendancy in the second half of the nineteenth century, the rise of socialism at
the beginning of the twentieth century and the economic depression of the 1920s and
1930s.

365 **The national question again: Welsh political identity in the 1980s.**
Edited by John Osmond.   Llandysul, Wales: Gomer Press, 1985. 325p.
maps.

The rejection of the proposal to establish an elected Welsh Assembly by the
overwhelming majority of the Welsh electors is widely considered to be a significant
watershed in the development of Welsh politics. This important collection of essays, by
political scientists and professional politicians, presents an informed guide to the
sociology of Welsh politics as well as to the state of the political parties in Wales in the
aftermath of the 1979 general election. This volume provides a valuable contribution to
an understanding of Welsh politics today.

366 **The new working class and political change in Wales.**
David Adamson.   *Contemporary Wales*, vol. 2 (1988), p. 7-28

This article shows that the significant restructuring of the Welsh economy since the
1960s has had an enormous effect on the Welsh working class which in turn has
brought about shifts in party allegiances and ideologies. The author sees this shift as
being one of the reasons for declining support for the Labour Party and strong support
for Plaid Cymru in some industrial constituencies in South Wales during the 1960s and
1970s. The main characteristic of working-class allegiances in the current social and
economical climate is its fluidity.

367 **A political and electoral handbook for Wales.**
Denis Balsom, Martin Bunch.   Farnborough, England: Gower, 1980.
195p. maps. bibliog.

A practical reference book on contemporary Welsh politics for 'practitioners,
academics and interested citizens'. The volume includes sections which describe the
basic features of Welsh politics at national and local level, together with statistical data
on parliamentary elections held between 1950 and 1979, the organisational structure
and staffing of the Welsh Office, government agencies and the nationalised industries
and public corporations in Wales and various aspects of county and district councils
between 1974 and 1979.

368 **The politics of rural Wales: a study of Cardiganshire.**
P. J. Madgwick, Non Griffiths, Valerie Walker.   London: Hutchinson,
1973. 272p. bibliog.

A detailed study of the sociology of politics in a rural Welsh constituency, with
particular reference to the 1970 general election campaign. Although this book is an

examination of the influence of religious, cultural, social, linguistic and other factors on political attitudes and voting patterns in one constituency, the study does provide some valuable insights into Welsh rural politics in general.

369 **The radical tradition in Welsh politics: a study of Liberal and Labour politics in Gwynedd 1900-1920.**
Cyril Parry. Hull, England: University of Hull Publications, 1970. 89p. bibliog.
An examination of the decline of the Liberal Party and the rise of Labour in north-west Wales during the first two decades of the twentieth century. The study attempts to explain the factors which led to the decline of support for the Liberals and the social and economic background which explained the growing support for a socialist party.

370 **The rise of Labour: Llanelli, 1890-1920.**
Deian Hopkins. In: *Politics and society in Wales 1840-1922: essays in honour of Ieuan Gwynedd Jones.* Edited by Geraint H. Jenkins, J. Beverley Smith. Cardiff: University of Wales Press, 1988, p. 161-82.
An examination of the growth in support for the Labour Party in Wales during this period. The author provides a detailed analysis of the situation in one urban constituency in Carmarthenshire which returned a Labour candidate to Westminster for the first time in 1922.

371 **Union to reform: a history of parliamentary representation of Wales 1536 to 1832.**
Arnold J. James, John E. Thomas. Llandysul, Wales: Gomer Press, 1986. 472p. bibliog.
A reference book which consists of information on all Welsh constituencies during the period between the Act of Union in 1536 to the 1832 Reform Act, as well as the results of all the elections held during this period and an alphabetical list of parliamentary candidates. In addition to raw data, the work also includes comments on some of the major features of parliamentary representation for Wales during this three hundred year period, such as the strong political influence wielded by a handful of wealthy land owning families.

372 **Wales and the quest for peace: from the close of the Napoleonic Wars to the outbreak of the Second World War.**
J. Goronwy Jones. Cardiff: University of Wales Press, 1969. 187p.
A study of the part played by Wales in the search for peace and the prevention of war from the establishment of the London Peace Society in 1816 up to 1939.

373 **Wales at Westminster: a history of the parliamentary representation of Wales 1800-1979.**
Arnold J. James, John E. Thomas. Llandysul, Wales: Gomer Press, 1981. 284p.
A reference book on parliamentary elections held in Welsh constituencies from 1800 to 1979 which includes: details of all the candidates' names; party allegiances and results for each constituency, including the size of the electorate and turnout; and the author's

interpretation of the significance of the results in specific elections, or constituencies. In order to demonstrate the changed nature of representation during the period under investigation, short biographical notes and a summary of the occupation and education of members elected in the elections of 1832, 1892, 1923, 1945 and 1979 are given. The authors have also included detailed results and an analysis of referenda held in Wales on Sunday opening and entry into the European Economic Community. An indispensable tool for students of Welsh politics during the nineteenth and twentieth centuries.

374 **Wales and British politics 1868-1922.**
Kenneth O. Morgan.   Cardiff: University of Wales Press, 1980. 3rd ed. 363p. bibliog.

A study of the political history of Wales between the landmark elections of 1868 and 1922. The author demonstrates the nature and limitations of the political nationalism which grew in Wales during the latter part of the nineteenth century as well as the growing awareness outside Wales of the distinctive needs of the people and illustrates how this was reflected in the policies of the British political parties towards Welsh affairs. In a penetrating analysis Morgan shows that for a short period the forces of radicalism and nationalism were forged into a single campaign for national recognition. He also reveals how, once some of the distinctly Welsh issues had been resolved, the majority of political leaders could not see any distinction between Welsh politics and those of the rest of the United Kingdom. This period is seen by the author as the first phase of Welsh political nationalism. An epilogue traces the fortunes of political nationalism in Wales from 1922 to 1970.

375 **Welsh politics: Cymru Fydd to Crowther.**
Kenneth O. Morgan.   In: *Anatomy of Wales*. Edited by R. Brinley Jones. Peterston-super-Ely, Wales: Gwerin Publications, 1972, p. 118-144.

A short essay which outlines the developments in Welsh politics during the period 1870 to 1970. The author argues that the main feature of Welsh politics during this period was its continuity, as no other part of the United Kingdom showed such consistent support of the political left and so little encouragement for the Conservative Party. Morgan demonstrates that, during these years, Welsh politics fall into three distinct periods: the Liberal ascendancy 1868-1919; the Labour ascendancy 1919-1966; and the upsurge of Plaid Cymru 1966-1970. These three periods are briefly examined in the essay.

376 **The 1987 general election in Wales. Etholiad cyffredinol 1987 yng Nghymru.**
Denis Balsom.   Aberystwyth, Wales: Welsh Political Archive, National Library of Wales, 1989. 90p. illus. tables.

This bilingual pamphlet offers a detailed analysis of the results of the 1987 general election in the thirty-eight constituencies in Wales, together with the author's interpretation of the significance of these results when compared with voting patterns in the rest of the United Kingdom. Although an examination of the results clearly shows that, unlike the rest of the United Kingdom, Wales showed a swing towards the Labour Party, the author believes that the Labour hegemony of an earlier period will not be re-established in Wales because of deep-seated socio-economic changes. Consequently, it will only be the Welsh-speaking heartland of Wales which will be distinct from the general trends in Westminster politics.

Political nationalism

377 **Internal colonisation: the Celtic fringe in British national development, 1536-1966.**
Michael Hechter. London: Routledge & Kegan Paul, 1975. 361p.

Using the British Isles as a case study, the author investigates the rôle of ethnicity in the politics of industrial societies. Sociologists have developed two models of core-periphery relationships in an industrial setting, a diffusion model and an internal colonial model. Theoretically, the former model leads to ethnic homogenization and the latter can heighten ethnic conflict. This examination of the relationship of Scotland, Ireland and Wales with England, from the time of the Act of Union of England and Wales to 1966, lends support to the internal colonial model.

378 **The nature and distribution of support for Plaid Cymru.**
Denis Balsom. Glasgow: Centre for the Study of Public Policy, University of Strathclyde, 1979. 25p. (Studies in Public Policy, no. 36).

An analysis of the social and cultural background of Plaid Cymru supporters based on four sample surveys conducted in 1978 and 1979. The findings show that support for the party is strongest amongst Welsh-speakers, and that those under fifty-five are twice as likely to vote for Plaid Cymru as those over that age. Two-thirds of the party's support is amongst the working classes. These findings, together with the referendum defeat over the proposals for devolution and greater self-determination, suggest to the author that on the 'grounds of political issues as well as social support, Plaid Cymru, faces very real constraints upon future electoral success'.

379 **The Party of Wales, Plaid Cymru: populist nationalism in contemporary British politics.**
Thomas Olivitt Combs. PhD thesis, University of Connecticut, 1978. (Available from University Microfilms, Ann Arbor, Michigan, order no. 7813846).

Traces the origins of Welsh political nationalism, the development of Plaid Cymru from 1922 to 1976 and examines that party's political programme in relation to economic, social and political problems. The thesis also includes a review of Plaid Cymru's electoral strategy and progress as well as an analysis of the nature of nationalist sentiment in Wales today.

380 **The political consequences of Welsh identity.**
Denis Balsom, Peter Madgwick, Denis van Mechelen. Glasgow: Centre for the Study of Public Policy, University of Strathclyde, 1982. 27p. (Studies in Public Policy, no. 97).

An examination of the influence of language, identity and attitude factors on political behaviour in Wales. Although the investigation demonstrated the existence of a strong feeling of national identity amongst the majority of Welsh people, there was no consistent commitment either to Plaid Cymru (the Welsh Nationalist Party), to devolution or to self-government.

381 **Separatism and the mobilisation of Welsh national identity.**
Colin H. Williams. In: *National separatism*. Edited by Colin H.
Williams. Cardiff: University of Wales Press, 1982, p. 145-201.
Examines the 'socio-spatial variations' in Welsh nationalist support and demonstrates
that the demand for political autonomy in Wales is a response to the fear that the
Welsh national identity is under threat. Williams also traces the steps taken by Plaid
Cymru (the Welsh Nationalist Party), to persuade non-Welsh speakers to suppport
their goal of self-government.

382 **The Welsh extremist.**
Ned Thomas. Talybont, Dyfed, Wales: Y Lolfa, 1973. 139p. illus.
This work was first published by Victor Gollancz in 1971. The aim of the book is to
discuss the 'pressures on the Welsh-language community, the response to those
pressures, and the record of what is happening' during the cultural crisis facing Wales
during the second half of the twentieth century. The author describes the nature of the
Welsh national consciousness as it has been manifested in twentieth-century literature
and political activity. Aimed primarily at non-Welsh people, Thomas's objective is to
provide the reader with a greater understanding of the commitment and passion of
many Welsh people towards their language and national identity. The volume is
written from the standpoint of a Welsh socialist who strongly supports the idea of an
elected Welsh assembly.

383 **Welsh and Scottish nationalism: a study.**
Reginald Coupland. London: Collins, 1954. 426p.
An examination of the survival of the Welsh and Scottish nations within the British
state. The author outlines the history of Welsh nationhood from Roman times to the
present, and includes a detailed account of the home rule debates of the nineteenth
century and the struggle for self-determination during the first half of the present
century. Although the author claims that the absence of statehood need not threaten
the national identity and distinct culture of a people, he does appear to support some
form of political devolution for Scotland and Wales.

384 **The Welsh dilemma: some essays on nationalism in Wales.**
Edited by W.J. Morgan. Llandybie, Wales: Christopher Davies, 1973.
128p.
A series of short essays by acedemics and political figures discussing various aspects of
Welsh nationalism, including one essay on the historical background to Welsh national
consciousness as well as essays presenting the case for, and against, some form of self-
determination. Other contributors discuss economics and nationalism in Wales and the
relationship between Welsh nationalism and religion, and between nationalism and
language.

385 **The Welsh Nationalist Party 1925-1945: a call to nationhood.**
D. Hywel Davies. Cardiff: University of Wales Press, 1983. 286p.
bibliog.
A study of the first twenty-five years of the history of the Welsh Nationalist Party
based on a higher degree dissertation. The author claims that, for much of this early
period of its development, the party was more of a cultural and educational movement
rather than a political party campaigning to gain popular support for the aim of Welsh

self-government. Davies examines the views and activities of the early leaders, particularly Saunders Lewis who was the president of the party and dominated its policies for most of this early period of its history.

386   **The Welsh question: nationalism in Welsh politics 1945-1970.**

Alan Butt Philip.   Cardiff: University of Wales Press, 1975. 367p. bibliog.

An important contribution to an understanding of Welsh political nationalism between 1945 and 1970. The author examines the composition of Plaid Cymru (the Welsh Nationalist Party), and indicates the sections and groups in Welsh society which provide the party with its base. He also traces the impact of Welsh nationalism on the general political life of Wales. The growth of Welsh nationalism since the end of World War II is discussed in its social and political context and the book also considers the influence of Welsh nationalism on Welsh institutions and pressure groups.

Constitution, Administration, Local Government and the Law

Administrative devolution: historical development and the present position

387 **Beyond the doomsday scenario: governing Scotland and Wales in the 1980s.**
Barry Jones, Michael Keating. Glasgow: Department of Politics, University of Strathclyde, 1988. 35p. (Strathclyde Papers on Government and Politics, no. 58).

This pamphlet discusses the problems which face the major British political parties who could find themselves in government but with limited representation in certain regions of the United Kingdom. This is a particularly acute problem in Scotland and Wales where there is a degree of administrative devolution and distinct parliamentary organisations. The authors examine the problems which faced the Conservative Party in relation to this issue following the 1987 General Election when they returned a very small number of Members of Parliament in Scotland and Wales.

388 **The creation of the Welsh Office: conflicting purposes in institutional change.**
Ian C. Thomas. Glasgow: Centre for the Study of Public Policy, University of Strathclyde, 1981. 80p. bibliog. (Studies in Public Policy; no. 91).

The Welsh Office was established by the Labour Government in 1964 as a separate department of state headed by a cabinet minister. This development was a departure from the previous organisation of the British government's executive as it was established on a territorial, rather than a functional, basis. This report examines the attitudes of politicians towards administrative decentralisation, with particular reference to the conflicting views concerning the impact of the establishment of the Welsh Office.

Constitution, Administration, Local Government and the Law. Administrative
devolution: historical development and the present position

389 **Creative conflict: the politics of Welsh devolution.**
John Osmond. London: Routledge & Kegan Paul; Llandysul, Wales:
Gomer Press, 1977. 305p.
An examination of why, and how, Welsh devolution appeared on the agenda of British
politics during the 1970s together with an investigation of the Labour Government's
proposals for a Welsh Assembly. In part two, the author deals with the constitutional,
financial and economic policy aspects of Welsh devolution.

390 **The development of Welsh territorial institutions: modernization theory
revisited.**
Barry Jones. *Contemporary Wales*, vol. 2 (1988), p. 47-61.
An examination of four dissimilar institutions in Wales (namely the Welsh Office, the
Select Committee on Welsh Affairs, the Welsh Arts Council and the Wales TUC) in
order to determine to what extent, if any, these institutions have reinforced the Welsh
national identity. The author concludes his review by stating that 'Given the weak
autonomy of many Welsh institutions, they may simply serve to integrate Wales more
fully into the British State'.

391 **Devolution.**
Vernon Bogdanor. Oxford: Oxford University Press, 1979. 246p.
An analysis of the political and constitutional aspects of devolution in Britain from
1886 to the 1970s, which is aimed at historians, political scientists, lawyers and the
general reader. The book was published at the time of the devolution referenda for
Wales and Scotland and therefore its main thrust is the impact that the changes
proposed in the devolution bill would have on British politics and the concept of the
British state. Having analysed the profound effect that such changes would have, the
writer, a Fellow and tutor in politics at Brasenose College, Oxford, endorses the
federal solution as the most appropriate answer.

392 **Early campaigns to secure a Secretary of State for Wales 1890-1939.**
J. Graham Jones. *Transactions of the Honourable Society of
Cymmrodorion*, (1988), p. 153-75.
This article was originally delivered as a lecture to the Society of Cymmrodorion at a
meeting held in the House of Commons in 1988. It examines the campaign for a
Secretary of State for Wales, both in Parliament and outside, between the first
appearance of such a demand in 1890 and the outbreak of World War II in 1939. The
author shows that, initially, the idea was conceived as a preliminary stage to the wider
concept of Welsh self-government, but by the 1930s the creation of this office was seen
as the only goal of devolutionists within the British political parties.

393 **Government by consultation: the case of Wales.**
P. J. Madgwick, Mari James. Glasgow: Centre for the Study of Public
Policy, University of Strathclyde, 1979. 43p. (Studies in Public Policy,
no. 47).
The aim of this report is 'to explore the functions of the Welsh Office in the system of
central and local government as it effects Wales; to assess the extent and limits of
central control; and to examine the nature and significance of the key processes of
consultation'. The research for the paper was based on interviews and documentary

Constitution, Administration, Local Government and the Law. Administrative devolution: historical development and the present position

evidence and the authors illustrated the issues through case-studies in the areas of health, housing, roads and finance.

394 **Government in Wales in the twentieth century.**
Ivor Gowan. In: *Welsh studies in public law*. Edited by J. A. Andrews. Cardiff: University of Wales Press, 1970, p. 50-64.
Examines the main developments regarding the machinery of government in Wales from the time of the first measure of administrative devolution which was introduced by David Lloyd George in 1913 when he established the Welsh Health Insurance Commission of 1913. This review traces the significance of subsequent developments, particularly the pressure for a Secretary of State for Wales and for the formation of the Welsh Office. The essay also includes a brief evaluation of the achievements of the Welsh Office during its first few years.

395 **Limited power and potential influence: the Committee of Welsh Affairs and the policy process.**
J. Barry Jones. In: *Parliamentary Select Committees: a symposium*. Edited by Dilys M. Hall. Glasgow: Department of Politics, University of Strathclyde, 1984. (Strathclyde Papers in Government and Politics, no. 24).
In the aftermath of the devolution referendum of 1979 the Conservative Government established a parliamentary select committee for Wales which was charged with the responsibility of examining the expenditure, administration and policy of the Welsh Office and associated public bodies. This pamphlet discusses to what extent this body has brought about a degree of public accountability to government in Wales.

396 **Our changing democracy: devolution to Scotland and Wales.**
London: HMSO, 1975. 72p. (Cmnd. 6348).
This White Paper presents details of the central government's proposals on devolution for Scotland and Wales in the light of the proposals of the Royal Commission on the Constitution, 1969-1973 (Cmnd. 5460) [The Kilbrandon Report], and the reaction to its findings in Parliament and elsewhere. The report explains 'how the new institutions would work, what subject areas would be developed and how the financial arrangements would work'. The section dealing with the position in Wales consists of the following parts: background to devolution; constitutional arrangements; financial arrangements; devolved subjects; and a summary of the scheme proposed for Wales.

397 **Parliament and territoriality: the Committee on Welsh Affairs 1979-1983.**
J. Brinley Jones, R.A. Wilford. Cardiff: University of Wales Press, 1986. 102p.
The Committee on Welsh Affairs is an all-party departmental select committee of the House of Commons which was established in the aftermath of the devolution referendum of 1979. The chief aim of the committee was to achieve a degree of accountability for the Welsh Office and its associated bodies. This study is an attempt to examine whether the Committee has succeeded in representing Welsh interests, as well as to evaluate to what extent it has made the Welsh Office more accountable to the Welsh people. The methodology adopted was to interview Members of Parliament, civil servants and those bodies which have presented evidence to the committee.

Constitution, Administration, Local Government and the Law. Administrative devolution: historical development and the present position

398 **Royal commission on the constitution 1969-1973.**
Commission on the Constitution.   London: HMSO, 1973. 2 vols. (Cmnd. 5460).

Volume one presents the main report of the Royal Commission set up by the Labour government in 1969 'to examine the present functions of the central legislature and government in relation to the several countries, nations and regions of the United Kingdom' following the electoral successes of the Scottish and Welsh nationalist parties during the 1960s. This report, with its recommendations for an elected Welsh Assembly, was the basis for further debate both within, and outside, parliament which eventually led to the devolution referendum of 1979. In addition to providing a detailed discussion of the alternative forms of government which were available to the nations and regions of Britain, the commission also included information on the historical background to the Welsh national movement and existing administrative devolution to Wales. Volume two consists of a memorandum of dissent by two members of the Commission.

399 **Territorial ministries: the Scottish and Welsh Offices.**
James G. Kellas, Peter Madgwick.   In: *The territorial dimension in United Kingdom policies*. Edited by Peter Madgwick, Richard Rose. London: Macmillan, 1982, p. 9-33.

A short, descriptive account of the historical development, and current rôles, of the Scottish and Welsh Offices with special emphasis on their relationship with Whitehall and local authorities, together with an assessment of their effectiveness. The authors demonstrate that both offices have adopted similar approaches to enable them to integrate into the British government framework, despite being territorial, rather than functional, departments of state.

400 **Wales: a separate administrative unit.**
David Foulkes, J. Barry Jones, R. A. Wilford.   In: *The Welsh and their country: selected reading*. Edited by I. Hume, W. T. R. Pryce, Llandysul, Wales: Gomer Press, 1986, p. 273-90.

A short essay which outlines the development of administrative devolution to Wales from the central government during the modern period and briefly describes non-government national institutions.

401 **The Welsh Office today: a description of its function.**
Welsh Office Information Division.   Cardiff: Welsh Office, 1988. 8p.

Since it was established in 1965, the range of responsibilties which have been devolved to the Secretary of State for Wales and the Welsh Office have grown enormously. Accordingly, the Welsh Office is now a multi-functional department which administers and implements a wide range of government policies. This handbook briefly describes these activities.

402 **The Welsh veto: the Wales Act of 1978 and the referendum.**
David Foulkes, J. Barry Jones, R. A. Wilford.   Cardiff: University of Wales Press, 1983. 238p.

The result of the devolution referendum of 1979, which showed that only one in four of the electorate in Wales supported an elected Welsh Assembly, has been considered by many to be an important landmark in twentieth-century Welsh politics. This detailed study traces the emergence of Wales as an administrative unit, analyses the political debate on Welsh devolution with particular reference to the period after the publication of the Kilbrandon Report (Royal Commission on the Constitution, 1969-1973 Cmnd. 5460) in 1973, and also examines the issues raised during the devolution campaign. Other contributors to this book discuss the rôle and influence of the broadcasting media and press during the course of the campaign, and considers the parliamentary passage of the Wales Act of 1978.

403 **Written evidence: commission on the constitution; 7. Wales.**
Commission on the Constitution. London: HMSO, 1972. 151p.
This is one of a series of seven volumes containing evidence submitted by various organisations and individuals to the Royal Commission on the Constitution. This volume deals exclusively with evidence concerning the position in Wales.

Local government

404 **Local government.**
In: *Digest of Welsh historical statistics. Crynhoad o ystadegau hanesyddol vol. II.* John Williams. Cardiff: Welsh Office, 1985, p. 171-94.
A collection of raw statistics, gathered from a number of sources, for the benefit of research workers and scholars. This section of the work deals mainly with statistics on local government finance in counties and county boroughs from the eighteenth century up to 1974, but it also includes details of expenditure and receipts under the Poor Law in Wales from 1748 to 1937.

405 **Local government and administration in Wales 1536-1939.**
Harold Carter. In: *Welsh studies in public law.* Edited by J. A. Andrews. Cardiff: University of Wales Press, 1970, p. 30-49.
A short essay which traces the development of local government in Wales from the Act of Union to the outbreak of World War II. The author observes two major trends which tend to dominate this period: firstly, that local government in Wales tends to adopt the structures and reforms established in England; and secondly, following the development of a national consciousness from the second half of the nineteenth century onwards, we see the emergence of distinct Welsh bodies and legislation which only effects Wales.

406 **Local government finance (Wales): the Welsh rate support grant report.**
Welsh Office. London: HMSO. 1988-. annual.
Provides explanatory material regarding the support grants and supplementary grants for transport purposes and national parks to be paid to local authorities in Wales.

407 **The reform of local government in Wales: consultative document.**
Welsh Office.   Cardiff: HMSO, 1971. 31p. map.

Most of the changes which took place as a result of the re-organisation of local government in England and Wales in 1974 were based on the proposals found in this document. The only significant exception was that the old county of Glamorgan was eventually re-organised into three, rather than two, county authorities. The document presents the proposals regarding the new county and district authorities together with a list of the responsibilities which were to be delegated to each tier of local government. In addition, it includes a short account of the historical background to local government in Wales from the end of the nineteenth century onwards.

408 **Welsh local government financial statistics. Ystadegaeth ariannol llywodraeth leol yng Nghymru.**
Cardiff: Welsh Office, 1977-. annual.

Most of the statistics in this volume have been compiled from the various financial returns made by local authorities to the Welsh Office and to the Department of the Environment. The statistics cited relate to the rate fund services, housing revenue, trade services, capital expenditure, borrowing, rating and housing benefit, local government manpower; and local authority expenditure and exchequer contributions.

Medieval Welsh laws and the legal system in Wales

409 **Cambrian Law Review.**
Aberystwyth, Wales: Department of Law, University College of Wales, Aberystwyth, 1970-. annual.

A journal devoted to general, rather than technical, aspects of the legal system which is aimed both at lawyers and the layman. Although the articles and reviews are not specifically confined to the Welsh dimension of the legal system, most issues of the journal include items with a Welsh connection.

410 **Law and government in Wales before the Act of Union.**
Dafydd Jenkins.   In: *Welsh studies in public law*. Edited by J.A. Andrews. Cardiff: University of Wales Press, 1970, p. 7-29.

Presents a general background introduction to law and government in Wales during the medieval period.

411 **The law of Hywel Dda: law texts from medieval Wales.**
Compiled and translated by Dafydd Jenkins.   Llandysul, Wales: Gomer Press, 1986. 425p. illus. map. (The Welsh Classics).

A selection of the texts, translated into English, of some of the most important and interesting material found in medieval Welsh lawbooks. The work includes a general introduction, source references and textual notes, and a glossary of terms. The volume has been designed so that it can both provide the general reader with an introduction

Constitution, Administration, Local Government and the Law. Medieval Welsh laws and the legal system in Wales

to the nature of medieval Welsh law but at the same time also act as a valuable guide for the student and scholar. In his introduction, the author explains that the texts were produced by, or for, lawyers between the thirteenth and sixteenth centuries although they are based on much earlier material.

412 **Lawyers and laymen: studies in the history of law presented to Professor Dafydd Jenkins.**
Edited by T. M. Charles-Edwards, Morfydd E. Owen, D. B. Walters.
Cardiff: University of Wales Press, 1986. 395p.
A collection of legal studies with particular emphasis on Welsh law. The first part of the book deals with Suretyship, a major area in medieval Welsh law, whilst the second part contains studies on a number of topics in legal history in Wales and elsewhere.

413 **The solicitors regional directory: Clwyd, Dyfed, Gwent, Gwynedd, Mid-Glamorgan, Powys, South Glamorgan, West Glamorgan.**
Law Society.   London: Law Society, 1986-. annual.
A directory of solicitors practising in Wales, including duty solicitors and members of the Child Care and Mental Health Review Tribunal Panel. The directory provides an entry for all solicitors' offices in Wales together with details of the individual solicitors in those offices. It also includes information about legal aid, organisations providing legal services, legal advice centres and Citizens Advice Bureaus, for example.

414 **Studies in the Welsh laws.**
Hywel D. Emmanuel.   In: *Celtic studies in Wales.* Edited by Elwyn Davies. Cardiff: University of Wales Press, 1963, p. 73-100.
A critical review of the main investigations into the textual and other studies of medieval Welsh laws which have been undertaken during the first sixty years of the twentieth century.

415 **The Welsh language in the courts.**
J. A. Andrews, L. G. Henshaw.   Aberystwyth, Wales: University College of Wales, Aberystwyth, 1984. 116p.
Following a report commissioned during the 1960s into the legal status of the Welsh language, a Welsh Language Act was passed in 1967 which changed the status of the language in the courts and in public administration. Subsequently, provisions were made to facilitate the use of Welsh in the law courts. This short report presents the findings of an examination undertaken in the early 1980s to find out what use is made of the Welsh language in magistrates', crown and county courts. It is asserted that the facilities offered by the courts are effective, particularly in traditional Welsh-speaking areas, but few cases are conducted in the Welsh language.

416 **The Welsh laws.**
T. M. Charles-Edwards.   Cardiff: University of Wales Press on behalf of the Welsh Arts Council, 1989. 105p. bibliog. (Writers of Wales).
Examines the texts of Welsh laws from the tenth to the fifteenth centuries and shows that during the twelfth and thirteenth centuries the Law of Hywel Dda came to be seen as an important badge of nationhood due to the political and military struggle between Edward I and Llywelyn ap Gruffudd. The volume reappraises some earlier interpretations of variants of Welsh law found in medieval manuscripts.

Economy

Economic and social history

417 **After the mines: changing employment opportunities in a South Wales valley.**
Stephen W. Town. Cardiff: University of Wales Press, 1978. 138p. maps. (University of Wales, Board of Celtic Studies, Social Science Monographs, no. 4).
A study undertaken between 1972 and 1974 in the Amman Valley at the western end of the South Wales coalfield. It covers employment expectations, patterns of unemployment, the growth, albeit slow, of alternative employment opportunities, and women in employment. Town also links changes in employment structure with social attitudes and shows how a process of structural change has influenced, and interacted with, social behaviour to produce a distinctive and articulate set of beliefs about employment in the valley.

418 **Industrial South Wales 1750-1914: essays in Welsh economic history.**
Edited by W. E. Minchinton. London: Frank Cass, 1969. 264p.
An introductory study by the editor, which indicates the paucity of studies in this area, is followed by essays by prominent scholars divided into five subject areas: population; industry; banking; labour; and housing.

419 **Modern South Wales: essays in economic history.**
Edited by Colin Baker, L. J. Williams. Cardiff: University of Wales Press, 1986. 324p. maps.
A collection of seventeen essays dealing with the economic development of South Wales during the period 1780 to 1950. The essays are grouped chronologically into three sections: 1790-1840; 1840-1914; and the twentieth century. They deal with a wide range of subjects including canals, farming, banks, railways, public health, the coal industry, trade and shipping, the ports of South Wales, power and energy, and the effect of wars. This is a significant and particularly useful volume.

420 **South Wales.**
Graham Humphreys. Newton Abbot, England: David, Charles, 1972.
253p. maps. bibliog. (Industrial Britain series).

A study of the changes that have taken place in the industries and the economy since 1943, and of the forces which have brought about those changes: rationalisation; modernisation; outside investment; and nationalisation. The work also offers further perspectives on the impact of change on housing, leisure and educational opportunities. The study concludes with an assessment of trends as they relate to six sub-regions, and by offering arguments in favour of the development of a coherent and wide-ranging plan for the South Wales economy.

421 **South Wales in the sixties: studies in industrial geography.**
Edited by Gerald Manners. Oxford: Pergamon Press, 1964. 265p.

A collection of nine essays dealing with a range of subjects: regional economy; the coal industry; the steel industry; employment; diversification; regional economic policies; transport; and regional planning. A work intended to record industrial achievement and progress, and offering new perspectives in economic planning.

422 **The South Wales valleys: a contemporary socio economic bibliography.**
Teresa Baggs, Paul H. Ballard, Paul Vining. Aberfan, Wales: Tŷ Toronto, 1974. 122p.

Lists materials published after 1960, with a few standard works dating from an earlier period. The bibliography is organized in two parts: a subject order; and an author sequence. The subjects listed are community studies, economy, education, environmental studies, geography, health, social welfare, housing, industry, language, leisure, recreation and tourism, planning, politics and government, population and migration, regional policy, sociological trends, transport and communications.

423 **The Welsh economy.**
Graham L. Rees. In: *Anatomy of Wales*. Edited by R. Brinley Jones. Peterston-super-Ely, Wales: Gwerin Publications, 1972, p. 55-83.

A concise essay which traces and explains some of the predominant characteristics of, and influences on, the Welsh economy since the beginning of the nineteenth century. Particular attention is paid to population, the metallurgical industries, agriculture, employment patterns, transport and the impact of government policies on the Welsh economy.

424 **The Welsh economy: studies in expansion.**
Edited by Brinley Thomas. Cardiff: University of Wales Press, 1962. 217p.

An anthology of ten essays, written at a time of an expanding economy and of great optimism. The first essay traces economic growth in Wales in the post-war period; subsequent essays consider unemployment, agriculture, coal, steel, transport, income and consumer expenditure, and population. All the essays reflect optimism but also isolate structural tensions and weaknesses which became so apparent in the ensuing decades. A work intended for both the general and specialist reader.

Economic development

425 Contemporary Wales: an annual review of economic and social research.
Cardiff: University of Wales Press, 1987-. annual.
This work is published under the auspices of the Social Science Committee of the University of Wales, Board of Celtic Studies, with the aim of developing an 'understanding of what is happening in Wales and which thereby improves the quality of public debate', and of providing an annual review of major social and economic research. Each volume has an important analysis of Welsh social and economic research, together with shorter discussions of issues of current concern and debate. The annual review of the Welsh economy (see item 431) is particularly useful.

426 Development Board for Rural Wales. Bwrdd Datblygu Cymru Wledig. Annual Report.
Newtown, Wales: The board, 1977-.
Based in Newtown, central Wales the Board was modelled on the Highlands and Islands Board in Scotland and was established in 1977. It has a wide remit to effect industrial, economic, cultural and social growth and developments. It has a wide range of responsibilities which influence industrial economic, cultural and social growth and developments. Its geographical area covers Powys, part of Dyfed and part of Gwynedd, an area which is essentially the rural heartland of Wales. The Board offers business advisory services, a factory building programme, a social and cultural development programme and finance to support such activities.

427 Economic and social consequences of rationalization in the South Wales coal industry.
Victoria Wass, Lynn Mainwaring. *Contemporary Wales*, vol. 3, (1989), p. 161-85.
A study of the coal industry after the miners' strike of 1984 and a retrospective assessment of the issues propounded at that time. Amongst the subjects considered are productivity, the local labour market, and the nature and extent of the higher unemployment levels which ensued after the end of the strike. These themes are developed in a case study of Markham colliery. The study is concluded by an assessment of the prospects for the South Wales coal industry in the context of privatisation and the European single market.

428 An economic plan for Wales.
Cardiff: Plaid Cymru Research Group, 1970. 288p. maps.
Issued by the Welsh Nationalist Party, the plan outlines the party's strategy for solving the economic problems of Wales. The plan covers employment problems, selected locations for development, selected industries, the development of the infrastructure, the machinery to sustain growth, and housing and finance. This is an ambitious programme, which basically argues that all governments have failed to produce a coherent economic plan for Wales.

429 The structure of the Welsh economy.

E.T. Nevin, A.R. Roe, J.I. Round. Cardiff: University of Wales Press, 1966. 41p. (Welsh Economic Studies, no. 4).

This significant study is divided into two parts: the first being a summary and discussion of income and output between 1948 and 1964, and documenting the growth of the Welsh economy during that period; and the second being a description of an input-output model of the Welsh economy and its rôle in the specific planning of the whole, or components, of that economy.

430 Survey of the Welsh economy.

Graham L. Rees. London: HMSO, 1973. 183p. illus. maps. (Commission on the Constitution Research Papers, no. 8).

The report of a survey undertaken in 1970 primarily to provide a closer understanding of the economic relationship between Wales and the rest of the United Kingdom. The report provides comparisons at most points in the analysis. Sections of the report deal in turn with employment and unemployment, housing, consumer durables, household expenditure, the nature and development of new industries, transport, industry policy, social accounts, and public finance. A summary and conclusions are also offered, and these are aimed specifically at the deliberations of the Commission on the Constitution i.e., the Kilbrandon Report (see item no. 398).

431 Wales in 1988: an economic survey.

Dennis Thomas. *Contemporary Wales*, vol. 3, (1989), p. 199-243.

The second in a proposed series of annual reviews (the first being for 1987 in *Contemporary Wales*, vol. 2, 1988, p. 131-72). The survey commences with a brief comment on the British economy, how it performed and how it related to forecasts, and then moves on to consider the performance of the Welsh economy in terms of some key economic and social indicators and sectors. Sections consider output, employment, unemployment, earnings, agriculture, tourism, industrial development and regional comparisons.

432 Wales, the modernising of an economy, a report compiled for the WDA.

Bowles Research. [Cardiff]: Welsh Development Agency, 1987. 20p.

A short but significant report, which is a study of selected indicators against which the economy of Wales is compared for evidence of growth and improvement. The report also seeks to prove how the economy of Wales has performed better in some respects than other regions of Britain in recent times. The indicators used are GDP per head, employment, employment structure (diversification from the old traditional heavy industry base), the electronics industries, self-employment, company performance, industrial relations and productivity.

433 Wales: the way ahead.

Cardiff: HMSO, 1967. 137p. Cmnd. 3334.

A government White Paper (a consultative document), of great significance when issued, which examines 'the economy of Wales and the environment of its people . . . the first occasion when . . . the Government have brought together all the issues which affect the economic, social and cultural background of life in modern Wales'. Essentially a macro planning document, it analyses prospective employment, new industry and investment, government support and interventionist policies, development area status, transport, new technology, tourism, housing, urban and rural planning, health, education and the special local problems experienced within Wales, with an appraisal of the main issues.

434   **The Welsh Development Agency Corporate Plan 1984-1990.**
Cardiff: Welsh Development Agency, 1984. 28p.
A statement, in two parts (the first part describes the context of the plan, the economic prospects and opportunities, and the second part forms the plan itself) which considers operating strategies, features of the business plans, key actions, implementation, investment plans, construction and building development, land development, marketing and sales, and special projects. Tables of expenditure are also included.

435   **The Welsh Development Agency: Report and accounts.**
Cardiff: Welsh Development Agency, 1977-. annual.
Established in 1976, the Agency has a wide remit and significant powers in terms of social, industrial and economic development and regeneration. It offers an extensive range of services by means of a central office and a wide network of regional offices, tendering advice on commercial and industrial development, investment, business promotion, the construction of factories and workshops, urban renewal, land reclamation and environmental improvements, rural enterprise and support for community enterprise groups, planning, and research and marketing. The annual report reflects and quantifies the Agency's activities, listing strategies, individual projects and activities.

436   **Welsh Economic Review.**
Cardiff: Institute of Welsh Affairs, 1988-. twice per year.
A journal which: 'aims to provide an up-to-date, authoritative and objective critique and analysis of the Welsh economy, summarising recent developments in economic variables, and suggesting areas of future change'; and 'to provide a meaningful and intelligible summary of the Welsh economic environment in a way that promotes understanding and acts as a decision aid to both private and public policy-makers'. A typical issue will be thematic, with feature articles (tourism, for example) with primary data and commentary offered in three surveys, i.e., social, business and economic.

437   **Welsh economic trends. Tueddiadau'r economi.**
Cardiff: Welsh Office, 1977-. biennial.
A major source of primary data which is gathered from a range of sources, but predominantly governmental. Tabulated statistics are provided for population, the working population, regional income and expenditure, earnings and hours worked, personal incomes, household incomes and expenditure, industrial activity, aid to industry, capital expenditure, and public expenditure. There are 133 tables in all, with appendices.

438   **The Welsh economy.**
Edited by K. D. George, Lynn Mainwaring.   Cardiff: University of Wales Press, 1988. 301p.
This volume represents a major modern survey of the Welsh economy, and it examines developments that have taken place since the early sixties. There are twelve essays by various specialist contributors, and following an introduction to what are perceived as

being the main issues and an outline of the Welsh national accounts, there are studies of population trends, housing, standards of living, the labour market, agriculture, manufacturing, the coal and steel industries, the service sector and regional policy. A work suitable for both general and specialist audiences.

439   The Welsh economy in the 1980s.
  Kenneth D. George, Lynn Mainwaring.   *Contemporary Wales*, vol 1, (1987). p. 7-37.

A review of a seven-year period, which examines developments and changes in the Welsh economy against the background of the fortunes of the United Kingdom economy as a whole. Various sections of the review are devoted to an analysis of specific economic sectors, such as mining, construction, the utilities, manufacturing, steel, agriculture, the service industries and tourism and attention is paid to turnover, foreign investment, new technology and innovation. Further analysis is also provided of economic and social welfare factors, including labour and earnings, regional problems, and government policies.

Finance and banking

440   Finance for business in Wales.
  Cardiff: Welsh Committee for Economic and Industrial Affairs, 1989. 54p.

The report of a study undertaken over a period of twelve months, setting out the findings, with a list of the major public and private sector sources of finance for business in Wales, with addresses and contacts for further information.

441   Personal wealth and finance in Wales.
  Jack Revell, Cyril Tomkins.   Cardiff: Welsh Council, 1974. 71p. bibliog.

This is probably the first comprehensive study of this subject undertaken for Wales, which is viewed as a region of the United Kingdom. Accordingly, the study is comparative and relational. Sections are devoted to: the place of Wales in the United Kingdom financial system; personal finance research; personal wealth and savings; and finally to the financial system of Wales, its institutions, local authorities and companies.

442   Wales and the enterprise culture.
  Caerffili, Wales: Wales Council for Voluntary Action, Community Initiatives Unit, 1987. 51p. bibliog.

A study of an important priority of regional and national economic policy, illustrating the complex nature of initiatives and enterprise at regional and local levels. It argues the case for local initiatives where historical antecedents of business and enterprise exist.

Trade

443 Export Wales.
Cardiff: Welsh Office in conjunction with the British Overseas Trade Board, 1989.

A journal which considers, for example, trade initiatives, information of value to exporters, European regulations, and awards. It also includes, a list of sources of information, advice and useful contacts.

444 Inter-regional input-output tables for Wales and the rest of the UK, 1968.
Richard Ireson, Cyril Tomkins.   Cardiff: Welsh Council, 1978. 94p. bibliog.

A detailed study and analysis of the inter-relationships between Welsh industries and those in the rest of the United Kingdom, reflecting the fact that more statistical data relating to, and emanating from, Wales was facilitating such studies by the late sixties. The study offers analyses of industries and commodities in thirty-three groups. This is a significant document for those seeking an analysis of the structure of the Welsh economy.

Industry and Energy

Historical development

445 **Glamorgan County History. Volume V. Industrial Glamorgan from 1700 to 1970.**
Edited by Arthur H. John, Glanmor Williams. Cardiff: Glamorgan County History Trust, 1980. 671p. maps.
A major study of the most significant industrial area of Wales, encompassing essays on each of the industries, labour issues, banking and financial organization, transport, ports and shipping, the economy, and economic development after 1945.

446 **The growth and decline of the south Wales iron industry, 1760-1880.**
Michael Atkinson, Colin Baber. Cardiff: University of Wales Press, 1987. 101p. (Board of Celtic Studies Social Science Monographs no. 9).
A study of the factors which brought about the growth, prosperity and eventual decline of the region's first major industrial sector, iron smelting. Particular attention is paid to the availability of raw materials, the impact of technology, enterprise and finance, markets and distribution.

447 **A history of the north Wales slate industry.**
Jean Lindsay. Newton Abbot, England: David & Charles, 1974. 376p. maps. bibliog.
A comprehensive study of what was once the primary industry in North Wales. Lindsay's approach is chronological, commencing with a review of the industry to 1731; thereafter chapters are devoted: to the industry's history prior to 1918; individual quarries; mechanisation and technical developments; transport; and social and cultural activities. The volume is concluded by two studies: one concerned with the changes between 1918 and 1945, and the other to the decline of the industry since 1945.

Industry and Energy. Historical development

448 **The industrial development of South Wales 1750-1850.**
A. H. John. Cardiff: University of Wales Press, 1950. 201p. bibliog.
The standard study of the history of the industrial economy in South Wales, which of course, was dominated by coal and steel. The work also traces the impact of industry on social and economic life. Chapters are devoted to the financing of industry, the labour force, the markets, production techniques and to industrial processes.

449 **The Industrial Revolution in North Wales.**
A. H. Dodd. Cardiff: University of Wales Press, 1971. 439p. maps. bibliog.
First published in 1933, this outstanding work remains the primary account of industrial activity in North Wales. It commences with a study of conditions and influences up to 1760, and then traces the history of early entrepreneurship, enclosures, communications, the metal industries, collieries and quarries, the woollen industry and other textiles. It also considers the new social order brought about by the Industrial Revolution and discusses owners, capitalists, labourers, and industrial unrest.

450 **Industry before the Industrial Revolution.**
William Rees. Cardiff: University of Wales Press, 1968. 2 vols. maps. bibliog.
Whilst not exclusively devoted to the study of Wales, these volumes are the major reference source for the history of the early development of industry in Wales. Sections are devoted to mining, coal mining, metal mining, timber supplies, the migration of industry, the impact of civil wars and strife, and the effect of crown rights and chartered companies.

451 **Industry in Wales.**
D. Morgan Rees. In: *Anatomy of Wales.* Edited by R. Brinley Jones. Peterston-super-Ely, Wales: Gwerin Publications, 1972, p. 85-104.
Describes the predominant industrial activities in Wales from the second half of the sixteenth century to the present time. Consideration is given for the following industries, iron, steel, tinplate, coal, transport and quarrying, and the development and diversification that has occurred during the twentieth century is also discussed.

452 **Lead mining in Wales.**
W. J. Lewis. Cardiff: University of Wales Press, 1967. 415p.
This is the standard study of an industry which was of considerable significance to Wales. It commences with two essays on mining, one dealing with the period up to 1568 and the other the period 1569 to 1690. These are followed by studies of activities in the eighteenth century, mining since 1800, the conditions of labour, transport, trade and the techniques deployed.

453 **The Welsh woollen industry.**
J. Geraint Jenkins. Cardiff: National Museum of Wales Welsh Folk Museum, 1969. 409p. maps. bibliog.

An outstanding and comprehensive study which discusses the early development of the industry and the techniques employed in five geographical areas. The work is fully illustrated and has copious appendices and a significant bibliography.

Contemporary studies

454 **A bibliography of the coal industry in Wales.**
John Benson, Robert G. Neville. *Llafur*, vol. 2, no. IX (1979), p. 78-91.

A list of the major secondary works (books, pamphlets, articles and theses) dealing with the industry, and the social and labour history of the Welsh coalfield from the earliest times to 1979. The bibliography lists materials relating to: the General Strike of 1926; biography and autobiographies of prominent personalities; industry in Wales, with sub-divisions for North and South; social and working conditons; and labour, again in Wales generally and in North and South Wales in separate sections. For a more comprehensive bibliography see the 'Wales sections' of the *Bibliography of the British coal industry: secondary literature, parliamentary and departmental papers, mineral maps and plans and a guide to sources* compiled and occasionally annotated by John Benson, Robert G. Neville and Charles H. Thompson (Oxford: Published for the National Coal Board by Oxford University Press, 1981. 760p.).

455 **Commercial and industrial floorspace statistics: Wales. Ystadegau arwynebedd llawr masnachol a diwydiannol: Cymru.**
Cardiff: Welsh Office, 1979-. annual.

Provides data with an introductory commentary. Tables offer data on floorspace and hereditaments, gross changes in total areas since the preivious year, and data by economic or industrial activity, with further analysis by county.

456 **Economic regeneration in industrial South Wales: an empirical analysis.**
Jonathan Morris, Roger Mansfield. *Contemporary Wales*, vol. 2 (1988). p. 63-82.

Examines the change in the industrial base of South Wales, with reference to its new diversified manufacturing and service based economy, the decline in coal and metal manufacture, the rise of the consumer-based manufacturing sectors and the large increase in service sector employment. Attention is also given to investment in Wales by foreign companies and companies located elsewhere in the United Kingdom, expanding firms, restructured plants and the new business sector.

Industry and Energy. Contemporary studies

457 **From cradle to reincarnation.**
Allan Williams. In: *The new Wales*. Edited by David Cole. Cardiff:
University of Wales Press, 1990, p. 11-26.
An overview of the contemporary nature of industry in Wales, its major characteristics
and recent changes, with particular emphasis on employment patterns, finance for
industry, and a short assessment of key factors, environmental issues, communications,
the labour force and regional policy.

458 **Industrial growth Wales: a sector by sector analysis of Wales' leading
companies.**
London: Industrial Growth Wales, ICC Information Group, 1988.
397p. maps.
As well as supplying very detailed data and statistics for 500 companies in twenty
industrial sectors, this work also presents very useful studies in the form of three
preliminary essays which provide a review of the Welsh economy, a study of the coal
industry, and a consideration of the tourist industry. A fourth essay offers commentary
on the salient features, figures and findings of the analysis of the companies and
industrial sectors. It is intended that this analysis should be published annually.

459 **Industrial Wales.**
Graham Humphreys. In: *Wales: a new study*. Edited by David
Thomas. Newton Abbot, England: David & Charles, 1977, p. 154-89.
Analyses the nature and effect of the economic and industrial changes that occurred in
the 1970s. Humphreys discusses the structure of industry, the primary influences for
change, and reviews the state of major industries (coal, metal, engineering, vehicles,
and chemicals) and the distribution of industrial growth. He concludes with a brief
overview of the main industrial sub-regions: South Wales, north-east Wales and the
'rural remainder'.

460 **Industry in rural Wales.**
Roy Thomas. Cardiff: University of Wales Press, 1966. 45p. (Welsh
Economic Studies, no. 3).
An important study which examines the manufacturing sector in outlying rural areas
which usually have a sparse and declining population. It offers an important assessment
of growth, the means and methods of achieving growth, and the nature of
manufacturing industries which are in existence and which could be developed.
Reference is also made to the Development Area status initiative granted to a large
part of rural Wales, and to the establishment of the Development Board for Rural
Wales.

461 **Japanese manufacturing investment in Wales.**
Max Munday. Cardiff: University of Wales Press for the Institute of
Welsh Affairs, 1989. 198p.
An analysis of a notable characteristic of industry in Wales in recent times; Japanese
investment and manufacturing expansion schemes having contributed significantly to
the recent re-structuring of the manufacturing base in both South Wales and north-east
Wales.

114

462 Manufacturing industry in Wales: prospects for employment growth.
D. H. Simpson. Cardiff: Wales TUC, 1987. 138p. bibliog.
An assessment of the state of the contemporary manufacturing industry, its inherited problems, its potential, its trading patterns, its employment profiles, and the effectiveness of aid schemes, small firms and new ventures. Simpson argues that there is a need for a reassessment of the contraction in the Welsh manufacturing industry.

463 The mineral wealth of Wales and its exploitation.
T. M. Thomas. London: Oliver & Boyd, 1961. 248p. maps. bibliog.
This remains the only convenient and fairly comprehensive review of this subject, which encompasses coal, slate, limestone, rock quarrying, clay shales and marles for the building industry, specialist minerals, iron and non-ferrous, gold, copper and other precious metals.

464 The textiles of Wales.
Ann Sutton. London: Bellew Publishing Company in association with Dyfed County Council and the Wales Craft Council, 1987. 96p. maps.
An illustrated work which offers a history, a resource book, and a guide to the background, traditions and present directions of the textile industry of Wales. It also includes a directory of contemporary textile producers in Wales.

465 Welsh industry and commerce. Diwydiant a masnach Cymru.
Manchester, England: Wealthstream, February 1989-. monthly.
An independent business journal which 'aims to provide a point of contact for businessmen and industrialists throughout Wales'. Each issue presents information about, and an analysis of, the main business centres within Wales and regular updates in government legislation and regulations affecting industry and commerce. Some of the articles and news items are in Welsh. Recent issues have included studies of small companies, information technology, innovation awards, work environments, training, manpower issues, industry and the environment in Wales, property and development studies, law and accounting in Wales, incentives for rural Wales, venture capital, transport, and Wales in Europe.

Energy

466 Energy resources in Wales.
Cardiff: Welsh Council, 1977. 51p.
Considers the nature and scale of energy reserves, identifies the production and marketing features of each energy resource, and examines possible areas of change in future energy provision. A study of the energy context, its use and production, is followed by studies of coal, electricity, gas, liquid fuels and off-shore exploration. The work concludes with a brief study of conservation issues.

467 **A history of gas production in Wales.**

Richard Jones, Cyril G. Reeve. Cardiff: Wales Gas Printing Centre, 1978. 248p. maps.

A chronological history covering the period from 1821 to nationalization in 1949, of both the production of gas and the companies producing it. Reference is made to the structure of the industry, advances in technology, legislation, the advent of natural gas and a history of gas in mines, and coke oven gas.

468 **Nuclear power and Wales.**

G. R. H. Jones, E. A. Parry. Connah's Quay, Wales: North East Wales Institute, 1979. 95p.

Presents papers delivered at a forum organised by the Institute and the Council of Churches for Wales and others. The contributions range over technical and moral issues, a review of power needs, and offer alternative strategies.

469 **Small-scale hydro-electric potential of Wales.**

[Salford], England: Department of Energy and University of Salford, Department of Civil Engineering, 1980. 60p. maps.

Provides the results of a survey undertaken in 1979 which identified over 500 suitable sites, having given due regard to environmental impact, amenity value, ease of access, the topography of each site, engineering difficulties and waterflow conditions. The report is fully illustrated with a large number of maps, drawings and photographs.

Agriculture and Rural Life

History

470 **The agricultural community in south west Wales at the turn of the twentieth century.**
David Jenkins.   Cardiff: University of Wales Press, 1971. 291p. bibliog. maps.

A study of a community in pre-mechanization times and in the early years of mechanization with an assessment of the impact of agricultural change on rural society. Chapters are devoted to farm practice and social structure, farm organisation, houses and household organisation, the family (youth, marriage, age and succession), kinship, religion and religious revival, and the integration of the community into the nation at large.

471 **Agriculture in Wales during the Napoleonic Wars: a study in the geographical interpretation of historical sources.**
David Thomas.   Cardiff: University of Wales Press, 1963. 196p. bibliog. maps.

A study of agriculture during this era in its economic, political and social context, with a consideration of statistical and census evidence as well as cartographic (estate and farm plans, enclosure awards) and written evidence (the Board of Agriculture reports 1794-1814).

472 **The agriculture of Wales and Monmouthshire.**
A. W. Ashby, I. L. Evans.   Cardiff: University of Wales Press, 1944. 300p.

A survey of the main characteristics of Welsh agriculture with special emphasis upon the period immediately preceding the outbreak of World War II. Chapters deal with crops, livestock, prices, markets, labour, ownership and occupation, types of farming,

117

co-operation, the State and agriculture, education and administration, regional surveys, and an overall assessment of agriculture and its transition.

473 **The Welsh cattle drovers: agriculture and the Welsh cattle trade before and during the nineteenth century.**
Richard J. Colyer.   Cardiff: University of Wales Press, 1976. 155p. maps. bibliog.
A work which seeks to piece together from many scattered sources various aspects of the Welsh cattle trade and also to illustrate the vital rôle of the drovers in the cultural, intellectual and social life of Wales. Particular attention is paid to technical aspects of droving and to the finances and general conduct of the trade. The work also includes studies of the wide range of cattle available to the drovers and the technical and financial aspects of cattle production in nineteenth-century Wales.

Modern agriculture

474 **The classification of agricultural holdings in Wales.**
T. N. Jenkins.   Aberystwyth, Wales: University College of Wales, Department of Agricultural Economics, 1982. 258p. maps. bibliog.
Analyses the structure and the various types of agricultural holdings in Wales, the characteristics of an ideal classificaiton for holdings in Wales, the nature of the growing number of part-time holdings, and the value of data concerning holdings currently available.

475 **Complexities of modern farming.**
Rowland Brooks.   In: *The new Wales*. Edited by David Cole. Cardiff: University of Wales Press, 1990, p. 27-32.
A short assessment of the precarious state of contemporary agriculture in Wales in European context and in a changing consumer market.

476 **Dairy farming in Wales: a study of structure, output and problems of seasonality.**
W. Dyfri Jones, A. M. Sherwood.   Aberystwyth, Wales: University College of Wales, Department of Agricultural Economics, 1980. 241p.
The report of a research study on the industry which examines its structure, its estimated output specializations and production. It also analyses herds by size, the seasonality of production, the economic characteristics of farms, and their profitability. Conclusions and recommendations are also included.

477 **Farm incomes in Wales.**
Welsh Office.   Cardiff: Welsh Office, 1987-. annual.
A relatively new statistical publication, which brings together into a single integrated source various data previously published separately. It provides a comprehensive

picture of the economic state of the farming industry in Wales. Data is offered in three sections: reviews of the national and economic environment and structure of the industry: the results of the *Farm Business Survey* in Wales, providing an analysis according to farm type and business size; and output and input and farming incomes, with aggregate net incomes.

478 **Farmers together: Golden Jubilee volume of the Welsh Agricultural Organisation Society.**
Edited by Elwyn R. Thomas.   Aberystwyth, Wales: WAOS, 1972. map.

An anthology of twelve essays on the development of farmer cooperatives, which are an important characteristic of the industry in Wales. Three of the essays are in Welsh. The range of subjects is wide and include biographical studies of early pioneers, the concept of farming cooperatives, future prospects and past achievements. The appendix listing cooperatives is particularly useful, although a number of them have merged in recent years.

479 **Farming in Wales.**
Roscoe Howells.   London: David Rendell, 1967. 127p. maps.

An introductory work, originally aimed at those contemplating entering farming, but also useful for the general reader. It offers a general overview of land, climate, growth, finance and a seasonal chronology of activities in various sectors. Marketing and other activities are explained, as are aspects of rural life and an awareness of rural issues.

480 **Hill and upland cattle and sheep farming in Wales.**
T. N. Jenkins.   Aberystwyth, Wales: University College of Wales, Department of Agricultural Economics, 1983. 35p. (Agricultural Enterprise Studies in England and Wales, Economic Report, no. 88).

A sample survey of herds, flocks and farms, their composition and output together with a labour classification, and a consideration of tenure characteristics, stocking levels, land use, breeds and markets.

481 **Hill and upland farming in Wales: an economic study for 1973-74 and 1974-75.**
A. Lloyd, W. Dyfri Jones.   Aberystwyth, Wales: University College of Wales, Department of Agricultural Economics, 1978. 69p. bibliog. (Agricultural Enterprise Studies in England and Wales, Economic Report, no. 58).

This is an important study because upland farming constitutes a large percentage of agricultural activity in Wales and more than half the land devoted to agriculture qualifies for special financial support. The report offers an overview of beef and sheep enterprises, financial results and other data.

482 **Hill farming in Wales: manpower and training needs.**
J. L. Lees, R. J. Colyer. Aberystwyth, Wales: University College, Department of Agriculture, 1973. 152p.

This study for the Agricultural, Horticultural and Forestry Industry Training Board, is concerned with sustaining and improving the total pool of skill and expertise available to the hill farming industry. It refers to the bearing which social factors have upon the subject and describes: the physical background; the manpower structure; the scope of jobs; the extent of cooperation on upland farms; rates and levels of recruitment and wastage; education and training. In addition, it offers an assessment of training needs.

483 **Present farming patterns.**
H. John R. Henderson. In: *Wales: a new study*. Edited by David Thomas. Newton Abbot, England: David & Charles, 1977, p. 121-53.

An introductory study of agricultural land use, farm size and distribution, small farm and tenure problems, farmers and farm-workers and farm type classification, illustrated and exemplified by thematic maps, diagrams and statistics.

484 **Sheep production and management in Wales.**
A. Lloyd. Aberystwyth, Wales: University College of Wales, Department of Agricultural Economics, 1977. 85p. (Agricultural Enterprise Studies in England and Wales, Economic Report, no. 43).

Presents the results of a survey carried out in 1974 with a summary of findings, and an analysis of lambing, breeding, replacement rates, breed types and characteristics, markets, feeding requirements and new initiatives and possible future developments.

485 **Y Tir and Welsh Farmer.**
Aberystwyth, Wales: Farmers Union of Wales, 1956-. bi-monthly.

Originally issued as a monthly news bulletin for members of the Farmers Union of Wales, this publication gradually took on a newspaper format during 1957 although it was issued less regularly (some three months elapsed between each issue until 1962). The publication then adopted its present title, *Welsh Farmer*, and is now a bi-monthly journal offering union news, advice, articles on Welsh agriculture and notes and contributions from Welsh county associations. Recent issues have featured a section on European Community publications. Its language is predominantly English with occasional Welsh contributions.

486 **Welsh agricultural statistics. Ystadegau amaethyddol.**
Cardiff: Welsh Office 1979-. annual.

Based on the Annual Agricultural Census conducted in June, this volume provides data for agricultural area, livestock, agricultural holdings, labour and machinery, production and marketing, livestock prices, land prices and rents, grants and subsidies, farm structures and less favoured areas. It also includes comparisons with other countries in the United Kingdom.

487 **Welsh ponies and cobs.**
Wynne Davies. London: J. A. Allen, 1985. 2nd ed. 516p.

This is the first book relating to the history of Welsh ponies and cobs ever to have been written. The author has selected certain Welsh mountain pony and Welsh cob families which he considers to have had the gretest influence on the development of the Welsh pony and cob breeds. The work is lavishly illustrated.

Forestry

488 **Environmental aspects of plantation forestry in Wales.**
Edited by J. E. G. Good. Grange-over-Sands, England: Institute of Terrestrial Ecology, 1987. 77p.
The proceedings of a symposium held in 1986. The papers consider the influence of afforestation on aquatic fauna, soils, surface water chemistry, soil water, birds, the recreational potential of forests and the factors influencing the future of plantation forestry in Wales.

489 **Forestry Commission Conservancy: North Wales; census of woodlands and trees. 1979-82. Comisiwn Coedwigaeth: Gwarchodaeth Gogledd Cymru. Cyfrifiad coedlannau a choed. 1979-82.**
Edinburgh: Forestry Commission, 1983. 58p.
Presents the results of the census for the counties of Gwynedd, Clwyd and the northern parts of Dyfed and Powys, which include an assessment of the environmental status of trees in the rural and urban landscape. It records woodlands and trees owned by the Forestry Commission and by private owners in Dedicated and Approved Woodland schemes, and other woodlands not within these first categories. It should also be noted that, in addition, reports for individual counties were issued and that a report for Wales was also published offering less detailed analysis than the regional reports.

490 **Forestry Commission Conservancy: South Wales; census of woodlands and trees. 1979-82. Comisiwn Coedwigaeth: Gwarchodaeth De Cymru. Cyfrifiad coedlannau a choed. 1979-82.**
Edinburgh: Forestry Commission, 1983. 57p.
Provides the results of the census for the counties of Dyfed (south), West and Mid Glamorgan, South Glamorgan, Gwent and Powys (south), including an assessment of the environmental status of trees in the rural and urban landscape. The volume includes woodlands and trees owned by the Forestry Commission and by private owners in Dedicated and Approved Woodland schemes, and other woodlands not within these first categories. Reports for individual counties were also published and a report for Wales was also issued but this offered less detailed analysis than the regional reports.

491 **Forestry in Wales.**
J. W. Ll. Zehetmayr. Edinburgh: Forestry Commission, 1985. 15p.
A concise guide to forestry in Wales, which includes: a history of indigenous and plantation trees; an assessment of the resource value of trees in the economy; a description of forestry operations; a brief account of conservation, natural history and forest recreation; and a description of the forest tree species to be found in Wales.

492 **Welsh woods and forests: history and utilization.**
William Linnard. Cardiff: National Museum of Wales, 1982. 203p.
maps. bibliog.
A comprehensive illustrated account of the history and importance of the woodlands
and forests of Wales from the earliest times to the twentieth century which includes a
consideration of the establishment of the Forestry Commission. The work studies in
detail: woodlands from the Ice Age to the Norman Conquest; the significance of
forests in the Norman Conquest; medieval forests and woods; monastic woods; the
decline of forests and estate building; forest based industries; conifer nurseries and
planting; professional foresters and private estate management in the nineteenth
century; and the advent of a national forest service.

Rural life

493 **Give me yesterday.**
James Williams. Llandysul, Wales: Gwasg Gomer, 1971. 154p.
A book of reminiscences about a country upbringing in west Wales, and a way of life
which has, to all intents and purposes, disappeared. It describes childhood in the early
years of the twentieth century in an agrarian environment which had remained largely
unchanged for almost a century, with particular reference to education, religion, farm
life, social custom and practice.

494 **Life and tradition in rural Wales.**
J. Geraint Jenkins. London: J. M. Dent, 1976. 192p. maps. bibliog.
A lavishly illustrated study of life in rural Wales; a 'living past which still exerts its
influence on the daily life of the people'. Various chapters study life on the land, farm
implements and tools, sleds and wheeled vehicles, the use of local raw materials,
agriculture meeting local needs, woollen manufacturing, leather working, cottage and
farmhouse homes, folk-customs and beliefs, food and drinks and fishing.

495 **Life in a Welsh countryside.**
Alwyn D. Rees. Cardiff: University of Wales Press, 1950. maps.
A much respected study based on a survey of Welsh life as it existed in 1950 in the
parish of Llanfihangel-yng-Ngwynfa in northern Powys. At the time this parish was still
largely Welsh-speaking and was relatively secluded from most major external
influences, and retaining many features of the traditional way of life. This illustrated
work studies the local economy, house and hearth, farmsteads, the family and family
relationships, youth, neighbours, religion, recreation and entertainment, status and
prestige, and politics.

496 **My own folk.**
D. Parry-Jones. Llandysul, Wales: Gwasg Gomer, 1972. 182p.
A portrait of Welsh rural society at the turn of the century, noting the many changes
that have taken place in agriculture, its methods and customs, and in traditional social
patterns. It is also a study of religion and the churches, and of the lighter side of Welsh
rural life.

497 A North Wales village: a social anthropological study.
Isabel Emmett.   London: Routledge & Kegan Paul, 1964. 154p.
bibliog. maps.

A study of the observation of life in the parish of Llan in Merionethshire between 1958 and 1962, recording everyday life. The main theme is the way in which in a Welsh-speaking parish the conflicts and antagonisms between various groups, i.e. country folk and town dwellers, officials and the man in the street, upper and middle class, are seen by the inhabitants in terms of the Welsh against the ruling English.

498 A strategy for rural Wales.
Cardiff: Welsh Council, 1971. 52p. maps.

A study which considers the merits of various proposals and suggestions that might contribute to a better use of the resources available for the development of the area. The author also offers a possible strategy and framework for future action. Sections of the report consider the land and its primary uses, the social and economic framework, tourism, recreation and the landscape.

499 Welsh country characters.
D. Parry-Jones.   London: Batsford, 1952. 74p.

A series of character sketches and stories in which the author recalls a representative few of the old Welsh country people of Cardiganshire and Carmarthenshire: '. . . how they lived and laboured, how they loved and hated, how they triumphed (or succumbed) in their hard struggle for existence. They belong to an age that is over for ever, to a way of life that is no more'.

500 Welsh country upbringing.
D. Parry-Jones.   London: Batsford, 1949. 2nd ed. 144p.

Considers the ways of the countryside including the customs, the seasonal work on the farm, the influence of school and the impact of religion. The work is composed of memories, recollections and reminiscences covering a twenty-five-year period from 1891 onwards. The book represents 'an endeavour to portray a society that had in it elements – communal, agricultural, religious and cultural – that had survived from a remote past, but which before the impact of a mechanical age and a materialistic education are undergoing radical and accelerated change'.

501 Welsh rural communities.
David Jenkins, Emrys Jones, T. Jones Hughes, Trefor M. Owen.
Edited by Elwyn Davies, Alwyn D. Rees.   Cardiff: University of
Wales Press, 1960. 254p.

This volume is the product of four studies in four locations undertaken in the period 1945 to 1950, describing a theme in each case. The study of Aberporth reveals a dichotomy in the social pattern as indicated by contrasting codes of behaviour and social values; the Aberdaron study describes aspects of material culture and the imprint of society on the land; the Tregaron investigation covers the social structure and the economic development and functions of a small market town; and the Glan-llyn study analyses the functions of a nonconformist chapel dominated settlement in both religious and secular life.

502 **Welsh rural forum 1985: keynote papers and reports.**
Edited by Paul Cloke.   Lampeter, Wales: St David's University
College, Department of Geography, 1985. 90p.

Presents the proceedings of the forum with the Chairmen's reports on discussions. The subjects presented and discussed are the problems associated with contemporary rural life in Wales, rural deprivation, the costs and benefits of economic development programmes in rural areas, and society, economy and conservation in the National Parks.

503 **Welsh rural life in photographs.**
Elfyn Scourfield.   Barry, Wales: Stewart Williams, 1979. 116p. illus.

A collection of 185 photographs depicting different aspects of the work and leisure of Welsh country people. Rural life is presented by a multiplicity of formal functions and events and informal representations of habits and customs.

Transport

General studies and planning

504 The communications systems.
A Moyes. In: *Wales: a new study*. Edited by David Thomas. Newton Abbot, England: David & Charles, p. 226-51. maps.
An introductory survey of the historical development of communications systems and services in Wales which covers roads, railways, road passenger services, and includes an analysis of contemporary transport problems. The text is illustrated by a series of thematic maps.

505 The economic problems of rural transport in Wales.
G. Clayton, J. H. Rees. Cardiff: University of Wales Press, 1969. 44p. maps. (Welsh Economic Studies, no. 5).
A study based on the results of two research studies, one on transport problems in Wales, and the other on the problems of coordinating and integrating transport in west Wales. Both studies originated as an attempt to investigate the full economic and social impact of the closure of passenger and other rail services in predominantly rural areas. This is a significant study which elucidates the problems inherent in the provision of public transport in sparsely populated areas characterised by difficult terrain.

506 The extent of public transport decline in rural Wales.
S. D. Nutley. *Cambria* vol. 9, no. 1, 1982, p. 27-48.
A description of the changes in public transport that have taken place since 1929, including the withdrawal of services, notably bus services, and the closure of railways. Nutley also analyses various transport indicators, such as frequency, the quality and perception of service, the success of services in meeting actual and perceived needs, and also assesses the growth of car ownership.

125

Transport. General studies and planning

507   **Rural transport: a symposium 1977.**
Cardiff: Welsh Office, 1977. 137p.
A collection of papers presented at a symposium held at the University College of Wales, Aberystwyth, in June 1977, to consider issues relating to the provision of rural transport. Among the issues considered are: the expected standards of accessibility among transport users; conventional transport services; problems and challenges of offering a railway service in rural areas; community buses; car schemes; postbus services; and the rôle of central and local government. Several of these issues have not been addressed in publications sharing the same title.

508   **A study of the passenger transport needs of rural Wales.**
Graham Rees, Richard Wragg.   Cardiff: The Welsh Council, 1975.
139p. maps.
A comprehensive study undertaken in 1973 to consider: the problem of transport in rural areas, the value of the rail network and bus transport; alternative means of transport; roads and the use of cars; and the use made of transport in rural areas. The work also provides an evaluation of networks, considers some policy options and their resource implications and includes various detailed studies as appendices. Developments, both foreseen and sought, are listed.

509   **A study of the passenger transport needs of urban Wales.**
Richard Wragg.   Cardiff: Welsh Council, 1977. 281p. maps.
A comprehensive study which examines buses in urban Wales, the rail system of South Wales, future trip forecasts and land use planning, transport costs, the rôle of public transport and its alternatives, administrative and structural policies; and the transport situation in Cardiff and other centres.

510   **Supplementary transport: papers presented at a symposium . . . 1978.**
Cardiff: Welsh Office, 1979. 66p.
An interesting collection of papers concerning the lesser-studied aspects of public transport in Wales: community bus services: postbus services; voluntary car schemes; the integration of supplementary services; experiments and specific studies; market-day services; and Sunday buses. All of these are described in the introductory comments as 'unconventional' means of transport.

511   **Welsh transport statistics. Ystadegau trafnidiaeth Cymru.**
Cardiff: Welsh Office, 1985-. annual.
This publication, illustrated with numerous charts and maps, brings together information on roads, railways, ports and airports. There is also a section on the transport economy which considers areas of public and household expenditure, employment, tourism and petrol and oil prices. Tabulations are provided for road lengths, the licensing and registration of vehicles, road freight, public service vehicles, road traffic, road accidents, motoring offences, rail transport, sea transport, air transport and the transport economy.

Roads

512 **Agricultural transport in Wales.**
J. Geraint Jenkins.   Cardiff: National Museum of Wales, National
Folk Museum, 1962. 107p.
A study 'concerned with the construction and design of those devices which man in
Wales has adopted in an attempt to solve his transport problems'. It commences with a
study of human porterage and sledges, and then proceeds to describe carts, wagons,
pack and draught animals and the wheelwright's craft. The work is well illustrated and
contains a highly detailed catalogue of the National Folk Museum's collection of realia
relating to transport, a collection which has increased significantly in size since this
catalogue was issued.

513 **The drovers' roads of Wales.**
Fay Goodwin, Shirley Toulson.   London: Whittet Books, 1977. 240p.
maps. bibliog.
An illustrated study in four parts: the first discusses the drovers and their work; the
second analyses the work necessary to trace the drover routes through the Welsh
countryside; the third studies major route concentrations – the routes to Wrexham and
Shrewsbury, Birmingham and Hereford; and the fourth provides a brief overview of
drovers in England, examines some of the natural dangers encountered by drovers and
modern day walkers, and provides a glossary of Welsh terms.

514 **History of British bus services: South Wales.**
David Holding, Tony Moyes.   London: Ian Allan, 1986. 128p. maps.
An illustrated study of fleet histories in South Wales, and of the operators, staff and
customers, places and politics which all provided a context within which bus services
operated. The growth and eventual decline of fleets and services are traced. The area
considered is the South Wales Traffic area – Gwent, Glamorgan, Dyfed and Powys –
which includes a large portion of central Wales. The study commences with early urban
entrepreneurs, and with a study of early services in rural areas, and then considers the
services in their heyday, the development of a national bus company and the recent
growth of independent operators.

515 **Minor rural roads in Wales.**
Gareth W. Edwards.   Lampeter, Wales: St. David's University
College Centre for Rural Transport, 1984. 160p. bibliog. maps.
An introductory study of roads and road transport in Wales. It includes a statement of
trends in traffic and road maintenance, followed by a detailed study of structures,
maintenance programmes, the effect of the physical and climatic environment, and a
study of public policies relating to rural roads.

516 **Road accidents: Wales. Damweiniau ffyrdd Cymru.**
Cardiff: Welsh Office, 1979-. annual.
Statistical data, with brief reviews of some topical subjects and a number of
commentaries and maps and diagrams, augment the tabulations, which include: review
topics (seat belts, drinking and driving and similar subjects which are examined on a

127

regular basis); trends and detailed analysis (accidents, casualties, locations, daylight or darkness, accident severity); breath tests; and analyses by county and comparisons of accidents in the Welsh counties and the United Kingdom as a whole.

517 **Roads and trackways of Wales.**
Richard J. Colyer.   Ashbourne, England: Moorland Publishing, 1984.
192p. maps.

An illustrated introduction 'to aspects of the history of the Welsh road network between Roman times and the development of the turnpike system'. This is a popular work which is also the product of scholarly research and investigation. Its treatment is limited to the network of mid- and North Walian roads which exemplify Roman roads, medieval trackways, pre-turnpike roads, drove roads and turnpikes.

518 **Roads for Wales: the 1990's and beyond. Ffyrdd Cymru. 1990'au ac wedyn; a Consultation Paper.**
Cardiff: Welsh Office, 1986. 31p. maps.

A document outlining strategies for road development involving central and local government and encompassing strategic routes, small schemes and maintenance programmes.

519 **Roads in Wales: progress and plans for the 1990's. Ffyrdd yng Nghymru. Cynnydd a chynlluniau ar gyfer y 1990au.**
Cardiff: Welsh Office (publicity unit), 1989. 52p. maps.

The most recent in a series of Welsh Office statements on road programmes, noting: objectives; achievements; a forward programme; proposals for specific projects; road renewal schemes; road maintenance; road safety aspects; and considering the effect of the road programme on the landscape and the environment. The publication is augmented by tables of statistics which indicate expenditure, mileage, improvement scheme costs, studies in progress, and lists of supplementary grants.

520 **Stage coaches in Wales.**
Herbert Williams.   Barry, Wales: Stewart Williams, 1977. 120p.

A popular illustrated history of the stage coach system in Wales, its development, characteristics and decline. The volume provides a fascinating insight into the growth of the road network in Wales and the rôle of the stage coach companies in the agitation for improvements to the road system.

521 **Welsh bus handbook.**
Chris Taylor, Alan Witton.   Harrow Weald (Middlesex), England:
Capital Transport Publishing, 1987. 160p.

A detailed study of fifty-two bus and coach companies operating in Wales, with fleet lists, the routes operated and other data. The book also presents a history of the growth and development of each company, and considers mergers, purchases, and the take-overs that have taken place. Also included is an assessment of the services provided by the various companies and activities since deregulation.

522   **The Welsh post towns before 1840.**
Michael Scott Archer.   London: Philimore, 1970. 136p. maps. bibliog.
A study of the postal service in Wales from the sixteenth century to the introduction of
the uniform Penny Post in 1840. It offers a historical summary, an alphabetical list of
post towns with tabulated data, a number of appendices, a glossary of terms and
illustrations.

523   **Wheels within Wales: rural transport and accessibility issues in the
Principality.**
Edited by Paul J. Cloke.   Lampeter, Wales: St. David's University
College Centre for Rural Transport, 1984. 145p. maps. bibliog.
A collection of essays encompassing primary contemporary transport issues such as:
traditional attitudes to rural transport; accessibility; the mobility of the population;
managing rural buses; the perspectives of the development agencies on transport and
regional development, local authority policies, consumer perspectives, and changing
patterns of needs and provision.

Railways and trams

524   **The Cambrian Railways: volume I, 1852-1888.**
Rex Christiansen, R. W. Miller.   Newton Abbot, England: David &
Charles, 1967. 178p. maps.
A study of the railways of mid-Wales (north of Brecon and south of Wrexham), their
development, variety, eventual decline and their resurrection as tourist attractions.

525   **The Cambrian Railways: volume II, 1889-1968.**
Rex Christiansen, R. W. Miller.   Newton Abbot, England: David &
Charles, [n.d.]. 218p. maps.
A companion volume to the work, listed in item 524 above.

526   **Forgotten railways: North and mid Wales.**
Rex Christiansen.   Newton Abbot, England: David & Charles, 1976.
160p. maps. bibliog. (Forgotten Railways Series).
A companion volume to that for South Wales (item 527) which concentrates on
standard gauge lines. A gazetteer lists what remains of the lines. Seven lines are
studied in detail; those offering passenger services and some which were goods lines,
such as the terra cotta and coal line at Ruabon.

527   **Forgotten railways: South Wales.**
James Page.   Newton Abbot, England: David & Charles, 1988. 2nd
ed. 207p. maps. bibliog. (Forgotten Railways Series).
A work which studies remnants and traces of former lines which were part of the dense
and complex railway network of Wales. Chapters are devoted to various locations

throughout South Wales, and deal with passenger and goods services. A gazetteer summarising the main details of each line supplements the ten chapters of descriptive text which is fully illustrated.

528 **An illustrated history of The Vale of Rheidol Light Railway: the little line along the Rheidol.**
C. C. Green.   Didcot, England: Wild Swan Publications, 1986. 264p.
A full and detailed survey of this railway which opened in 1902. The work is based on an extensive photographic archive in the author's possession, which was created to record examples of every feature. The volume documents the material in various chapters which deal with the administrative history; running the line; the journey along the line and its features; stations; halts and sidings; the locomotives; the rolling stock; timetables; special events and occasions; and the management of the railway by London Midland region, of British Rail. Interesting appendices are also included. This is an example, probably the most detailed, of the many published histories and studies of individual lines in Wales.

529 **The little wonder: 150 years of the Festiniog Railway.**
John Winton.   London: Michael Joseph 1986. rev. ed. 238p. maps. bibliog.
A history of a railway originally built to convey slate to the coast for export, which declined as that industry declined, but which has been revived by experts and amateurs and is now both a social amenity and part of the transport network as well as being a tourist attraction of great significance. As well as giving the early history of the line, this work traces the work of renewal and rebuilding, the rôle of railway societies in the restoration of the railway. This is a revised edition of a work first published in 1975, and therefore brings the story of the restoration of the Festiniog Railway up to the late 1980s.

530 **North Wales tramways.**
Keith Turner.   Newton Abbot, England: David & Charles, 1979. 176p. maps. bibliog.
A study which represents the only substantial attempt made to record the history of this mode of transport in Wales. It includes studies of the horse and electric tramways of Wrexham, Pwllheli and Llanbedrog, the Great Orme tramway, the Llandudno and Colwyn Bay electric railway and minor lines. The book is illustrated with extensive appendices for each service.

531 **Railways of Wales.**
Stuart Owen-Jones.   Cardiff: National Museum of Wales, 1981. 48p. maps.
A concise illustrated history of the railways of Wales, covering their growth and development, their influence on commercial, industrial and social life, their decline and contraction, and their situation today.

532   **Rheilffyrdd Cymru. The railways of Wales.**
R. Emrys Jones.   [Caernarfon], Wales: Welsh Library Association, 1979. 154p.

The subject matter of this illustrated bi-lingual publication is arranged chronologically tracing the most significant dates and events in the history and development of railways in Wales. The starting date is 1802, the date of the establishment of the first public railway in Wales (and the second in Britain) and the author ends his account in 1948, the year in which Welsh railways were regionalized following nationalisation the previous year.

533   **The Welsh narrow-gauge railways.**
Peter Johnson.   Weybridge, England: Ian Allan, 1985. 56p. maps.

An illustrated history and contemporary assessment of the narrow-gauge railways of Wales – the Festiniog, Talyllyn, Vale of Rheidol, Welshpool and Llanfair, Snowdon Mountain, Padarn Lake, Bala Lake, Brecon Mountain, Welsh Highland and Fairbourne Railways – as well as other lines, such as the Rhiw Valley, Rhyl miniature and Great Orme lines. The introduction analyses their attraction and fascination, their location amid spectacular scenery, and provides a brief historical account of their development, their current situation and how they are marketed as tourist attractions.

534   **Welsh railways in the heyday of steam.**
H. C. Casserley.   Truro, England: D. Bradford Barton, [n.d.]. 96p.

This volume, which is part of a series (embracing Ireland and Scotland), describes the railways of Wales from ca. 1920 to the 1960s, with particular reference to the resurrection of steam trains such as the Talyllyn and Vale of Rheidol Railway as tourist attractions often described as the 'great little trains of Wales'. An illustrated study which seeks to describe trains and rolling stock, surroundings, landscapes and terrains as well as services and goods.

535   **Western region in Wales.**
James McGregor.   London: Ian Allan, 1983. 112p. maps.

An illustrated study of contemporary railway activity in Wales, including the routes, services, rolling stock and traffic volumes. It also includes a short introduction indicating the significance of the railway system to industrial and economic life and the particularly interesting aspects that can be observed by the railway enthusiasts.

Water and air transport

536   **Air services in Wales: report of a consultancy. . .**
Cardiff: Welsh Office, Welsh Development Agency and others. 1985. 10p.

A summary report which lists only the main conclusions and recommendations of a much larger detailed report (not published) of the consultancy. It assessed the need and demand for intra-Wales services, scheduled and chartered and the potential for international growth.

537 **Cambrian coasters: steam and motor coaster owners of north and west Wales.**
R. S. Fenton.   Kendal, England: World Ship Society, 1989. 200p. bibliog.

A short, illustrated history of a significant aspect of Welsh maritime activity, with an introductory essay which places the Welsh coastal shipping industry in an appropriate social and economic context. It includes all known owners of powered coasters from St. David's head in the south to the Dee estuary in north-east Wales, as well as selected Liverpool-based companies operating steam packet services to Wales. However, it excludes pure passenger vessels serving the Welsh coast. This is an important study of some of the smaller Welsh coastal ports and harbours.

538 **Canals in Wales.**
Ian L. Wright.   Truro, England: Barton, 1977. 96p.

A pictorial study designed to 'provide the first visual record of all the canals in Wales, and of some of the people whose working lives were bound up with them'. The work includes a brief history of the development of the canals and their distribution, their eventual decline and their recent revival as tourist amenities.

539 **Cardiff shipowners.**
J. Geraint Jenkins, David Jenkins.   Cardiff: National Museum of Wales, 1986. 87p.

A study of the inter-relationship between the growth of Cardiff as a port, its principal shipowners, its trade, and its growth as a commercial centre. The work pays particular attention to the Bute family and to the export of coal. The author's treatment, though predominantly historical, also has a contemporary perspective.

540 **Cymru a'r môr. Maritime Wales.**
Caernarfon, Wales: Gwynedd Archives Service, 1976-. annual.

An illustrated journal aimed 'at recording the story of the ships of Wales through the ages, the men who owned them, and the men (and women) who sailed in them'.

541 **Early aviation in north Wales.**
Roy Sloan. Llanrwst, Wales: Gwasg Carreg Gwalch, 1989. 167p. maps.

An illustrated work which chronicles the history of aviation in North Wales from the time of the early nineteenth-century balloon flights to the outbreak of war in 1939. The subjects discussed range from exhibition flights, to attempts to cross the Irish Sea, aeronautical research, and anti-submarine patrols during World War I. Illustrated.

542 **The maritime heritage of Dyfed.**
Cardiff: National Museum of Wales, 1982. 59p.

An illustrated exhibition catalogue, which provides an interesting, extensively researched pictorial history of maritime life and activity in south-west Wales. It covers fishing, seafaring, the growth of trade in a range of commodities, piracy and smuggling, the major ports, major ships and owners, ship-building, the impact of world and local trade conditions and provides an assessment of the contemporary scene.

543 **Maritime heritage: the ships and seamen of southern Ceredigion.**
J. Geraint Jenkins.   Llandysul, Wales: Gwasg Gomer, 1982. 265p.

An illustrated work which traces the history of maritime activity in south west Wales from the earliest times. Amongst the subjects considered are Viking marauders, the arrival of Celtic saints, seafaring, fishing, the transportation of goods, emigration, the ship owners, builders and trading patterns.

544 **Maritime industry and port development in South Wales.**
Graham Hailett, Peter Randall.   Cardiff: University College Department of Economics, 1970. 122p. maps. bibliog.

A comprehensive study outlining general principles for investment in port facilities, the economics of development, and the history of South Wales ports, as well as studies of Newport, Cardiff, Barry, Port Talbot, Swansea and Milford Haven. It also contains studies of iron ore imports, considers the scope for developments, as well as offering conclusions.

545 **National atlas showing canals, navigable rivers, mineral tramroads, railways and street tramways. Volume Four. Wales and the Welsh Marches. Atlas Cenedlaethol yn dangos camlesi, afonydd mordwyol, rheilffyrdd ceffyl ac agerbeiriant a thramlinoedd stryd. Cyfrol IV. Cymru a'r Mers.**
Preston, England: G. L. Crowther, 1986. 70p. maps.

The atlas includes cliff railways, rail served docks and quays in addition to the categories listed in the title. The maps are cumulative and cover the period from the Roman dykes and canals to May 1984. This volume for Wales includes a glossary of commonly occurring place-names and terms.

546 **Reardon Smith Line.**
P. M. Heaton.   Risca, Wales: The Starling Press for the author, 1984. 133p.

An illustrated account of the best-known shipping company based in Wales, which also provides a further study which indicates the significance of Cardiff as a port. The work traces the origins and development of the line and its trade (in coal and other commodities), particularly to the Pacific coast of north America. It also carefully relates the line's fortunes in response to prevailing economic conditions, wars, depressions, and to technical developments.

547 **Ships and seamen of Gwynedd.**
Aled Eames.   Caernarfon, Wales: Gwynedd Archives Service, 1976. 67p.

A pictorial history of seafaring life in north-west Wales issued to accompany a travelling exhibition of the same title organized in 1976 by Gwynedd Archives Services. The introduction is a succinct account of the importance of the area and its ports.

548 **Ventures in sail. Aspects of the maritime history of Gwynedd, 1840-1914, and the Liverpool connection.**
Aled Eames. [Caernarfon], Wales: Gwynedd Archives and Museums Service, Merseyside Maritime Museum, National Maritime Museum, 1987. 315p.
A study 'which indicates aspects of the part played by ships and their owners in the history of north west Wales, and some of the ways in which the wealth that came from the sea . . . in turn influenced the social, political, religious and educational life of Gwynedd'. Major chapters study builders, owners, captains and major ships. In addition, lengthy appendices list fleets, owners, operators and charter parties.

549 **The Welsh ports.**
Cardiff: Welsh Council, 1973. 46p. maps.
A report which examines the facilities and advantages offered by ports in Wales, reviews contemporary trends in their use and development, and considers their prospects, particularly as regards the scope which they offer for the development in their hinterland areas of related industrial enterprises. The study includes the oil terminal at Milford Haven and the ferry ports of west and North Wales as well as freight services, contemporary trade patterns and users.

550 **Welsh sail: a pictorial history.**
Susan Campbell-Jones. Llandysul: Gomer Press, 1976. 103p. bibliog.
An illustrated introductory study which provides an outline history, and a study of the main ports, shipbuilding, rigs, mariners, wrecks and mysteries.

551 **Welsh shipping forgotten fleets.**
P. M. Heaton. Risca, Wales: Starling Press for the author, 1989. 91p.
A study of five small and lesser-known shipping companies which operated out of Cardiff and other Welsh ports in their heyday: Duncan Sisters (1889-1959); Seagers (1904-63), Pardoe-Thomas' White Cross Line (1910-36); Claymore Shipping (1919-62); and Lovering's coasters (1936-67). The work includes much valuable information on trade and ports and is well illustrated.

Employment and Manpower

552 Regional trends 1988.
London: HMSO, 1988. 160p. maps.
Provides a regional profile of Wales and presents employment statistics in tabular form. The statistics relate to the number of employees, the number of men and women in employment, the civilian labour force (with components of change), the economic activity rate, the self-employed, employment by households, occupational groupings, educational qualifications, overtime, sickness absences, industrial disputes, redundancies, training and employment measures, restart counselling, Community Programme activity, and unemployment.

553 Training Agency in Wales. Annual Report.
Cardiff: The Training Agency, 1988-. annual.
Set up in 1988, the Training Agency was established within the Department of Employment Group, and took over the rôle of the Training Commission and the Manpower Services Commission. A network of autonomous and self-funding Training and Enterprise Councils were created under the auspices of the Training Agency in 1990. The Agency offers Employment Training, Business Growth Training, a Youth Training Scheme and two educational programmes in schools and colleges, – i.e., the Technical and Vocational Educational Initiative (TVEI), and Work Related Further Education (WRFE). The annual reports consider activities, achievements, plans, new initiatives, and income and expenditure.

554 Wales: employment and the economy.
Cardiff: Welsh Council, 1972. 23p.
A report submitted to the Secretary of State for Wales, surveying growing unemployment, patterns of employment and changes in the labour requirements of Welsh industry. It assesses demand and growth, the impact of regional incentives and long term employment factors, and provides a summary of recommendations.

Labour Movement and Trade Unions

555 **Bibliography of Welsh labour history.**
Llafur vol. 1, no 1 (1972), p. 16-26.
A list of publications which deal with the following aspects of Welsh labour history: economic and social history; trade union and friendly societies; political history; industrial conditions; industrial disputes; rural conditions; rural disorder; Chartism; the Poor Law; and health and sanitation.

556 **The Fed: a history of the South Wales miners in the twentieth century.**
Hywel Francis, David Smith.   London: Lawrence & Wishart, 1980.
530p. illus.
This is a significant contribution to the history of trade unionism in the South Wales coalfield which was officially commissioned by the South Wales area of the National Union of Mineworkers. It traces the history of the South Wales Miners' Federation in its social and ecnomic context from its foundation in 1898 up to the 1970s.

557 **The great strike: a history of the Penrhyn quarry dispute 1900-1903.**
Jean Lindsay.   Newton Abbot, England: David & Charles, 1987.
256p.
A detailed account of the struggle between the owners and workers during the Penrhyn Quarry Strike at the beginning of the twentieth century. This strike is still considered to be one of the bitterest disputes in Welsh working-class history. In this study the author begins by examining the history of industrial relations in the quarry during the years preceding the dispute and concludes with the aftermath of the struggle, particularly the continued animosity between those who returned to work and those who stayed out to the bitter end. This volume is suitable for the student of Welsh labour history and for the general reader.

558 **The last rising: the Newport insurrection of 1839.**

David J. V. Jones. Oxford: Clarendon Press, 1985. 273p.

On 4 November 1839 soldiers shot and killed some twenty miners who were involved in armed insurrection outside the Westgate Hotel in Newport. This event was a landmark in Welsh working-class history. In this detailed, but highly readable, study of the rising and its aftermath, the author analyses the impact of the insurrection on the social and political climate. Although much of the study deals with the events during the days leading up to the rising and the march and attack on Newport, it also contains a survey of the working and social conditions in the South Wales coalfield during the 1830s so that the rising can be placed in its true context.

559 **Llafur: Journal of Welsh Labour History.**

Aberystwyth, 1972-. annual.

Contains short articles on various aspects of the study of labour history and related topics, together with reports on the activities of the Welsh Labour History Society, the South Wales Miners' Library and the Welsh Political Archive. This journal is suitable for the the scholar, the student and the interested layman.

560 **Mabon (William Abraham 1842-1922): a study in trade union leadership.**

E. W. Evans. Cardiff: University of Wales Press, 1959. 115p. bibliog.

A study of the career and achievements of one of the best known leaders in the history of Welsh trade unionism during a critical period in its development.

561 **The Merthyr rising.**

Gwyn A. Williams. Cardiff: University of Wales Press, 1988. 237p. maps. tables.

This book was first published by Croom Helm in 1978. By the early 1830s, Merthyr Tydfil had become the first major town of the Welsh Industrial Revolution and in 1831, Merthyr was the scene of a serious insurrection led by the ironworkers. Although the disturbance was eventually crushed by the militia it is considered by the author to be a key event in working-class history in South Wales. This study presents a dramatic account of the incidents leading up to the rising as well as the social, political and economic context of the disturbance. Williams also provides a perceptive analysis of the significance of the insurrection. Although the book is written by a professional historian for students of Welsh and labour history, his vivid descriptions of the events mean that it is highly readable and would appeal equally to the general reader.

562 **The North Wales quarrymen 1874-1922.**

R. Merfyn Jones. Cardiff: University of Wales Press, 1988. 360p. bibliog.

A study of the efforts of the quarrymen to organise a trade union in the slate quarries and mines of North Wales with particular reference to the giant Penrhyn Quarry in Bethesda, which witnessed one of the longest and most dramatic events in the history of the working-class struggle for better pay and conditions. This book also provides a detailed account of the main tensions which existed in the slate villages and quarries culminating in the Penrhyn lock-outs of 1896-97 and 1900-03.

563 **The rural revolt that failed: farm workers trade unions in Wales 1889-1950.**

David A. Pretty. Cardiff: University of Wales Press, 1989. 291p. illus. bibliog.

The struggle of rural society against injustices in nineteenth-century Wales has received considerable attention amongst Welsh historians and special attention has been focussed on the Rebecca Riots, the Tithe War and the Land Question. Generally speaking, these disturbances reflected the grievances of middle-class farmers. There was, however, a further class, the agricultural labourers, who were generally poor and badly exploited by their employers. Towards the close of the nineteenth century, the living conditions of this class had improved very little since feudal times. Notwithstanding this, in the 1890s the agricultural workers became more assertive. The chief aim of this detailed study is to reclaim the lost history of this underprivileged group by tracing the growth and development of rural trade unionism in Wales from the 1890s to 1950.

564 **Society and trade unions in Glamorgan 1800-1970.**

Hywel Francis. In: *Glamorgan County History Vol VI: Glamorgan society 1780-1980.* Edited by Prys Morgan. Cardiff: Glamorgan History Trust, 1988, p. 89-107.

The growth of the iron and coal industries, particularly in the county of Glamorgan, was the dominant feature in the social and political life of Wales for almost a century after 1850. This survey of trade unionism in Glamorgan, describes the emergence of trade unions from the last decade of the eighteenth century to the present day. It provides a useful overview for students and the general reader who wish to understand the history of the trade union movement in Wales.

565 **South Wales miners. Glowyr De Cymru: a history of the South Wales Miners Federation, (1898-1914).**

R. Page Arnot. London: George Allen & Unwin, 1967. 390p. illus.

A study of the formation and early history of the South Wales Miners' Federation in which the author records the struggles and sacrifices of the miners and their leaders to safeguard and improve the colliers' living conditions. This volume covers the period up to the beginning of World War I and shows the key rôle played by the 'Fed' in shaping the social, political and industrial life of the people of South Wales.

566 **South Wales miners. Glowyr De Cymru: a history of the South Wales Miners' Federation (1914-1926).**

R. Page Arnot. Cardiff: Cymric Federation Press, 1975. 356p. illus.

This is part two of the official history of the South Wales Miners' Federation and a companion volume to item no. 565 in which the same author traced the early history of the Federation. Although this volume presents the history of just twelve years of the union's activities, these were amongst the most eventful in the whole history of labour relations in Wales and they culminated in the seven-month lock-out of 1926. The study presents a detailed account of the bitter conflicts between the union, the colliery owners and the government during World War I, the lock-out of 1921 and examines the causes of the 1926 strike.

567 **Wales T.U.C. Cyngor Undebau Llafur Cymru annual report.**
Cardiff: Wales Trade Union Council, 1974-. annual.
A report on the activities of the General Council of the TUC and the annual conference of the Wales TUC, including details of the main speeches and the motions passed at the conference. The volume also includes the names and addresses of trade unions affiliated to the Wales TUC, together with their membership figures, the names of General Council members, ballot results and the rules and standing orders.

568 **The Welsh dockers.**
Philip J. Leng. Ormskirk, England: G. W. & A. Hesketh, 1981. 124p.
Presents the story of the devlopment of the Dock, Wharf, Riverside and General Labourers Union in South Wales from its foundation in 1889 until its amalgamation with other organisations to form the Transport and General Workers Union in 1922. The work also includes a general introduction to the development of the South Wales ports and their trade during the course of the nineteenth century, together with an examination of the system of employment adopted on the waterfront and the characteristics of the labour force engaged.

Statistics

569 Digest of Welsh historical statistics. Crynhoad o ystadegau hanesyddol Cymru.

John Williams.   Cardiff: Welsh Office, 1985. 2 vols.

Data is enumerated for population, labour, wages, earnings and consumer expenditure, agriculture, iron and steel, lead, copper, slate, transport, housing, tourism, social services, care, parliamentary elections, local government, education and religion. The work seeks to offer a statistical service for those working on the history of modern Wales, in the belief that 'the quantitative element is a necessary and important part of the historical record' and because 'it was an aspect that was particularly inaccessible for scholars of Welsh history'.

570 Digest of Welsh statistics. Crynhoad o ystadegau Cymru.

Cardiff: Welsh Office, 1954-. annual. maps.

Prepared in collaboration with the statistics divisions of other government departments, this publication is the primary source of Welsh statistical data. It offers tabulations in the areas of: population; vital statistics (birth, marriages, divorces, deaths etc); health and personal social services; social security; law, order and protective services; housing; new towns; the Welsh language; the electorate; areas of recreation; schools; higher and further education; labour; industrial production; energy; construction and investment; agriculture; forestry; fishing; distribution (retail outlets); transport and communications; national income; finance; personal incomes; expenditure and the environment. It also includes various appendices.

Environment

571 **Acid rain in Wales. a report with particular reference to the constituency of Brecon and Radnor.**
London: Friends of the Earth, 1985. 15p. bibliog.
Based on data gathered from numerous sources, trusts, associations and councils, this work has a particularly useful bibliography which lists articles and published and unpublished studies relating to Wales. The report considers the nature of acid rain in Wales, the onset of acidification, and the effects on forestry, fisheries, wildlife and agriculture.

572 **Annual Report.**
Centre for Alternative Technology. Canolfan y Dechnoleg Amgen.
Machynlleth, Wales: The Centre, [1973-]. annual.
Relates the activities of a centre established in mid-Wales for the purpose of 'experimenting with and demonstrating ways in which individuals, families and small communities can have a sustainable, whole and ecologically sound way of life'.

573 **Chernobyl accident data for Wales: compilation of the results of environmental measurements in Wales.**
Cardiff: Welsh Office, 1986. 36p.
The nuclear accident in the USSR in April 1986 had a profound effect on the environment, and particularly on agriculture in North Wales. This report offers data concerning radioactivity concentrations in the air, in rivers, streams and lakes, and reservoirs and on grasses, and in milk, leafy vegetables and other foods.

574 **Council for the Protection of Rural Wales. Annual report.**
Welshpool, Wales: CPRW, 1928-. annual.
A report of the Council's activities since its establishment in 1928. reports have become more significant and lengthier since 1980.

575 **Countryside Commission: Comisiwn Cefn Gwlad. Annual report.**

Cheltenham, England: Countryside Commission. 1967-. annual.

A bi-lingual publication describing the Commission's work largely, but not exclusively, in Wales. It contains reports on conservation and environmental protection ventures, strategies on recreation and access to sensitive areas, work in specific locations and the general promotional and publicity activities undertaken. The Commission has a permanent office in Wales which is located in Newtown, Powys.

576 **Current information on the environment.**

Cardiff: Welsh Office Library, 1986-. monthly.

A current awareness bulletin which has three sections: new books, pamphlets and official publications; on-line search material; and the contents pages of relevant periodicals. Normally it lists all the materials relevant to environmental issues in Wales.

577 **Environmental bibliography of Wales, 1900-1976.**

J. N. M. Firth, C. V. Caine. Cardiff: HMSO, 1978. 282p. maps.

A bibliography listing some 4,000 items from over 300 journals and other sources which is produced 'in an attempt to bring together all those papers with an environmental science aspect published between 1900 and 1970 that refer specifically to the Welsh environment'. The subjects included are agricultural science, biology, botany, entomology, environmental chemistry, epidemiology, geochemistry, hydrology, marine studies, meteorology, oceanography, ornithology, parasitology, pollution studies, soil science and zoology. Works are listed in three sections: by subject; by author; and within a cross reference sequence.

578 **Environmental digest for Wales. Crynhoad o ystadegau'r amgylchedd.**

London: HMSO. 1984-. annual.

Statistical analyses of aspects of environmental matters in Wales. Tables of data are presented for land and human activity, water use and resources, atmosphere, and radio activity. There are also cartographic representations of demographic features, specific areas of environmental concern or interest, areas of natural beauty or special scientific interest, rainfall patterns, estuaries and reservoirs, as well as appendices relating to particular issues in a given year.

579 **Land drainage, fisheries and aquatic environment bibliography.**

A. Neville Jones. Brecon, Wales: Welsh Water Authority, 1980. 20p.

This publication is intended primarily for the use of fishery, recreation and amenity staff, to assist them to develop an appreciation of the ecology of rivers and to provide information on habitat improvement. The works listed are divided into the following categories: stream morphology and hydrology; land drainage practice; and environmental impact (particularly on fisheries, and habitat improvement). A significant number of the items refer to Wales as do the suggestions for basic texts offered in the introduction.

580 **Nature Conservancy Council. Report.**

Peterborough, England: Nature Conservancy Council, 1974-. annual.

The Council's report refers to its activities, sites and projects in Wales, the sites of special scientific interest, the land management agreements, and the nature reserves offices and staff. However, there is no separate section devoted to Wales as such, data and references being interspersed with that for England and Scotland.

581 **Nature conservation in Wales.**
Chris C. Park. *Cambria*, vol. 3, no. 2, (1976), p. 135-44.

A short but valuable overview which lists the bodies, organisations and agencies involved in conservation work and planning in Wales. It also examines their activities, sites and responsibilities and highlights particular issues and areas of conflict, such as tourism and economic development in National Park areas. The article also has a very useful bibliography.

582 **Regaining the wastelands.**
Gwyn Griffiths. In: *The new Wales*. Edited by David Cole. Cardiff: University of Wales Press, 1990, p. 61-8.

A study of the progress of land reclamation in Wales which considers the agencies undertaking the schemes, the characteristics of particular schemes, and the controversial issues involved.

583 **Rural Wales magazine for a green environment: official magazine of the Council for the Protection of Rural Wales.**
Welshpool, Wales: Council for the Protection of Rural Wales. 1928-.
three times per year.

A periodical whose main language is English which discusses environmental issues in a Welsh context, and which includes comment, news, lengthy articles, natural history sections, correspondence, and illustrated sections on reserves and areas of conservation significance. It covers contemporary issues and developments, international relations, and all issues relating to rural Wales and country life. The journal commenced as a news bulletin for members and then it became *CPRW news* . The magazine had a chequered early history when publication patterns were very *ad hoc*.

584 **Survey of contaminated land in Wales.**
Cardiff: Welsh Office, 1984. 80p. bibliog.

The report of survey work undertaken between 1983 and 1984 which was funded by the Welsh Office and the Welsh Development Agency. Sources of contamination are listed (as are the sites in an appendix), and the trends are indicated.

Education

General and historical development

585   **'Certain scholars of Wales': the Welsh experience in education.**
R. Brinley Jones.   Llanwrda, Wales: Drovers Press, 1986. 92p.
bibliog.

A collection of essays in which the author presents the history of the efforts made by the Welsh people from the earliest times to the twentieth century to take advantage of educational opportunities both in Wales and elsewhere. One chapter describes the connection between Wales and the University of Oxford up to 1600. The volume also includes brief assessments of grammar schools from the sixteenth century, the Society for the Promotion of Christian Knowledge (SPCK) schools, Griffith Jones' circulating schools, and the British and National schools of the nineteenth century.

586   **Education.**
John Williams.   In: *Digest of Welsh historical statistics. Crynhoad o
ystadegau hanesyddol, vol. 2.* Compiled by John Williams. Cardiff:
Welsh Office, 1985, p. 195-221.

A collection of raw statistics gathered from a large number of sources in order to assist researchers and scholars who require quantitative data on aspects of education in Wales in the nineteenth and twentieth centuries. Also included is a short essay which surveys the educational statistics available in various nineteenth-century reports. In addition to statistical data on schools, this section of the book also includes data on teacher numbers, trainee teachers, expenditure on education, public examinations and on activities in the university sector.

587 **Education in a new era.**

R. Brinley Jones. In: *The new Wales*. Edited by David Cole. Cardiff: University of Wales Press, 1990, p. 191-204.

A general survey of Welsh education provision at all levels at the beginning of the 1990s. Changes in the social and economic climate have brought about educational developments and innovations such as Technical and Vocational Education (TVEI) and the Education Reform Act and these and other issues are dealt with briefly.

588 **Education in a Welsh rural county, 1870- 1973.**

J. A. Davies. Cardiff: University of Wales Press, 1973. 278p. bibliog.

A detailed study of the development of educational provision and its administration in Montgomeryshire from the Elementary Education Act of 1870 to 1973 after which local government was reorganized. Many of the issues and controversies which are dealt with in this book would also have been experienced in most other rural local educational authorities in Wales during the same period.

589 **Education in industrial Wales 1700-1900: a study of the works schools system in Wales during the industrial revolution.**

Leslie Wynne Evans. Cardiff: Avalon Books, 1971. 362p. bibliog.

A detailed history of the efforts of employers to provide a basic education for working-class children in developing industrial areas in Wales before the advent of state education. The book is arranged by the types of industry found in Wales during the period under investigation. In assessing the achievements of these schools, the author shows that their efforts were dictated to a large extent by industrial demands for labour and by contemporary social attitudes towards education.

590 **The education of Welshmen.**

R. Brinley Jones. In: *Anatomy of Wales*. Edited by R. Brinley Jones. Peterston-super-Ely, Wales: Gwerin, 1972, p. 146-70.

A short essay which provides the general reader with an outline history of developments in the education of the Welsh people from the Roman period to 1970.

591 **The history of education in Wales Vol. 1.**

Edited by Jac L. Williams, Gwilym Rees Hughes. Swansea, Wales: Christopher Davies, 1978. 144p.

A collection of eight essays which traces the history of Welsh education from the earliest times to the middle of the nineteenth century. Although written initially to provide students in colleges of education and university departments of education with an insight into the development of education in Wales, the book will also be of interest to the general reader. The essays discuss the following topics: education and culture to the sixteenth century; the Puritan contribution; eighteenth-century charity schools; Welsh circulating schools; the Sunday school; the British Schools movement; the contribution of the established church to education; and the 'Blue Books' of 1847.

Education. General and historical development

592 **Pioneers of Welsh education.**
Swansea, Wales: Faculty of Education, University College Swansea,
[1964]. 100p. bibliog.
A collection of essays on four Welsh education leaders from the eighteenth century to
the first quarter of the twentieth century. The four figures who are featured in the
volume are: Griffith Jones (1683-1761); Thomas Charles (1755-1814); Hugh Owen
(1804-81); and Owen M. Edwards (1858-1920).

593 **Review of educational provision in Wales: a report.**
Cardiff: Welsh Office, 1988-. annual
Reviews aspects of educational provision, as well as teaching and learning at all levels
of education in Wales. The reviews are based on the extensive visits made to schools
and colleges by members of the HM Inspectorate of Schools in Wales.

594 **Studies in Welsh education: Welsh educational structure and
administration 1880-1925.**
Leslie Wynne Evans.   Cardiff: University of Wales Press, 1974. 427p.
bibliog.
This book consists of six interrelated studies which deal with aspects of the evolution of
Welsh educational administration between 1880 and 1925. This was a crucial period in
the development of a semi-autonomous administrative system of education for Wales
and the author provides a detailed account of the genesis of the Welsh Department of
the Board of Education and the contentious issues of this period.

595 **The Sunday school.**
T. M. Bassett.   In: *The history of education in Wales 1.* Edited by Jac
L. Williams, Gwilym Rees Hughes. Swansea, Wales: Christopher
Davies, 1978, p. 70-87.
A short essay on the history of the Sunday school movement in Wales from the 1790s
to the end of the nineteenth century. The author presents a balanced evaluation of the
weaknesses, as well as the strengths, of these schools and maintains that their main
achievement was to create a public eager to read materials in the Welsh language.

596 **The Welsh Journal of Education. Cylchgrawn Addysg Cymru.**
Cardiff: School of Education, University of Wales College Cardiff,
1989-. biannual.
This new journal publishes articles, surveys of research in progress, official reports and
book reviews on all aspects of education but with particular relation to Wales. The
publication is aimed at those concerned with education in Wales in a professional or
lay capacity.

146

Schools

597   Control and conflicts in Welsh secondary education 1889-1944.
Gareth Elwyn Jones.   Cardiff: University of Wales Press, 1982. 248p.
bibliog.

A study of the Welsh secondary school system from the Welsh Intermediate Act of
1889 to the 1944 Education Act. The author sets out to examine the contribution of
various parties in moulding the nature of the education provided in these schools as
well as the tensions which arose between the distinctly Welsh educational philosophy
of Owen M. Edwards, the Chief Inspector of Schools in Wales, and others involved in
the decision making process at local level.

**598   The curriculum and organization of county intermediate schools
1880-1926.**
Wynford Davies.   Cardiff: University of Wales Press, 1989. 299p.
bibliog.

The Welsh Intermediate Education Act of 1889 presented Wales with an opportunity
to experiment with the development of secondary education. In this study of the
period, the author examines the nature, organisation and the curriculum of these
schools and assesses their contribution to the development of secondary education.

**599   Curriculum and organisation of primary schools in Wales. Cwrs addysg
a threfniadaeth ysgolion cynradd Cymru.**
Welsh Office.   [London]: HMSO, 1984. 43p. (HMI Wales Educational
Issues, no. 7).

This bilingual report, based on HM Inspectors visits to most of the primary schools in
Wales, attempts to provide an overview of the life and work of these schools. The
report includes sections on aims, planning and the staffing of the curriculum, as well as
the standard of work produced in languages, maths, humanities, arts and crafts, music,
physical education and science.

600   Directory of resource providers (Wales).
Compiled by Geraint Evans, Hywel James.   Council for Educational
Technology & College of Librarianship Wales, 1982. 447p.

This directory was produced as a result of a research project jointly funded by CET
and the College of Librarianship Wales and is aimed at teachers in primary and
secondary schools. The volume provides information on 395 organisations in Wales
which supply resources which could be of value to schools for project work etc. The
entries contain the following details: name; address; name of contact; description of
organisation; main subjects; resources; availability; services; publications; and
educational value. Some eight years have elapsed since this work was published and
therefore care needs to be taken in using some of the data. Nonetheless, this volume
remains the only comprehensive guide of its kind in this field.

601 **Perspectives on a century of secondary education in Wales, 1889-1989.**
Edited by W. Gareth Evans. Aberystwyth, Wales: Centre for
Educational Studies, Faculty of Education, University College of
Wales, 1990. 240p.

A collection of twelve essays on aspects of secondary education in Wales written by academic and educational administrators. Part one consists of three essays which examine aspects of the Welsh Intermediate and Technical Education Act of 1889; the second part looks at aspects of secondary education during the past one hundred years (technical education and bilingual education, for example); and the papers in the final part consider current issues in the secondary education scene in Wales such as tertiary education, examinations and assessments, and the problems of small rural schools.

602 **Primary education in rural Wales. Addysg gynradd yn y Gymru wledig.**
HMI (Wales). Cardiff: Welsh Office, 1978. 122p. illus. maps.
(Education Survey, no. 6).

A bilingual survey undertaken by HM Inspectors of Schools in Wales to investigate the organisation and the curriculum found in small rural primary schools in Wales and to evaluate to what extent, if any, these schools are disadvanatged in meeting the needs of their pupils. Part one consists of an analysis of the demographic and linguistic changes which took place in rural Wales during the 1960s and 1970s. Part two provides an evaluation of the findings of the inspectors in relation to the nature, staffing and organisation of the schools, the curriculum and provision for the under fives.

603 **Secondary education in rural Wales. Addysg Uwchradd yn y Gymru Wledig.**
Aberystwyth Policy Group. Aberystwyth, Wales: University College
of Wales Faculty of Education, [1986]. 65p

This report examines rural secondary schools with particular reference to their demographic, economic and socio-cultural background and identifies the problems facing these schools at present in regard to the curriculum and organisation. Two aspects which are considered in some detail are bilingual education and in-service training. The report includes a list of recommendations for local education authorities and the Welsh Office regarding the development of such schools.

604 **Some trends in Welsh secondary education, 1967-87.**
Peter Ellis Jones. *Contemporary Wales*, vol. 2 (1989), p. 99-118.

A short review of recent trends in secondary education in Wales chiefly based on an analysis of the statistics of the Welsh Joint Education Committee's public examinations. The main developments of the period such as the introduction of CSE examinations, curriculum initiatives, gender differentiation and the greater commitment to teaching Welsh are briefly discussed.

605 **Statistics of education in Wales: schools. Ystadegau addysg yng Nghymru: ysgolion.**
Welsh Office. Cardiff: Welsh Office, 1988-. annual.

A collection of official statistics relating to nursery, primary and secondary education in Wales. The volume provides data on the number of schools, teaching staff and pupils in each sector together with statistics on the number of candidates and an analysis of the results in GCSE and A level examinations. The work also includes statistics on Welsh-language teaching, school leavers, school services, finance and unit costs, together with a helpful glossary of terms. It supersedes *Statistics of education in Wales. Ystadegau addysg yng Nghymru* which was published annually between 1976 and 1987 and covered schools, further and higher education.

606 **Two centuries of Anglesey schools 1700- 1902.**
David A. Petty. Llangefni, Wales: Anglesey Antiquarian Society, 1977. 383p. bibliog. (Studies in Anglesey History, no. 5).
This book is a study of the development of primary and secondary education in a Welsh rural county during the eighteenth and nineteenth centuries. The central theme is the struggle for the control of education between rival religious sects. The author also examines other aspects of education including the status of the Welsh language within the schools of the county. Although this is a study of one county many of the themes and issues were applicable to other Welsh counties.

607 **What are schools in Wales for? Wales and the Education Reform Act.**
Gareth Elwyn Jones. *Contemporary Wales*, vol. 2 (1988), p. 83-97.
Discusses the need to identify the rôle of education in Wales, particularly the part it has to play in maintaining the linguistic, cultural and other distinctive features of the Welsh people. The author expresses concern at the current obsession with examinations and assessment and sees a parallel with the conflict on this issue between the Welsh Department of the Board of Education and teachers during the first two decades of this century.

Further and higher education

608 **Prifysgol Cymru: Calendar. Calendar: University of Wales.**
Cardiff: University of Wales, 1897-. annual.
This is the standard guide book on the administration, the committee structure and the rules and regulations of degree and diploma courses. It also provides the names and qualifications of officers and teaching staff of constituent colleges and includes the charter, statutes and ordinances of the University and details of fellowships, scholarships, prizes and awards.

609 **Statistics of education in Wales: further and higher education.**
Ystadegau addysg yng Nghymru: addysg bellach ac uwch.
Welsh Office. Cardiff: Welsh Office, 1988-. annual.
A collection of official statistics relating to further and higher education in Wales based mainly on returns made to the Welsh Office and the Department of Education and Science by colleges and local education authorities, as well as data published by universities. The volume presents statistics on the number of students enrolled on various courses in further and higher educational institutions of various kinds in Wales, together with data on staff-student ratios, efficiency indicators and finance. The work also includes similar information on Open University and adult education students. It was originally published in one volume, which covered schools, further and higher education (q.v.).

610   **The University College of North Wales: foundations 1884-1927.**
J. Gwynn Williams.   Cardiff: University of Wales Press, 1985. 499p.

A detailed history of the University College of North Wales at Bangor written by a former student and the head of the college's Welsh History department for over twenty years. The study traces the story of the College from its foundation in 1884 to the year of the retirement of its first Principal, Sir Harry Reichel. As well as describing the relationship between the College and the wider community and with the federal university, it describes the major academic achievements of the institution and its members.

611   **The University College of Wales Aberystwyth 1872-1972.**
E. L. Ellis.   Cardiff: University of Wales Press, 1972. 353p.

The University College at Aberystwyth is the senior constituent of the federal University of Wales and therefore its history is vital to those who wish to understand the early development of higher education in Wales. This volume traces the story of the college during the first one hundred years of its history and, in addition to describing the developments and achievements which took place, the author discusses its significance in the wider educational, social and political context.

612   **The University of Wales: a historical sketch.**
D. Emrys Evans.   Cardiff: University of Wales Press, 1953. 176p.

The University of Wales was granted a Royal Charter in 1893 a few years after the first three constituent colleges of the federal system had been founded. This study focuses on the events which led to the granting of the charter to the larger institution and its development during the following decades.

Bilingual education

613   **Aspects of bilingualism in Wales.**
Colin Baker.   Clevedon, Philadelphia: Multilingual Matters, 1985. 209p. bibliog. maps.

An examination of the future prospects of the Welsh language and the rôle of education in its struggle for survival. The author describes developments to promote the language in educational research, curriculum development, education policy and provision and also examines the significance of the mass media and the microelectronics revolution to Welsh and other minority languages. One of the conclusions is that the survival of the language depends on political decisions and it is the author's hope that this publication will be seen as a contribution to that debate.

614   **Bilingual education: evaluation, assessment and methodology.**
Edited by C. J. Dodson.   Cardiff: University of Wales Press, 1985. 183p.

A collection of papers on the Schools Council Projects conducted during the 1970s on bilingual education at primary and secondary-school levels in Wales. These papers will not only be of interest to teachers and education administrators in Wales who are involved in developing bilingual education, but also to educationalists in other countries who are anxious to introduce a sound methodology for developing a bilingual education in primary and secondary schools.

615 **Bilingual education in Wales or education for a bilingual Wales?**
Colin Williams.   Bangor, Wales: Language Studies Centre, 1988. 20p. maps. (Cai Lecture Series, no. 1).
A critical assessment of the development of Welsh medium education in Wales in recent years. Despite the advances which have been made, the author sees that the provision of bilingual education in Wales at present is fragmentary and underdeveloped. Moreover, he asserts that a much greater challenge faces Welsh educationalists in 'convincing all Welsh citizens that a "bilingual Wales" is theirs by right and not the private fiefdom of a cultural minority'.

616 **Bilingualism: a bibliography of 1,000 references with special reference to Wales.**
Cardiff: University of Wales Press, 1971. 95p. (Welsh Studies in Education, no. 3).
This bibliography was originally compiled for Welsh-speaking students 'concerned with the study and promotion of bilingualism in Wales' but this revised edition is seen as an aid to students and research workers concerned with bilingual education in Wales and elsewhere. However, twenty years have elapsed since this work was compiled so that its main value today is for those who wish to trace the history of bilingual education in Wales up to 1970.

617 **Bilingualism in Welsh education.**
W. R. Jones.   Cardiff: University of Wales Press, 1966. 202p.
This study, aimed at students of education in university departments of education and colleges of education, examines endeavours to provide a bilingual education in Wales and discusses the psychological and educational problems which exist. Part one, presents an outline of the historical background to the bilingual movement in Welsh education, with particular reference to the place of Welsh and English in schools from the sixteenth century up to 1960. Part two, reviews research into bilingual education in Wales during the 1950s and 1960s.

618 **The growth of bilingual education in the secondary schools of Wales.**
Colin Baker.   In: *Perspectives on a century of secondary education in Wales: 1889-1989.* Edited by W. Gareth Evans. Aberystwyth, Wales: Centre for Educational Studies, Faculty of Education, University College of Wales Aberystwyth, 1990, p. 77-96.
A survey of bilingual secondary education in Wales during the second-half of the twentieth century. The author discusses the contrast between the growth of bilingual education and the decline of the language, the significant rôle of bilingual education in the efforts to maintain the Welsh language and other related themes.

619 **The implementation of language policy in the schools of Wales.**
Phillip M. Rawkins. Glasgow: Centre for the Study of Public Policy,
University of Strathclyde, 1979. 108p. bibliog. (Studies in Public Policy,
no. 40).

A report based principally on interviews held in 1978 with education administrators, teachers, parents, pressure groups and politicians to examine the rôle of central government, local authorities and headteachers in determining the language policy of individual primary and secondary schools in Wales. The author has selected south Glamorgan, mid-Glamorgan, Clwyd, Dyfed and Gwynedd as case studies of the decision-making process and linguistic conflict in this field. This report should help education practitioners and other interested groups, such as parents and politicians, to understand the uneven pattern of Welsh-language provision in Welsh schools during the past two decades. However, recent education acts, and particularly the implementation of a national curriculum in England and Wales, will radically alter the position of the Welsh language in education during the 1990s.

620 **The right to a bilingual education in nineteenth century Wales.**
B. L. Davies. *Transactions of the Honourable Society of
Cymmrodorion*, (1988), p. 133-51.

Examines the 'processes of anglicisation imposed upon the day-schools of Wales' during the nineteenth century together with an outline of the events which led to the Cross Commission on Elementary Education (1886-88) recommending that Welsh could be used as a medium of education and taught as a subject. The article pays tribute to the individuals and associations which played a crucial part in achieving this major breakthrough for bilingual education in Wales.

621 **The Welsh language in education.**
Jac L. Williams. In: *The Welsh language today*. Edited by Meic
Stephens. Llandysul, Wales: Gomer Press, 1979, p. 93-111.

A short essay which outlines the place of the Welsh language in the history of education in Wales from the Middle Ages to the late 1970s. Despite the steady progress during this century, the author emphasises that only a small proportion of the pupils are currently offered the opportunity to become thoroughly bilingual through the education system.

622 **The Welsh language in education: a volume of essays.**
Edited by Merfyn Griffiths. Cardiff: Welsh Joint Education
Committee, 1986. 116p. bibliog.

A collection of sixteen essays by academics and practitioners which aims to explain the growth of Welsh-medium education and the place that the language has within the Welsh education system. The volume consists of essays on the following aspects of the topic: the historical development of Welsh education; the different types of school; the teaching of Welsh as a second language in schools; the teaching of Welsh as a second language to adults; the Welsh nursery school movement; Welsh-medium teaching in colleges; the language policy of local education authorities; central government policy; and the contribution of the Welsh Joint Education Committeee to Welsh education and language patterns in Wales. This publication provides an informative overview of Welsh-language teaching at all levels of education and is of value to students of education and the general reader who wishes to know about the position of the Welsh language in the education system of Wales.

623 **Welsh-medium work in secondary schools. Gwaith cyfrwng-Cymraeg mewn ysgolion uwchradd.**
HMI (Wales). London: HMSO, 1981. 83p. (Education Survey, no. 9).

This is a bilingual report of a survey undertaken by Her Majesty's Inspectorate of Schools in Wales on 'the development, the range and the significance of Welsh medium work' in the secondary schools of Wales together with an evaluation of the work undertaken through the medium of Welsh. It covers the policies of local education authorities towards Welsh-medium instruction, exisiting provision, the organisation and development of courses, and the provision of learning resources in the language. This work is particularly useful for teachers, headteachers, education administrators and others interested in developing Welsh-medium instruction in secondary schools.

Literature

General

624 **Literature in Wales in the twentieth century.**
Pennar Davies.   In: *Literature in Celtic countries: Taliesin congress lectures*. Edited by J. E. Caerwyn Williams. Cardiff: University of Wales Press, 1971, p. 61-76.
A short essay which traces some of the major features of Welsh and Anglo-Welsh literature during the first-half of the twentieth century including a discussion of the concept of Anglo-Welsh literature.

625 **The Oxford companion to the literature of Wales.**
Compiled and edited by Meic Stephens.   Oxford: Oxford University Press, 1986. 682p.
A major reference work on Welsh and Anglo-Welsh literature which provides the student and the intelligent layman with a general introduction to the two literatures of Wales. The volume consists of over 2,800 entries, of which about 1,200 provide biographical and bibliographical information on creative writers from the sixth century to the present century. It also includes entries on important 'antiquaries, lexicographers, almanackers, balladeers, scholars, historians, journalists, editors, translators, critics, and writers on miscellaneous subjects such as topography, religion, philosophy and politics' where there is some literary merit in their work. There are also entries on, for example, literary periodicals, publishing houses, literary genres, individual novels and anthologies.

626 **Of poetry, paradoxes and progress.**
R. Gerallt Jones.   In: *The new Wales*. Edited by David Cole. Cardiff: University of Wales Press, 1990, p. 148-60.
Presents a general overview of the two literatures of Wales in the last decade and assesses their significance in a social and cultural context.

627　The Penguin book of Welsh short stories.

Edited by Alun Richards.　Harmondsworth, England: Penguin, 1976. 358p.

An anthology of twenty-four short stories by twentieth century Welsh and Anglo-Welsh writers. Those stories, originally written in the Welsh language, have been translated into English. All have been carefully selected to provide an insight into life in both the rural and urban areas of Wales.

628　Profiles: a visitor's guide to writing in twentieth century Wales.

Glyn Jones, John Rowlands.　Llandysul, Wales: Gomer Press, 1980. 382p. illus. bibliog.

An introductory volume to twentieth-century Welsh and Anglo-Welsh literature for visitors to Wales, which was commissioned by the Welsh Arts Council. In addition to a short essay tracing the development of literature in Wales, the main part of the work consists of a collection of essays, or profiles, which deal with the lives and literary achievements of outstanding poets, novelists and playwrights. Each essay also includes a short extract from the author's work and a select bibliography. This is a useful introduction for any reader who wishes to become familiar with the two literary traditions in Wales.

629　Triskel one: essays on Welsh and Anglo-Welsh literature.

Edited by Sam Adams, Gwilym Rees Hughes.　Swansea, Wales: Christopher Davies, 1971. 197p. illus.

A collection of ten essays on aspects of twentieth-century Welsh and Anglo-Welsh literature produced primarily to meet the needs of sixth form pupils and students. The essays should also provide useful reading for all those who enjoy literature. In addition to the essays, which discuss the aspects of the work of Kate Roberts, David Jones, R. Williams Parry, Vernon Watkins, R. T. Jenkins, Edward Thomas, Euros Bowen and R. S. Thomas, there are two more general surveys; one on Welsh poetry from 1945 to 1970, and another on twentieth-century Anglo-Welsh literature.

630　Triskel two: essays on Welsh and Anglo-Welsh literature.

Edited by Sam Adams, Gwilym Rees Hughes.　Llandybie, Wales: Christopher Davies, 1973. 181p. illus.

A collection of eight essays on twentieth-century writers in the two languages of Wales, which were specially commissioned to meet the needs of students of literature. The authors discussed in this companion volume to item number 629 include Dylan Thomas, Saunders Lewis, T. H. Parry-Williams, Vernon Watkins, Pennar Davies, Alun Lewis and Gwyn Thomas.

631　Writers of Wales.

Edited by Meic Stephens, R. Brinley Jones.　Cardiff: University of Wales Press on behalf of the Welsh Arts Council, 1970-.

A major series of short critical essays on leading Welsh and Anglo-Welsh imaginative writers, both past and present. The aim of the series is to provide an introduction to the two literatures of Wales. Approximately seventy volumes have been published to date.

Welsh literature

General

632 The dragon's pen: a brief history of Welsh literature.
Bobi Jones, Gwyn Thomas. Llandysul, Wales: Gomer Press, 1986. 96p.

This concise volume by two distinguished Welsh scholars presents a short introduction to the main developments in Welsh literature from the sixth century to the present day. The first section deals with the literature in its social, cultural and political context up to the Act of Union of 1536 and the second part examines the finest writers and literary movements from 1536 onwards. The work was designed for those with no previous acquaintance with Welsh literature.

633 Highlights in Welsh literature: talks with a prince.
R. M. Jones. Swansea, Wales: Christopher Davies, 1969. 122p. illus.

In the summer of 1969, Prince Charles was enrolled for a term as a student at the University College of Wales, Aberystwyth. During the term he was introduced to the history, language and culture of the country by members of the college's Welsh History and Welsh Departments. The author of this book was responsible for introducing Prince Charles to some of the highspots in the history of Welsh literature. This volume is based on those tutorials and should provide the general reader with a useful introductory guide to the Welsh literary tradition.

634 A history of Welsh literature.
Thomas Parry, translated from the Welsh by H. Idris Bell. Oxford: Oxford University Press, 1955. 534p. bibliog.

This work was first published in the Welsh language in 1944 and the original work presented a comprehensive survey of Welsh literature from the sixth century to the end of the nineteenth century. This translation also includes an appendix by the translator which provides an equally scholarly account of the main developments between 1900 and 1950. This volume is recognised as the standard history of Welsh literature and is indispensable reading for students.

635 An introduction to Welsh literature.
Gwyn Williams. Cardiff: University of Wales Press on behalf of the Welsh Arts Council, 1978. 123p. bibliog. (Writers of Wales).

This booklet provides the general reader and the student with a short analysis of some of the major landmarks in the history of Welsh literature from the sixth century to the present day. The author shows that, despite the social and political changes which have occurred during the past fourteen hundred years, there exists an unbroken tradition and sense of continuity particularly in Welsh poetry between the warrior poet, Taliesin, and twentieth-century writers.

156

636 **Llyfryddiaeth llenyddiaeth Gymraeg.** (Bibliography of Welsh literature.)
Edited by Thomas Parry, Merfyn Morgan. Cardiff: University of Wales Press, 1976.

A Welsh-language publication which provides a select bibliography, arranged in broad chronological periods, of approximately 6,000 critical studies on Welsh literature. It is aimed particularly at students in schools and colleges. A substantial proportion of the items cited in the bibliography are in the Welsh language but it also includes references to studies on aspects of Welsh literature in English and other languages. A supplement covering the period 1976-80 was published in the *Bulletin of the Board of Celtic Studies*, vol. 30, no.1-2 (1982), p. 55-121.

637 **The Oxford book of Welsh verse in English.**
Gwyn Jones. Oxford: Oxford University Press, 1977. 313p.

An anthology of over 200 poems selected to acquaint the non-Welsh-language reader with the achievements of the Welsh poetic tradition from the sixth century to the present day. Most of the items found in the anthology are English translations of works originally published in the Welsh language, although it also includes a smaller selection of poems originally produced in English. A valuable feature of the book is the introductory essay on the development of poetry in Wales.

638 **To look for a word: collected translations from Welsh poetry.**
Gwyn Williams. Llandysul, Wales: Gomer Press, 1976. 278p.

An anthology of over 150 Welsh poems dating from the sixth to the twentieth centuries selected and translated into English by Gwyn Williams. This collection provides a useful introduction to the development of Welsh poetry for students and the general reader who has no previous knowledge of the Welsh language or its literature. Gwyn Williams has probably been the most prolific translator of Welsh verse during the past forty years and this authology brings together translations which have appeared in several of his many earlier volumes.

639 **Welsh verse.**
Tony Conran. Bridgend, Wales: Poetry Wales Press, 1986. 355p.

Originally published in 1967 as *The Penguin book of Welsh verse*, this anthology of Welsh poetry from the sixth century to the mid-twentieth century, provides an excellent introduction to the most flourishing branch of Welsh literature. The book also includes a scholarly essay on the important social rôle of Welsh poetry during the past fifteen centuries together with a short guide to the intricacies of Welsh strict verse.

Early Welsh

640 **The Cynfeirdd: early Welsh poets and poetry.**
A. O. H. Jarman. Cardiff: University of Wales Press on behalf of the Welsh Arts Council, 1981. 133p. bibliog. (Writers of Wales).

This short essay provides an evaluative survey of the content and milieu of Welsh verse written between ca. 580 AD and 1100. A sound introduction for the general reader and student to this early period in the history of Welsh literature.

641   The earliest Welsh poetry.

Joseph P. Clancy.   London: MacMillan, 1970. 223p.

An anthology of the finest Welsh poetry written between the sixth and fourteenth century, translated into English verse. This anthology provides those not previously acquainted with early Welsh literature with an excellent insight into the the themes and craft of the early Welsh poets.

642   Early Welsh poetry: studies in the Book of Aneirin.

Edited by Brynley F. Roberts.   Aberystwyth, Wales: National Library of Wales, 1988. 212p.

A collection of essays which was originally presented to an international colloqium on early Welsh poetry with special reference to the Book of Aneirin, organised jointly by the National Library of Wales and the Centre for Advanced Welsh and Celtic Studies. The aim is to present and discuss new developments in the textual, linguistic, literary and historical study of early Welsh poetry. The contributors were distinguished scholars representing these different approaches to the study of early poetry.

643   A guide to Welsh literature. Vol. 1.

Edited by A. O. H. Jarman, Gwilym Rees Hughes.   Swansea, Wales: Christopher Davies, 1976. 295p. illus map. bibliog.

A collection of essays which surveys the history and development of Welsh literature from the sixth century to the end of the thirteenth century. The essays also discuss the relationship between the literature and its historical and social background. This volume forms part of a series which was designed for higher education students and a broad spectrum of readers in Wales and elsewhere who are interested in literature.

Medieval Welsh

644   Dafydd ap Gwilym: a selection of poems.

Translated by Rachel Bromwich.   Harmondsworth, England: Penguin, 1985. new. ed. 207p.

Originally published by Gomer Press in 1982, this volume includes the original Welsh text and translations of fifty-six poems composed by Dafydd ap Gwilym, a fourteenth-century Welsh poet generally considered to be one of the finest European poets of the Middle Ages. The collection, selected and translated by a distinguished Welsh scholar, aims to assist students with little, or no, Welsh to understand and appreciate the poet's work and to introduce this figure to English readers who had not previously heard of Dafydd.

645   A guide to Welsh literature. Vol.2.

Edited by A. O. H. Jarman, Gwilym Rees Hughes.   Swansea, Wales: Christopher Davies, 1979. 400p. illus. bibliog.

A collection of essays by Welsh scholars which survey the development of Welsh literature from 1282 to 1550. Fourteen of the sixteen contributions deal with some aspect of poetry, or the bardic system – a fair reflection of the predominance of poetry over prose during this period. In addition to discussing the contribution of individual writers and the themes and content of the literary output, there are chapters on the historical background and an explanation of the intricacies of the metrical system. This work is a particularly useful publication for students of Welsh literature.

646   The Mabinogion.
Translated by Gwyn Jones, Thomas Jones.   London: J. M. Dent, 1989. rev. ed. 291p. maps. bibliog. (Everyman Classics).

This translation was first published by the Golden Cockerel Press in 1948 and in the Everyman's Library in 1949. The collection of eleven Welsh legends known as the Mabinogion have generally been considered to be one of the masterpieces of medieval European literature since they were first translated into English by Lady Charlotte Guest during the 1830s. This English translation, produced almost fifty years ago as the joint effort of two distinguished scholars, is acknowledged to be an authoritative translation which combines meticulous scholarship and a fine literary style. The Mabinogion is considered significant both in its own right and also because of its influence on other imaginative writers in many languages.

647   Medieval Celtic literature: a select bibliography.
Rachel Bromwich.   Toronto, Canada: University of Toronto Press, 1974. 109p. (Toronto medieval bibliographies, no. 5).

A select bibliography of approximately 500 items on medieval Welsh and Irish literature produced for students engaged in the study of medieval Celtic literature. The bibliography covers the period from the time of the earliest examples of the native literary tradition in Welsh and Irish up to the middle of the fifteenth century. As the bibliography is intended for students for whom English is their first language, the works cited are chiefly in English although it does also include a number of outstanding editions and critical works written in Welsh.

648   Medieval Welsh lyrics.
Joseph P. Clancy.   London: MacMillan, 1965. 289p.

An anthology of over 100 Welsh poems composed between the fourteenth and sixteenth centuries translated into English verse. The anthology includes a selection of over fifty poems by Dafydd ap Gwilym who is generally acknowledged to be one of the finest Welsh poets ever. Wherever possible the translator has attempted to reproduce the intricate verse techniques of the bard.

649   Poems of the Cywyddwyr: a selection of cywyddau c. 1375-1525.
Edited by Eurys I. Rowlands.   Dublin: Dublin Institute for Advanced Studies, 1976. 135p. bibliog. (Mediaeval and Modern Welsh Series, no. 8).

The later Middle Ages is generally considered to be a golden era in Welsh poetic tradition with the emergence of new themes and new forms such as the 'cywydd'. This volume consists of an anthology of twenty-five poems representing the work of some of the major protagonists of the new form such as Iolo Goch, Guto'r Glyn and Gutun Owain. Although the text of the poems is in the original Welsh, the volume includes a scholarly essay in English on the bardic order in the post-conquest era, the 'cynghanedd', a formal metrical order, and the 'cywydd' form. The detailed notes on the poems and the vocabulary are in English.

Twentieth century

650 Contemporary writing in the Welsh language.
R. Gerallt Jones. *Anglo-Welsh Review*, no. 77 (1984), p. 56-69.

Presents a brief survey of Welsh literature being produced today and a discussion of the motives of people who write for a minority audience. The author concludes that there has been significant development during the past twenty-five years as regards the scope and variety of this literary output.

651 Kate Roberts.
Derec Llwyd Morgan. Cardiff: University of Wales Press on behalf of the Welsh Arts Council, 1974. 97p. illus. bibliog.

A short introductory essay which analyses the contribution of the leading Welsh prose writer of the twentieth century. The author examines the novels and short stories published by Kate Roberts up to the 1970s and discusses their themes, style and content.

652 The literary revival of the twentieth century.
R. Gerallt Jones. Llandybie, Wales: Christopher Davies, 1967. 20p. (The Welsh Literary Tradition).

Examines the output of Welsh poets and prose writers during the first half of the twentieth century. This essay was originally delivered as a paper to a course on the Welsh literary tradition arranged by the Faculty of Education, University College Swansea. The author concludes that 'the development of Welsh writing towards modernity and twentieth-century relevance has been a spasmodic and irregular process but, largely in spite of established literary institutions, it has been achieved'.

653 Poetry of Wales 1930-1970: a selection of poems 1930-1970 with translations into English.
R. Gerallt Jones. Llandysul, Wales: Gwasg Gomer, 1974. 427p.

An anthology of Welsh poetry presented in parallel English and Welsh texts. The aim of the work is to provide non-Welsh speaking readers with a representative selection of Welsh poetry composed between 1930 and 1970.

654 Presenting Saunders Lewis.
Edited by Alun R. Jones, Gwyn Thomas. Cardiff: University of Wales Press, 1983. 361p. bibliog.

Saunders Lewis is widely recognised as one of the leading Welsh writers of the twentieth century as well as being a leading personality in the struggle for political changes in Wales. This volume is intended to introduce non-Welsh speakers to Lewis' contribution to Welsh literature and politics. Section one presents three short accounts of his personal influence, the second section consists of four short introductory essays on his achievements as a politician, dramatist, critic and poet. A final section provides translations of some of his literary and political writings, including three of his major plays – *Blodeuwedd, Siwan and Brâd*.

655 **Twentieth century Welsh poems.**
Joseph P. Clancy. Llandysul, Wales: Gomer Press, 1982. 253p.

An anthology of more than 200 twentieth-century Welsh poems selected and translated into English for non-Welsh speakers. In addition to selecting items which demonstrate the wide range of themes, styles and poetic forms of twentieth-century Welsh poets, the editor has also written a cogent introduction which discusses Welsh poetry of this century in its social, historical and literary context.

Anglo-Welsh literature

656 **Anglo-Welsh literature: an illustrated history.**
Roland Mathias. Bridgend, Wales: Poetry Wales Press, 1987. 142p.
illus. bibliog. (The Illustrated History of the Literatures of Wales, no. 4).

A brief illustrated history of English-language writing in Wales from the fifteenth century to the present day. The author, an acknowledged specialist in the field, provides a guide to literary movements and a brief evaluation of the contribution of individual writers to this branch of English literature. This attractive volume represents a suitable introduction for the general reader and the student of Anglo-Welsh literature.

657 **Anglo-Welsh poetry 1480-1980.**
Raymond Garlick, Roland Mathias. Bridgend, Wales: Poetry Wales Press, 1984. 377p.

An anthology of Anglo-Welsh poetry. Although it includes the work of Welsh poets writing in English during the past 500 years, well over half the poems belong to the twentieth century, i.e., the period when Anglo-Welsh literature has flourished.

658 **The bibliography of Anglo-Welsh literature 1900-1965.**
Brynmor Jones. Library Association, Wales and Monmouthshire Branch, 1970. 139p.

A select bibliography of creative writing and critical works on twentieth-century Anglo-Welsh literature. In the introduction, the compiler explains that the scope of the bibliography includes the work of writers of Welsh birth, or extraction, who write imaginative literature in English with a Welsh background and /or characters.

659 **The cost of strangeness: essays on the English poets of Wales.**
Anthony Conran. Llandysul, Wales: Gomer Press, 1982. 330p.

A collection of critical essays on Anglo-Welsh poets. The poets examined include Ernest Rhys, W. H. Davies, Edward Thomas, Idris Davies, Dylan Thomas, Brenda Chamberlain, Gwyn Williams, R. S. Thomas and Lynnette Roberts.

660 **The dragon has two tongues: essays on Anglo-Welsh writers and writing.**
Glyn Jones. London: J. M. Dent, 1968. 221p. bibliog.

A study of the Anglo-Welsh literary tradition of the twentieth century by an Anglo-Welsh writer of some distinction. The first part of the work is an autobiographical essay which attempts to explain how the writer became interested in language and literature. The remaining sections are devoted to an examination of three prose writers (Caradoc Evans, Jack Jones and Gwyn Thomas) and three poets (Huw Menai, Dylan Thomas and Idris Davies).

661 **Dylan Thomas collected poems 1934-1953.**
Edited by Walford Davies, Ralph Maud. London: J. M. Dent, 1988. 268p. illus.

Dylan Thomas, a native of Swansea, is generally ackowledged to be one of the major English-language poets of the twentieth century. Shortly before his death in 1953, he authorized a collection of ninety-one poems which he wished to preserve and they were published by Dent as *Dylan Thomas collected poems 1934-1952*. This work provides a scholarly edition of those poems together with two others on which Thomas was working at the time of his death. The findings of textual and bibliographical investigations by the editors are presented here in the form of notes which will be indispensable to all those studying the poems of Dylan Thomas.

662 **An introduction to Anglo-Welsh literature.**
Raymond Garlick. Cardiff: University of Wales Press on behalf of the Welsh Arts Council, 1970. 97p. bibliog. (Writers of Wales).

In addition to discussing the difficulties surrounding the use of the term 'Anglo-Welsh literature', this short essay outlines the history and development of imaginative literature in the English language by Welsh writers from the second-half of the sixteenth century onwards. It refers particularly to poets living during the eighteenth and nineteenth centuries who have received less attention than twentieth-century figures.

663 **The New Welsh Review.**
Lampeter, Wales: New Welsh Review, 1988-. quarterly.

This new literary quarterly is sponsored by the English-language section of Yr Academi Gymreig and the University of Wales Association for the Study of Welsh Writing in English. Its main, though not exclusive, concern is with Anglo-Welsh literature but it also welcomes more general contributions on English literature. In addition to providing an outlet for new poetry and prose, there are book reviews, critical articles, letters, profiles and interviews as well as news items.

664 **Poems of R. S. Thomas.**
Fayetteville, Arkansas: University of Arkansas Press, 1985. 196p.

R. S. Thomas is considered by many to be amongst the finest living poets writing in the English language. This personal selection by Thomas of 254 of his poems is meant to be representative of his work during the period since the publication of his first volume of poetry in 1946. Much of his early writing deals with the natural history and stark landscape of Wales and a number of poems feature the struggles of the farmer to make a living from the soil. Some examples of this genre of poem are published in this volume, together with poems in which Thomas expresses his bitterness at the decay of Welsh life and culture during the present century.

665   **Poetry Wales: cylchgrawn cenedlaethol o farddoniaeth newydd.**
Bridgend, Wales: Poetry Wales Press, 1965-. quarterly.
A literary journal, published with the financial support of the Welsh Arts Council, which has made a significant contribution to the development and status of Anglo-Welsh poetry during the past quarter of a century. In addition to providing new and established poets with an outlet for their work, it also includes critical essays and book reviews on past and present writers. A special feature of the journal is that occasionally it has produced special issues on individual Welsh and Anglo-Welsh poets.

666   **A ride through the wood: essays on Anglo-Welsh literature.**
Roland Mathias.   Bridgend, Wales: Poetry Wales Press, 1985. 320p.
A collection of eleven substantial essays which offer an insight into the background and quality of aspects of English writing in Wales from the seventeenth century onwards.

667   **The shining pyramid, and other stories by Welsh authors.**
Edited by Sam Adams, Roland Mathias.   Llandysul, Wales: Gomer Press, 1970. 163p.
An anthology of twelve short stories by Anglo-Welsh writers together with an introduction and notes on the authors.

668   **Twelve modern Anglo-Welsh poets.**
Edited by Don Dale Jones, Randal Jenkins.   London: University of London Press, 1975. 204p. bibliog.
An anthology of the work of twelve twentieth-century Anglo-Welsh poets, aimed at both the general reader and students in schools and colleges. The poets represented in the volume are Idris Davies, Vernon Watkins, R. S. Thomas, Dylan Thomas, Alun Lewis, Roland Mathias, Harri Webb, Leslie Norris, Harry Jones, John Ormond, Dannie Abse and Raymond Garlick.

The Arts

General

669   **The artist in Wales.**
    David Bell.   London: George G. Harrap, 1957. 208p. illus. bibliog.
The author claims that Wales does not have as rich a tradition in the fine and applied arts as it has in the fields of literature, and suggests reasons for this impoverishment. However, at certain times in its history, works of art have been created by the Welsh, or others living in Wales, which are of artistic merit. The aim of the book is to describe these and show how they fit into the Welsh environment and heritage. The volume covers paintings, architecture, crafts and fine printing. The author is aware of the absence of great works of art and so he has 'aimed not at selecting masterpieces, which might not stand as such in the glare of criticism, but at weaving a pattern from the past pointing a direction in the present'.

670   **Artists in Wales.**
    Editor: Meic Stephens.   Llandysul, Wales: Gomer, 1971-77. 3 vols.
Three volumes which consist of collections of essays produced by artists who live and work in Wales. The brief they received from the editor was to describe their background and to discuss the influences on their work and their view of contemporary Wales. The contributors represent the following activities: theatre, visual arts, literature, music, film, television, architecture, folk music and crafts.

671   **The arts in Wales 1950-1975.**
    Editor: Meic Stephens.   Cardiff: Welsh Arts Council, 1979. 342p.
    illus. bibliog.
A collection of essays which review the arts in Wales during the period 1950 to 1975. The volume includes contributions on music, the visual arts, architecture, literature, drama, film as well as on museums and art galleries and the housing of the arts in Wales.

672   **Welsh Arts Council Annual Report. Cyngor Celfyddydau Cymru adroddiad blynyddol.**
Cardiff: Welsh Arts Council, 1970-. annual.
Reviews the activities of the Welsh Arts Council which plays such a central rôle in artistic activities and events in present-day Wales. The report includes short sections on the work of the Council in relation to the visual arts, crafts, dance, drama, films, literature, music and the housing of the arts.

Crafts

673   **Crafts: a guide to craft shops and workshops open to visitors.**
Wales Tourist Board.   Cardiff: Wales Tourist Board, 1980. 3rd. ed. 36p.
illus.
A guidebook containing a selection of the craftsmen and women who have workshops in Wales today. The booklet has been arranged into the following sections: pottery; textiles and fabrics; wood, cane and wicker work; leatherwork; slate and stone; wrought iron and metalwork; candles and miscellaneous crafts. Although the booklet has been produced for the tourist trade, it can also be used as a quick reference guide for those who need information about Welsh crafts.

674   **Crefft: A quarterly Newsletter On The Crafts.**
Cardiff: Welsh Arts Council, 1976-. quarterly.
Each issue of this publication, which is prepared by the Department of Craft and Design of the Welsh Arts Council, includes news items, notices of forthcoming exhibitions, details about courses and lectures, previews and reviews of exhibtions together with a profile of a practising craftsman or woman.

675   **Davies brothers gatesmiths: 18th century wrought iron works in Wales.**
Ifor Edwards.   Cardiff: Welsh Arts Council & Crafts Advisory Council, 1977. 112p. illus. map.
This booklet describes the art and craft of Robert and John Davies of Croes Foel, near Wrexham, whose decorative wrought iron work, particularly their splendid iron gates, form a notable feature in the landscape of Clwyd and surrounding areas. The text is supported by a large selection of photographs which illustrate the fine craftsmanship of these two brothers.

676   **Gwaith haearn bwrw addurnol yng Nghymru. Decorative cast-ironwork in Wales.**
Ifor Edwards.   Llandysul, Wales: Gomer, 1989. 128p. illus. bibliog.
This bilingual booklet describes examples of decorative cast-ironwork which can be found in Wales. Although most of it was produced elsewhere, particularly in Scotland, the author considers it to be an important part of the artistic heritage of Wales and believes that every effort should be made to preserve the finest examples. The main

section of the work arranges the items described and illustrated according to their function e.g. railway stations, bridges, piers, gas lamps, clocks, balconies and verandas.

677 The Nantgarw porcelain album.

W. D. John with G. J. Coombes, Katherine Coombes. Newport, Wales: Ceramic Book Company, 1975. 29p. (plus 100 plates).

The quality and artitistic design of Nantgarw porcelain produced under the direction of William Billingsley between 1817 and 1822 is considered to be amongst the finest ever produced. The first part of this book presents a historical survey of the manufacture of the porcelain. The second part consists of large colour photographs of individual items from the collection, together with the following information regarding those specimens: size; description of decorations; name of designer; and the present owner.

678 The story of the lovespoon.

Edited by Trefor Owen. Swansea, Wales: Celtic Educational (Services), 1973. 97p. illus.

The presentation of wood-carved lovespoons as gifts to loved ones has been a widespread custom in Wales since the seventeenth century. The spoons were carved by the donors and this practice developed into one of the traditional crafts of Wales. In this book, the author introduces the reader to this tradition and also provides a fairly detailed description of how the spoons are made. There is also a short account of how the craft has been revived in recent times.

679 Swansea porcelain shapes and decorations.

A. E. Jones, Leslie Joseph. Cowbridge, Wales: D. Brown, 1988. 274p. illus. bibliog.

Porcelain of very high quality and artistic merit was produced in Swansea during the second-half of the eighteenth century and throughout the nineteenth century. This study, aimed at students and collectors of decorative porcelain, provides a comprehensive reference book on the shapes and decorations of these items. Part one, presents a general survey of the history and manufacture of porcelain at Swansea together with biographical essays on the professional and amateur artists who designed the decorations and shapes. The work also includes an illustrated catalogue of the shapes and designs of the items and a glossary of terms relating to the manufacture and design of porcelain.

680 Welsh crafts: an account of the historic crafts as they exist today.

Mary Eirwen Jones. London: Batsford, 1978. 160p. illus.

This book, written for the non-specialist, describes a wide range of traditional Welsh crafts, many of which have been practised continuously for over a hundred years, whilst others have only recently been revived. The origins, techniques and survival, or revival, of the craft are described. The crafts have been arranged according to the raw material used in their creation, for example, textiles, stone, wood, leather, metal and ceramics.

681 **Welsh crafts and craftsmen.**
J. Geraint Jenkins. Llandysul, Wales: Gomer Press, 1975. 86p. illus.
A survey, for the non-specialist, of traditional crafts found in rural Wales up to the early part of the twentieth century. The book includes sections on textiles, furniture, turnery, broth spoons, love spoons, willow baskets, straw baskets, coracles, slate work, pottery, iron work, leather work, clogs and saddles. In addition to describing the skills of the various craftsmen, the author also explains their social and economic importance.

Visual arts

682 **Art in Wales: an illustrated history 1850- 1980.**
Cardiff: University of Wales Press & Welsh Arts Council, 1985. 194p. illus.
A general survey of the fine arts in Wales during this period. The author claims that there is no distinctly national style to the output. The artists whose work is described were selected because they were born, or worked, in Wales and contributed to the general development of Western art. In total, the illustrations represent the works of approximately 100 Welsh artists.

683 **Art in Wales 2000 BC–AD 1850: an illustrated history.**
Edited by Eric Rowan. Cardiff: Welsh Arts Council & University of Wales Press, 1978. 127p. illus. bibliog.
This is the first of two books which present a general history of the visual arts in Wales (see also the companion volume, item no. 682). The books initially stemmed from an exhibition held at the Glynn Vivien Gallery, Swansea in 1964. This volume consists of the essays dealing with the following subjects: the evolution of art; the pre-Celtic and Celtic period; the Roman occupation; early Christian Wales; the medieval period and finally painting in Wales, 1550-1850.

684 **Art news. Newyddion celf.**
Cardiff: Welsh Arts Council, 1982-. three times per year
A bilingual newsletter for 'artists, art societies and art galleries in Wales' which contains news, views and information about visual arts events and activities in Wales.

685 **Y bryniau tywyll y cymylau trymion. The dark hills the heavy clouds.**
David Fraser Jenkins. Cardiff: Welsh Arts Council, 1981. 63p. bibliog.
This bilingual booklet is based on an exhibition of the work of seven expressionist artists, namely Josef Herman, Kyffin Williams, Will Roberts, Martin Bloch, George Chapman, Ernest Zobole and Peter Prendergast. The items selected for the exhibition showed common characteristics in their approach to the Welsh landscape which is radically different to the picturesque tradition of the eighteenth century and the work of the post-impressionist artists. All seven artists have worked in Wales and their works evoke a particular emotional mood. The work consists of a short biographical

essay, a list of major exhibitions, and a select bibliography of each of the artists represented in the exhibition, together with a description of the three examples of their work which have been reproduced in this publication.

686   **Cymru'r cynfas: pymtheg artist cyfoes. Wales on canvas: fifteen contemporary artists.**
Hywel Harris.   Talybont, Dyfed, Wales: Y Lolfa, 1988. 2nd ed. 96p. illus.

This book was originally published in Welsh in 1983, but this new edition includes an English-language text in the form of an appendix. The volume consists of a personal selection of the paintings and drawings of fifteen contemporary artists working in Wales who attempt to interpret the country and its people. In addition to reproducing a selection of their works, the author has also written short essays on their life and work and in some instances the artists themselves have provided personal comments on their work.

687   **"For Wales – see England".**
Roger Webster.   In: *Anatomy of Wales*. Edited by R. Brinley Jones. Peterston-super-Ely, Wales: Gwerin Publications, 1972, p. 228-47.

This short essay outlines the history of the visual arts in Wales from medieval times to the 1970s. It concludes that the fine arts have only played a minor part in Welsh life.

688   **Richard Wilson: the landscape of reaction.**
David H. Solkin.   London: Tate Gallery Publications, 1982. 251p. illus.

Richard Wilson, born in Penegoes in mid-Wales in 1713, is today considered to be one of the finest painters of the eighteenth century. This volume was prepared to coincide with an exhibition of his work at the Tate Gallery in 1983. Part one presents a scholarly reassessment of Wilson's work, whilst part two is an illustrated and annotated catalogue of the 147 items in the exhibition. This is a major study of Wilson's work which will be of interest to the art historian, the art student and all art enthusiasts.

689   **Stained glass in North Wales up to 1850.**
Mostyn Lewis.   Altrincham, England: John Sherratt, 1970. 137p. (72 plates). bibliog.

The first part of this volume consists of a general historical survey of stained glass in North Wales from the fourteenth century onwards. This is followed by a directory of churches with examples of decorated windows and a section describing the stained glass of the period before 1850 found in mansion houses and other secular buildings. Special attention is paid to the work of David Evans.

690   **A touch of magic on the road.**
John Petts.   In: *The new Wales*. Edited by David Cole. Cardiff: University of Wales Press, 1990, p. 92-110.

A general survey of the visual arts in Wales from the eighteenth century to the present day, with particular emphasis on the last forty years. The author concludes that during this latter period 'the story of art in Wales is the recital of steady, astonishingly varied and lively growth' with more practising artists, designers, sculptors and craftsmen than at any other time in its history.

168

Music and dance

691   **Caneuon cenedlaethol Cymru. The national songs of Wales.**
Edited by E. T. Davies, Sydney Northcote.   London: Boosey &
Hawkes, 1959. 146p.

A collection of approximately eighty Welsh songs which have gained widespread
popularity and are acknowledged as national airs and melodies. This book includes
music scores, and Welsh and English words.

692   **Caneuon llafar gwlad (Songs from oral tradition) 1.**
Edited by D. Roy Saer.   Cardiff: National Museum of Wales, Welsh
Folk Museum, 1974. 72p.

One of the activities of the Welsh Folk Museum has been to record the oral traditions
of Wales, including its traditional music. All but two of the thirty songs published in
this collection have been transcribed from field recordings undertaken by staff at the
Folk Museum. The aim of the series, of which this bilingual book is the only one to
appear to date, is to: 'recirculate among the Welsh people traditional material which is
no longer in general circulation'. In addition to presenting the music score and the
Welsh words, the author has produced background notes on each song.

693   **Canu Gwerin: Cylchgrawn Cymdeithas Alawon Gwerin Cymru. Folk
Song: Journal of the Welsh Folk Song Society.**
Welsh Folk Song Society, 1978-. annual.

The main aim of the journal and the society is 'the collection, preservation and
performance of Welsh folk-songs'. The contents of individual issues includes research
articles, the words and music of Welsh folk-songs, news, reviews, obituaries and
occasionally a list of the society members. Some of the articles are written in the Welsh
language.

694   **Canu'r Cymry.**
Edited by Phyllis Kinney, Meredydd Evans.   Welsh Folk-Song
Society, 1984-87. 2 vols.

Together, these bilingual volumes consist of a collection of over eighty traditional folk-
songs, a large number of which have not previously been published. In addition to
producing the music score and the words, the compilers have also included notes on
the social context and the derivation of each song at the back of the book. The editors,
who are recognised exponents of Welsh folk-singing, have deliberately not provided
arrangements for these songs as they are anxious to publish them in a form as near as
possible to the way in which they were originally presented. The two volumes are
aimed at folk-singers who wish to sing these songs in public, or in the home.

695 **Cerddoriaeth draddodiadol yng Nghymru: llyfryddiaeth. Traditional music in Wales: a bibliography.**
Wyn Thomas.   Cardiff: National Museum of Wales, Welsh Folk Museum, 1982. 160p.
This bibliography is comprehensive in its coverage of the more scholarly contributions to the study of traditional Welsh music. Section one consists of a chronological list of the main printed collections of Welsh traditional music published between 1621 and 1981. The remaining sections list books, periodical articles and dissertations relevant to this field of study. An indispensable tool for students and scholars of traditional music.

696 **Composers of Wales.**
Cardiff: University of Wales Press on behalf of the Welsh Arts Council, 1978-.
A series of introductory studies of individual Welsh composers which includes a short biographical sketch, an analysis of their major work and a comprehensive catalogue of their compositions. The composers featured in the first four volumes of the series are: William Mathias, Alun Hoddinott, David Wynne and Grace Williams.

697 **Cymdeithas Alawon Gwerin Cymru. The Welsh Folk-Song Society, 1908-1983.**
D. Roy Saer.   The Welsh Folk-Song Society, 1985. 47p. illus.
A bilingual booklet which presents a brief survey of the Welsh Folk-Song Society. This publication formed part of the society's seventy-fifth anniversary celebrations. In addition to the brief outline of the history and activities of the society, the booklet also includes a selection of photographs related to the society's history.

698 **Dawns. Cylchgrawn Cymdeithas Ddawns Cymru. The Welsh Folk Dance Society Journal.**
The Welsh Folk Dance Society, 1985-. annual.
This journal includes short articles and news items in English and Welsh about current activities and events in the field of Welsh folk-dancing.

699 **Dawnsio gwerin Cymreig. Welsh folk dancing.**
Barbara Denbury.   Welsh Library Association, 1982. 20p. (W.L.A. Bibliographies Series, no. 2).
This bilingual publication presents a bibliography of books, pamphlets and periodical articles in English and Welsh on Welsh folk-dancing for those who wish to take an active part in the art. Approximately half the items cited provide instructions for the dances.

700 **Famous songs of Wales I. Caneuon enwog Cymru I.**
Arranged by John Hywel.   Penygroes, Gwynedd, Wales: Gwynn, 1987. 31p. illus.
A collection of fourteen Welsh songs, including the national anthem. For each song there is a music score arranged for the piano, the original Welsh and English translation of the words and short background notes on the songs. The volume is designed for the visitor to Wales who wishes to learn something of the songs which belong to the Welsh people.

701 **Hanes y delyn yng Nghymru. The story of the harp in Wales.**
Osian Ellis. Cardiff: University of Wales Press, 1980. 91p. illus.
bibliog.

A bilingual booklet which traces the history of the harp in Wales. Although this study forms part of a series aimed at young people in secondary education, the volume is probably more suited to students of music in higher education and adult readers with a serious interest in the history of Welsh music or the harp. In addition to tracing the early references to the use of the harp in Wales, the author presents a detailed examination of some of the oldest surviving manuscripts of Welsh harp music as well as a description of the contribution of eighteenth and nineteenth-century Welsh harpists. Finally, there is a brief résumé of the contribution of twentieth-century Welsh composers to harp music.

702 **Music in Wales.**
Owain T. Williams. In: *Anatomy of Wales*. Edited by R. Brinley
Jones, Peterston-super-Ely, Wales: Gwerin, 1972, p. 208-26.

A short essay which describes the main developments in Welsh music from the sixteenth century to the present day. The author traces the emergence of two strands of Welsh music, one belonging to the educated gentry, and the other being the music of the ordinary people. He also discusses how these two traditions were brought together during the nineteenth century. The various forms of folk-music and the related instruments are briefly described.

703 **Musical life in the nineteenth century.**
Rhidian Griffiths. In: *Glamorgan county history vol. VI: Glamorgan society 1780-1980*. Edited by Prys Morgan. Cardiff: Glamorgan History
Trust, 1988, p. 367-79.

An introductory survey on the growth and development of music in Glamorgan during the nineteenth century. In the study, the author describes the decline in a tradition of folk-music supported by the gentry and the emergence of a new tradition linked to singing and playing at concerts and eisteddfodau. The essay also includes an examination of the development of choral singing in the new industrial communities.

704 **Praise the Lord! We are a musical nation.**
Geraint Lewis. In: *The new Wales*. Edited by David Cole. Cardiff:
University of Wales Press, 1990, p. 124-40.

A short essay which reviews developments in Welsh music during the 1970s and 1980s. The author examines the musical activities and institutions which were established, or flourished, and also assesses the stature of the major Welsh composers of the period under investigation.

705 **Seventh catalogue of contemporary Welsh music. Seithfed catalog o gerddoriaeth cyfoes Cymru.**
Compiled by Robert Smith. [Swansea, Wales:] Guild for the
Promotion of Welsh Music, 1981. 74p.

A catalogue of vocal and instrumental music composed by contemporary Welsh musicians. The items have been systematically arranged according to the musical form of the piece and the musical instrument, or instruments, the work was intended for.

Individual entries provide information regarding the title, duration, instrumentation, and whether the work is available in published or in manuscript form. The volume also includes short biographical notes on the composers whose works are listed. This volume cumulates earlier editions of the catalogue.

706 **Sir Geraint Evans: a knight at the opera.**
Geraint Evans with Noel Goodwin. London: Michael Joseph, 1984. 276p. illus.
The autobiography of a miner's son from Pontypridd who became an international opera star. This book traces his life from his days as an errand-boy to his farewell performance at Covent Garden in 1984. An appendix provides a chronological table of his rôles, as well as a discography and a list of the honours and awards presented to him.

707 **Tro llaw: 200 o bibddawnsiau Cymreig o Lyfrgell Genedlaethol Cymru. 200 Welsh hornpipe tunes from the National Library of Wales.**
Collected and edited by Robin Huw Bowen. Aberystwyth, Wales: National Library of Wales, 1987. 120p. illus.
A collection of the scores of traditional dance tunes published to meet the demand in Welsh folk-dance circles for more material. This volume is confined to the 'hornpipe' type of tune in the hope that the collection would be the first of many. The book also includes a short introduction to the history of traditional dance music in Wales, together with brief notes which include comments on the tunes and on the manuscript sources used in producing this collection.

708 **Wales.**
Peter Crossley Holland. In: *The new Grove dictionary of music and musicians*. vol. 20. Edited by Stanley Sadie. London: Macmillan, 1980, p. 159-71.
An outline survey of classical and folk-music in Wales from prehistoric times to the twentieth century. The article is divided into six sections: prehistoric and early Wales; from the tenth century to 1735; from 1735 to 1900; the twentieth century; the traditional heritage; and musical instruments. Together with the accompanying bibliography, this article offers students and others seriously interested in the history of Welsh music with a useful introduction to the field.

709 **The Welsh choral tradition: fact and myth.**
Gareth H. Lewis. *Welsh Music. Cerddoriaeth Cymru*, vol. 5, no. 4 (1976-77), p. 57-73.
A study of the history and development of choral singing in Wales which examines this phenomenon of Welsh musical activity in the nineteenth century in its social and cultural context. The author explains the decisive part played by Methodism in encouraging group singing as well as the rôle of the eisteddfod movement in developing these skills.

710 **Welsh folk-dances.**
Hugh Mellor.   Welsh Folk-Dance Society, 1976. 91p. illus.
This volume was originally published by Novello in 1932. It consists of a survey of traditional Welsh dances which survived the attempts to destroy them during the Methodist revival. It also includes short notes on musical instruments and dance tunes.

711 **A Welsh folk-dancing handbook.**
Alice E. Williams.   Rhydaman, Wales: Welsh Folk-Dance Society, 1985. 28p. illus. bibliog.
A practical manual aimed at teachers, instructors, dancers and musicians who are interested in promoting Welsh folk-dancing. The booklet also includes introductory material which traces the history of folk-dancing in Wales and discusses elements such as the music, costume and footwear. Also included is a short bilingual glossary of dancing terms.

712 **Welsh Music. Cerddoriaeth Cymru.**
Swansea, Wales: Guild for the Promotion of Welsh Music, 1959-. three times per year.
This is the official journal of the Guild for the Promotion of Welsh Music. It normally contains articles on composers and musical performances, reviews of recordings, performances and books, obituaries, letters, notes and news. This publication is aimed at professional musicians and the enthusiastic and informed layman.

713 **Welsh national music and dance.**
W. S. Gwynn Williams.   London: J. Curwen, 1971. 4th ed. 165p.
A standard survey of the history of Welsh music. Part one, outlines the devlopment of music making in Wales from earliest times to 1282. Part two, presents detailed descriptions of traditional Welsh harp airs, folk-songs, penillion singing [a traditional form of singing unique to Wales in which the singer produces a counter-melody to a tune being played on the harp] and Welsh dances. A major feature of the work is the bibliography of the main printed collections of Welsh national music published from 1621 onwards.

714 **Welsh National Opera.**
Richard Fawks.   London: Julia MacRae Books; Lane Cover, Australia: Franklin Watts Australia, 1986. 368p.
A history of the Welsh National Opera Company aimed at the non-specialist, and produced on the occasion of the Company's fortieth anniversary in 1986. The author presents a chronological account of the activities of the company from its humble beginnings in 1946 to the highly acclaimed company of today. The work considers the musical performances, the musicians who worked with the company and the everyday-life of running such a company. The appendices include lists of all the company's productions from 1946 to 1985 with the names of soloists, producers and designers together with a list of conductors and performances.

Theatre and film

715 Drama.
Elan Closs Stephens. In: *The arts in Wales 1950-1975*. Edited by Meic Stephens. Cardiff: Welsh Arts Council, 1979, p. 239-96.

A critical review of drama and the theatre in Wales from the end of World War II to 1975. The author explains that Wales experienced the demise of the long-standing amateur drama tradition immediately after 1945, which left a significant vacuum at the community level. This vacuum was gradually filled by two new developments, namely the advent of television drama and the emergence of professional companies and purpose-built theatres. Welsh and Anglo-Welsh dramatists of the period under review are also discussed.

716 The English theatre in Wales during the eighteenth and early nineteenth centuries.
Cecil Price. Cardiff: University of Wales Press, 1948. 202p. illus. bibliog.

The history of the English theatre in Wales from the days of the strolling players, whose productions were performed in inns, barns and warehouses, to productions in permanent playhouses. The author examines the rôle played by the gentry in promoting the theatre, particularly during the last quarter of the eighteenth century and the first quarter of the nineteenth, and the violent opposition of the Methodists to the theatre.

717 Miners cinemas in South Wales in the 1920s and 1930s.
Bert Hogenkamp. *Llafur*, vol. 4, no. 2 (1985), p. 64-76.

During the 1930s, the Labour movement in Britain attempted to use films as a medium of propaganda by producing their own films and by promoting films which supported left-wing ideas. In this short article, the author examines the cinemas of the Workingmen Halls and Miners' Institutes of South Wales in relation to this strategy.

718 The professional theatre in Wales.
Cecil Price. Swansea, Wales: University College of Swansea, 1984. 53p. illus. (The Mainwaring-Hughes Award Series).

An outline history of the professional theatre in Wales from the sixteenth century to the present day, describing the main developments and achievements and also the religious opposition to the theatre which curbed its progress for much of the nineteenth century. The booklet also discusses the impact of film and television on the growth of the theatre during the twentieth century, as well as the growth of purpose-built theatres during the 1960s and 1970s.

719 Rich: the life of Richard Burton.
Melvyn Bragg. London: Hodder & Stoughton, 1988. 533p. illus.

A biography of one of the most famous sons of Wales during the twentieth century who gained world-wide acclaim as an actor and film star. This book traces his life and career, describing the high and low points of his professional work and his personal relationships. The appendices consist of a list of Burton's performances in the theatre, film, television, radio and his sound records.

720   **Theatre (or not) in Wales.**
Carl Tighe.   In: *Wales: the imagined nation. Studies in cultural and national identity*. Edited by Tony Curtis. Bridgend, Wales: Poetry Wales Press, 1986, p. 241-60.
An examination of the theatre in Wales with particular reference to the period after 1970, together with a review of theatrical companies and dramatists in Wales between 1970 and 1985. Tighe explains why the period since 1970 should be considered as the 'birth' rather than the 'Renaissance' of the theatre in Wales and shows that the main developments have been in certain kinds of theatre such as experimental, community and theatre in education.

721   **Wales in the movies.**
Peter Stead.   In: *Wales: the imagined nation. Studies in cultural and national identity*. Edited by Tony Curtis. Bridgend, Wales: Poetry Wales Press, 1986, p. 159-79.
Although Wales was very much on the periphery of the history of film and the cinema, it made some notable contributions to its early development. This article includes a brief outline of the pioneering work of Walter Haggar of Aberdare and his contribution to the early history of the cinema. However, the main part of the article illustrates the different ways in which Wales was featured in documentary and feature films from the 1930s onwards.

Photography

722   **John Dillwyn Llewelyn 1810-1882: the first photographer in Wales.**
Richard Morris.   Cardiff: Welsh Arts Council, 1980. 48p. illus.
This booklet was prepared in conjunction with a Welsh Arts Council exhibition of the work of one of the early pioneers of photography, John Dillwyn Llewelyn of Swansea. The first part traces the life of Llewelyn, with particular reference to his technical and artistic achievements as a photographer. The publication also includes a catalogue to the 223 items in the exhibition with illustrations of some of them and a short note on the technical aspects of early photography.

723   **John Thomas 1838-1905: photographer.**
Hilary Woollen, Alistair Crawford.   Llandysul, Wales: Gomer Press, 1977. 81p. illus. bibliog.
John Thomas of Cellan in Cardiganshire earned his living as a travelling commercial photographer based in Liverpool. An important collection of photographs by Thomas, which forms an indispensable documentary record of Wales and the Welsh people during the second half of the nineteenth century, is now kept in the National Library of Wales. This booklet consists of a short study of the life and the technical and artistic merits of Thomas as a photographer, and is illustrated with approximately forty of the 3,000 items from the collection.

724 **Photography in Wales.**
Alistair Crawford. *Planet*, no. 44 (Aug. 1978), p. 13-27.
The author presents a case for establishing a Photographic Gallery in Wales in order to ensure that the country has a systematic historical archive of photography and an organisation to promote exhibitions of contemporary photography in Wales. To support his case, the author describes some of the notable contributions which have been made by Welshmen, or photographers working in Wales, to the development of photography and as such it offers a general survey of photography in Wales from its beginnings to the present day.

Eisteddfodau

725 **The eisteddfod.**
Hywel Teifi Edwards. Cardiff: University of Wales Press on behalf of the Welsh Arts Council, 1990. 83p. illus. bibliog. (Writers of Wales).
An essay on the history of the eisteddfod which particularly illustrates how it has evolved from being a medieval test for professional bards and minstrels into a popular annual festival. The main part of the study considers the contribution of the eisteddfod to literary activity in Wales during the nineteenth century and also evaluates the literary output of eisteddfodic competitions during the twentieth century.

726 **Eisteddfodau Caerwys. The Caerwys eisteddfodau.**
Gwyn Thomas. Cardiff: University of Wales Press, 1968. 117p. illus. bibliog.
A bilingual booklet which offers a description of the early eisteddfodau held at Caerwys during the second half of the sixteenth century to raise poetic and musical standards amongst the professional bards and musicians of the period.

727 **Gentle are its songs.**
Kenneth A. Wright. Birmingham, England: Sir Gerald Nabarro (Publications), 1973. 232p. illus. map.
This bilingual publication written, for the general reader, outlines the history of the Llangollen International Eisteddfod during the first twenty-five years of its history. The author traces the story of this unique folk-festival which was founded in the aftermath of World War II in order to create a better understanding between the nations of the world. It also describes the difficulties, and the achievements, of the event during the period from 1947 to 1972. In addition to providing a list of the successful contestants, the author provides an insight into related subjects such as the musical tradition of Wales and the history of Llangollen.

728 **Hanes yr eisteddfod a'r Eisteddfod Genedlaethol a'r orsedd. The story of the eisteddfod and the National Eisteddfod and gorsedd of bards.**

Thomas Parry and Cynan [A.E. Jones].   [Liverpool, England: Hugh Evans on behalf of the National Eisteddfod Court, 1963. 56p. illus.]

Two short essays on the eisteddfod. The first essay, by Thomas Parry, presents an outline history of the eisteddfod from medieval times to the present day, and the second describes the rôle of the Gorsedd of Bards, their ceremonies and officers. The booklet also includes a list of the winners of the major literary competitions at the National Eisteddfod from 1880 to 1962.

729 **The Royal National Eisteddfod of Wales.**

Dilwyn Miles.   Swansea, Wales: Christopher Davies, 1978. 170p. illus.

An outline description of this unique cultural festival, which forms one of the major events in the Welsh calendar, written for the interested non-Welsh speaking people of Wales and elsewhere. The author traces the history of the eisteddfodic tradition from the earliest times to the twentieth century and the book also includes a section on the origins of the bardic circle.

Architecture

730 **Architecture.**

John B. Hilling. In: *The arts in Wales 1950-1975*. Edited by Meic Stephens. Cardiff: Welsh Arts Council, 1979, p. 143-16.

A survey of the architectural achievements of Wales between 1950 and 1975. The author believes that the two main themes of this period were the discovery of a genuine Welsh architectural tradition and the importance of adapting buildings to their locality. The essay also includes an outline of historical studies on Welsh architecture which were published during the period, and a review of the progress in architectural education in Wales.

731 **The architecture of the Welsh chapel.**

John Bryan Hilling. *Transactions of the Honourable Society of Cymmrodorion*, (1983), p. 132-56.

Nonconformity replaced the Anglican Church as the main religious force in Wales during the nineteenth century and chapels displaced churches in the lives of the majority of the inhabitants in the rural areas and the new industrial centres alike. Consequently, the chapel achieved the status of the most important public building in many towns and villages. In this article, which is based on a paper delivered to members of the Cymmrodorion Society, the author presents the social and religious background to the growth of chapels and then discusses their architectural character. The main attributes of these buildings were the gable facade and the interior. Hilling shows, with the aid of illustrations, that most chapel designs are based on the classical style although there are examples of early gothic styles in some of the chapels of North Wales.

732 **Cardiff and the valleys: architecture and townscape.**

John Bryan Hilling. London: Lund Humphries, 1973. 184p. illus.

Examines the architecture of Cardiff and the Ely, Taf and Rhymni valleys together with their tributary valleys. Although the author's survey covers medieval and modern buildings, the main emphasis is on those built during the eighteenth and nineteenth centuries which was an era of rapid urban expansion in the area.

733 Clwyd (Denbighshire and Flintshire).

Edward Hubbard. Harmondsworth, England: Penguin; Cardiff: University of Wales Press, 1986. 518p. illus. (The Buildings of Wales).

A standard inventory of architectural works found in the historic counties of Flintshire and Denbighshire from earliest times to the present-day. An attempt has been made to provide comprehensive coverage of pre-1830 churches and all town, manor and country houses together with a selection of post-1830 churches, chapels and secular buildings. Where possible, buildings of architectural merit which have been destroyed, or mutilated, have been included. There is also an essays on prehistoric and Roman remains and on the development of architecture in Clwyd.

734 Getting better by design.

Dale Owen. In: The new Wales. Edited by David Cole. Cardiff: University of Wales, 1990, p. 70-90.

A review of developments in architecture in Wales during the past few decades. The author demonstrates the various influences on architectural design during this century and describes some of the major achievements of the period.

735 The historic architecture of Wales: an introduction.

John Bryan Hilling. Cardiff: University of Wales Press, 1976. 234p. illus. bibliog.

Presents an outline history of the architecture of Wales from the neolithic period to 1939. The main features of Welsh architecture during various historical periods are described, and attention is also paid to the author's interpretation of the link between these characteristics and the physical, social and cultural environment of Wales. The work also includes a series of appendices which list certain building forms and architectural features which can be seen in Wales.

736 The historical farm buildings of Wales.

Eurwyn William. Edinburgh: John Donald, 1986. 202p. illus. maps. bibliog.

This detailed survey is based on field examinations undertaken by the author of some 900 farmsteads throughout the length and breadth of Wales. As the form of buildings found on farms was subordinate to their function, the study also provides an insight into how a farm functioned in the days before full mechanisation.

737 Home-made homes: dwellings of the rural poor in Wales.

Eurwyn William. Cardiff: National Museum of Wales, 1988. 36p. illus.

An illustrated booklet for the non-specialist which traces the history, and describes the nature, of the homes of ordinary people in rural Wales during the eighteenth and nineteenth centuries.

Architecture

738 Houses of the Welsh countryside: a study in historical geography.
Peter Smith.   London: HMSO, 1988. 2nd ed. illus. maps. bibliog.
A comprehensive survey of domestic architecture in Wales from medieval times to the nineteenth century, presented in its geographical and historical context. In addition, this scholarly study also includes a series of distribution maps of architectural features found in houses, together with over 100 black-and-white photographs of buildings and associated features.

739 An inventory of the ancient monuments in Glamorgan IV: domestic architecture from the Reformation to the Industrial Revolution.
The Royal Commission on Ancient and Historical Monuments in Wales.   Cardiff: HMSO, 1981-88. 2 vols. illus. maps.
These two volumes offer a comprehensive and scholarly contribution to the study of domestic architecture in the County of Glamorgan. Part one consists of detailed descriptions of forty-two houses owned by the largest landowners in the county built between the sixteenth century and the second half of the eighteenth century. Part two is a comprehensive survey of the farmhouses of both the minor gentry and tenant farmers and a selection of the cottages inhabited by peasants, or village craftsmen, up to about 1760. Both volumes include essays providing an insight into the historical and architectural background of the buildings.

740 The lost houses of Wales: a survey of country houses in Wales demolished since c.1900.
Thomas Lloyd.   London: Save Britain's Heritage, 1986. 112p. illus.
An illustrated record of country houses in Wales which have disappeared from the landscape during the twentieth century because of neglect, fires or other reasons. In addition, the work includes a chapter which lists a number of important country houses which are also in danger of being destroyed.

741 Medieval churches of the Vale of Glamorgan.
Geoffrey R. Orrin.   Cowbridge, Wales: D. Brown, 1988. 514p. illus. bibliog.
A comprehensive survey of the architecture of the forty-five churches in the Vale of Glamorgan which were founded in medieval times. In addition to providing descriptions of the church buildings and their furnishings, the volume also includes general introductory essays on their history and architecture. The illustrated glossary of architectural and ecclesiastical terminology should enable the general reader, as well as enthusiasts, to benefit from this informative study.

742 The old cottages of Snowdonia.
Harold Hughes, Herbert L. North.   Capel Curig, Wales: Snowdonia National Park Society, 1979. 75p. illus. bibliog.
This book was originally published in 1908 after the authors, two well-known architects, had cycled around the area recording many of the small dwelling places in Snowdonia which had been built by ordinary people using local materials. Today, this short study is considered to be one of the pioneer works on vernacular architecture. In addition to reproducing the original text, this new and revised edition also includes additional material such as a survey of the present condition of the houses originally described by Hughes and North.

743 **Plans and prospects: architecture in Wales 1780-1914.**
John Hilling. Cardiff: Welsh Arts Council, 1975. 100p. illus.
An illustrated booklet produced to accompany a major exhibition of drawings to demonstrate the variety of architectural buildings built in Wales between 1780 and 1914. During this period, because of rapid industrialization, Wales experienced a radical transformation, not only of its villages, towns and cities, but also of its landscape. This work includes plans and/or drawings of over eighty buildings including mansions, smaller houses, and religious and other public buildings.

744 **Powys (Montgomeryshire, Radnorshire, Breconshire).**
Richard Haslam. Harmondsworth, England: Penguin; Cardiff: University of Wales Press, 1979. 436p. illus. maps. (The Buildings of Wales).
A standard inventory of architectural works of merit from the earliest times to the present day. It describes and critically assesses abbeys, churches, farms, chapels, castles and mansions together with the furnishings found in ecclesiastical buildings. The work is arranged according to the pre-1974 county boundaries and then alphabetically by placename and includes over 100 black-and-white plates.

745 **Rural buildings in Wales.**
Peter Smith. In: *The agrarian history of England and Wales. vol. 5, 1640-1750, ii. Agrarian change.* Edited by Joan Thirsk. Cambridge: Cambridge University Press, 1985, p. 686-813.
A survey of farmhouses and farm buildings built in Wales during the second half of the seventeenth and the first half of the eighteenth centuries. The author explains the significance of factors such as building materials, ethnic tastes and topography in the architectural styles and design found during that period. The essay is illustrated with a large number of diagrams, sketches, and distribution maps.

746 **Rural housing in Wales.**
Peter Smith. In: *The agrarian history of England and Wales vol. 4, 1500-1640.* Edited by Joan Thirsk. Cambridge: Cambridge University Press, 1967, p. 767-813.
A survey of the development of the architectural design of rural buildings in Wales between the beginning of the sixteenth and middle of the seventeenth centuries. The essay is illustrated with diagrams and sketches of buildings and architectural features.

747 **Society of Architects in Wales Year Book.**
Cardiff: SAW Publications on behalf of the Society of Architects in Wales, 1980-. annual.
In addition to being a directory of the members of the Royal Institute of British Architects and architects' practices found in Wales, this volume also includes reports on the activities of the previous year, including short descriptions of a selection of new buildings designed by Welsh architects.

Architecture

748 **Traditional farm buildings in north-east Wales 1550-1900.**
Eurwyn William. Cardiff: National Museum of Wales, Welsh Folk
Museum, 1982. 334p. illus.
Provides a detailed survey of traditional farm buildings in one of the richest
agricultural areas in Wales. The work is not an examination of farmhouses and
cottages, but of the various types of buildings which can be found on a farm, such as
barns, stables, cowhouses and smaller buildings, such as pig sties and dovecotes. In
addition to describing the design of these buildings, the work also refers to the siting,
layout and building materials used in their construction.

749 **Welsh chapels.**
Anthony Jones. Cardiff: National Museum of Wales, 1984. 87p. illus.
This booklet examines the religious buildings of the nonconformists in Wales built
between the end of the seventeenth century and the first decade of the twentieth
century. With the aid of over 100 illustrations it is possible to see the work and skills of
the little known 'architects' who transformed barns and designed large, purpose-built
buildings for the act of worship.

750 **Welsh country workers housing 1775-1875.**
Jeremy Lowe. Cardiff: National Museum of Wales, 1985. 49p. illus.
bibliog.
This booklet illustrates the homes of workers who lived in the countryside of Wales
during the first century of the Industrial Revolution. The first section shows the basic
housing types of the late-eighteenth and early-nineteenth centuries. Another section
illustrates the houses built for craftsmen and others in specialised occupations and the
final section examines the houses of the industrial age.

751 **The Welsh house: a study in folk culture.**
Iorwerth C. Peate. Liverpool, England: Hugh Evans, 1944. 204p.
illus. bibliog.
A seminal study of Welsh domestic architecture from the earliest known human
habitation in Wales down to the twentieth century. The author demonstrates that the
Welsh house is an expression of Welsh life and will vary according to the climatic and
geographical conditions of the locality as well as the social conditions and the economic
status of the occupant. The work discusses building materials and building
construction, as well as the main forms of domestic architecture traditionally found in
Wales.

752 **Welsh industrial workers housing 1775-1875.**
Jeremy B. Lowe. Cardiff: National Museum of Wales, 1977. 65p.
illus. bibliog.
This booklet illustrates the variety of house-forms which could be seen in the industrial
areas of Wales during the first-half of the Industrial Revolution. It also provides an
indication of the living conditions experienced by their inhabitants – the industrial
workers. The five sections of the work deal with the various developments in housing
design during this period.

Folklore and Customs

General

753 **Celtic heritage: ancient tradition in Ireland and Wales.**
Alwyn Rees, Brinley Rees.   London: Thames & Hudson, 1961.
bibliog.
A masterly reinterpretation of Celtic traditions based on recent studies in the areas of religion, mythology and anthropology. The study is based on an analysis of the content and the background of early Welsh and Irish tales.

754 **Crafts, customs and legends.**
Mary Corbett Harris.   Newton Abbot, England: David & Charles, 1980. 168p.
A study of the life and customs of the Welsh people written for the non-specialist. It contains chapters on a number of topics including the following: drovers and hill farms; crafts and skills; seasonal customs; witchcraft; and animals and saints in Welsh folklore.

755 **Popular beliefs in Wales from Restoration to Methodism.**
Geraint H. Jenkins.   *Bulletin of the Board of Celtic Studies*, vol. 27, no. 3 (Nov. 1977), p. 440-62.
Despite the efforts of religious leaders from the Elizabethan era onwards to erase Welsh people's views on supernatural powers and phenomena, the common folk clung to their traditional beliefs into the second half of the seventeenth century. Religious reformers in the period after 1660 attacked these beliefs strongly through the printed press but, with the exception of some of those who had received education and the sceptical gentry, superstition, apparitions and omens, witchcraft and magic, astrology and almanacs retained their credibility amongst the ordinary folk.

756 **Tradition and folk life: a Welsh view.**
Iorwerth C. Peate.   London: Faber, 1972. 147p. illus. bibliog.
An overview of Welsh folk-life aimed at the student and the general reader. The author, who was the first curator of the Welsh Folk Museum, defines folk-life as 'the study of man's material, mental and spiritual struggle towards civilisation'. The book consists of chapters on the following themes: the house; the hearth; the home; costume; music and dance; plays; folklore; the countryside; and the language.

757 **Welsh folk customs.**
Trefor M. Owen.   Cardiff: National Museum of Wales, Welsh Folk Museum, 1974. 3rd. ed. 197p. illus. bibliog.
An introductory handbook to the folk-customs of Wales, prepared by the Curator of the Welsh Folk Museum, which endeavours to collect and display material evidence relating to such customs. The descriptive account of the customs presented in this volume is based partly on the museum's collection of artefacts and partly on documentary evidence. No attempt is made to explain, or to trace, the origins of these customs. The arrangement of the customs follows the Christian calendar, starting with Christmas festivities, and also takes in customs connected to the various seasons. One chapter deals with customs associated with birth, marriage and death.

758 **Welsh folklore and folk-customs.**
T. Gwynn Jones.   Cambridge, England: D. S. Brewer, 1979. 255p. bibliog.
Originally published in 1930, this is a facsimile reproduction with a new introduction by Arthur ap Gwynn. It describes the chief features of the folklore and folk-customs of the Welsh people and the themes covered include: gods and culture heroes; ghosts and other apparitions; fairies; giants, hags and monsters; caves, mounds and stones; magic, divination and witchcraft; seasons; weather beliefs and practices; house and hearth; courtship, marriage and the family. The volume also includes illustrative examples of various types of folk-tales found in Wales.

Folk narrative

759 **Welsh folk tales.**
Robin Gwyndaf.   Cardiff: National Museum of Wales, 1989. 105p. bibliog.
This bilingual reference work is based on a national survey of the Welsh folk-narrative tradition. It aims to present a synopsis of a selection of legends and traditions. The introductory essay assesses the tradition of folk-narrative in Wales and also discusses the themes, function, meaning and value of the tales which have been included. The text is illustrated with drawings by Margaret Jones.

760 **Welsh legends and fairy lore.**

D. Parry-Jones. London: Batsford, 1988. New ed. 181p. illus. bibliog.

Traditional stories are no longer handed down from one generation to another. Fortunately, however, for the past hundred years or so, amateur enthusiasts and scholars have been active in collecting and publishing much of the folk-narrative which was only available in oral form. From these published collections, D. Parry-Jones here presents a selection of them for the general reader.

761 **Welsh walks and legends.**

Showell Styles. St. Albans, England: Granada Publishing, 1979. 205p. illus.

A collection of thirty-nine Welsh traditional stories together with practical information as to the routes of short walks in the areas featured in the individual stories. This book is aimed at the visitor to Wales who wishes to experience the fine scenery and also to become acquainted with some of the national traditions.

Food and drink

762 **Customs and cooking from Wales.**

Sian Llewellyn. Swansea, Wales: Celtic Educational, 1974. 112p. illus.

The first section of this book presents a popular introduction to a number of local and national customs such as the Mari Lwyd (a form of wassailing which flourished in the counties of Glamorgan and Monmouth during the mid-nineteenth century when the visiting party was led by a member holding an imitation horse's skull covered with a white sheet). The second section consists of a collection of recipes used for traditional Welsh dishes.

763 **First catch your peacock: a book of Welsh food.**

Bobby Freeman. Griffithstown, Pontypool, Wales: Image Imprint, 1980. 243p. illus. bibliog.

A well-researched contribution to the literature on traditional Welsh cookery written by one of the pioneers of the subject who began to publish traditional Welsh dishes during the 1960s. The introductory section analyses the history of various Welsh foodstuffs and examines the reasons for geographic and regional differences. The main section of the work is a selection of recipes with notes and direct quotations in support of their authenticity. These recipes are arranged under several headings including: river and sea fish, lake fish and shellfish; bread, oatcakes, bara brith (a traditional fruit loaf), mutton, lamb, goats; cheese; vegetables; puddings, pies, pancakes; and cakes.

764 **Lambs, leeks and laverbread: the best of Welsh cookery.**

Gilli Davies. London: Grafton Books, 1989. 336p. illus.

A personal selection of Welsh recipes which attempts to combine traditional fare with modern and healthier cooking methods. In preparing this collection, the author travelled extensively throughout Wales to gather information about dishes. Davies not only aims to demonstrate that some of the best traditional cooking is still alive, but also how contemporary cooks continue to use local produce to create new traditions. The volume deals with the following range of foodstuffs: fish; poultry; meat; vegetarian; puddings; baking; drinks; preservatives; and cheese.

765   **A taste of Wales. Blas ar Gymru.**
Richard Binns, Gilli Davies, Brenda Parry, edited by Roger Thomas, Antonia Hebbert.   Cardiff: Wales Tourist Board & Taste of Wales, 1989. 180p. illus.

A practical reference manual covering food and cooking in Wales which is aimed at the traveller, the cook and the good-food lover. Included in the volume are fifty recipes of traditional and new dishes which can be found in Wales, a guide to some of the finest eating establishments and a directory of the over 160 'Taste of Wales' members.

766   **A taste of Wales: Welsh traditional food.**
Theodora Fitzgibbon.   London: J. M. Dent, 1971. 123p. illus.

A personal selection of traditional Welsh dishes using ingredients such as sea-food, mutton and lamb, cheese and locally grown vegetables. Each recipe follows the normal practice of listing the ingredients and presenting the cooking instructions for the dish but it also includes background historical notes on each example.

767   **Welsh country cookery: traditional recipes from the country kitchens of Wales.**
Bobby Freeman.   Talybont, Dyfed, Wales: Y Lolfa, 1988. 79p. illus.

A selection of recipes for 100 authentic traditional Welsh dishes compiled by an author who has specialised in collecting and serving such dishes for over a quarter of a century. The nineteenth century photographs of rural Wales, and the lively anecdotes relating to the recipes, add to the book's appeal.

768   **Welsh fare: a selection of traditional recipes.**
S. Minwel Tibbott.   Cardiff: National Museum of Wales, Welsh Folk Museum, 1976. 84p. illus.

Food and drink form an important part of a nation's heritage and this volume was prepared with the objectives of keeping alive the memory of those dishes which were an integral part of the Welsh way of life and of reintroducing a selection of the foods for the Welsh people of today. The selection of recipes, based on oral evidence collected by staff of the Welsh Folk Museum throughout Wales, includes savoury dishes, griddle cakes, cakes, bread, cereal and milk dishes, puddings, fish, jam, toffee and drinks.

Costume

769 Costumes of the Welsh people.
Ilid E. Anthony.   Cardiff: National Museum of Wales, 1975. 40p.
illus.

Costumes present information about the people who wore them, and therefore clothes have been amongst the important items collected by the Welsh Folk Museum which is striving to build up a picture of Welsh life in the past. The policy of the Material Culture Department of the Museum is to collect, not only items worn on festive or formal occasions, but also those worn at work. From the collection, the author is able to trace the fashion in clothes from the elegant costumes of the eighteenth century to the age of designs and mass production in the second quarter of the twentieth century. There is also a chapter on the history of the traditional national costume of Wales and the part that Lady Llanover played in its creation.

770 Welsh costume in the 18th and 19th century.
Ken Etheridge.   Swansea, Wales: Christopher Davies, 1977. 112p.
illus.

The national costume of Wales is based on clothes which were worn by peasant women during the eighteenth and nineteenth centuries. This volume deals with the individual garments and costumes worn in Wales during the last two centuries and is based on original research undertaken by the author. In addition to describing the designs of the costumes, Etheridge provides information about the manufacture of garments. Other chapters describe the significance of the tall hat and men's clothes.

771 Welsh peasant costume.
F. G. Payne.   Cardiff: National Museum of Wales, Welsh Folk
Museum, 1969. 16p. illus.

A brief study of the origin and development of the Welsh national costume. This work was first published in 1964 as an article in *Folklife*, the journal of the Society for Folk Life Studies.

Sports and Recreation

General

772 **Changing times, changing needs: a 10 year strategy for sport in Wales 1986-1996. Amserau cyfnewidiol, anghenion cyfnewidiol: strategaeth 10 mlynedd i chwaraeon yng Nghymru 1986-1996.**
Cardiff: Sports Council for Wales, 1986. 85p. illus. maps. bibliog.

A report which presents a framework for the Sports Council for Wales, local authorities, governing bodies of sports, as well as statutory and voluntary bodies regarding the likely requirements for sport provision in Wales during the period 1986 to 1996 in view of changing needs. The report reviews the advancements made in this field since the Sports Council was established in 1972 and also discusses the factors which need to be considered in planning a strategy for the future, for example, increased leisure time and the growing needs of the disadvantages.

773 **The Sports Council for Wales Annual Report. Cyngor Chwaraeon Cymru adroddiad blynyddol.**
Cardiff: Sports Council for Wales, 1973-. annual.

Includes a review of the activities of the Council which are designed to preserve and safeguard 'the physical and mental health of the community' and 'to enhance the provision of facilities for physical recreation'. The report also lists both local projects which have been approved and the grants distributed by the Sports Council for Wales.

Rugby

774 **Fields of praise: the official history of the Welsh Rugby Union 1881-1981.**
David Smith, Gareth Williams. Cardiff: University of Wales Press, 1980. 505p. illus. bibliog.
The definitive history of the first century of the national game written by two professional Welsh historians. In addition to presenting a detailed analysis of famous matches, leading players and the administration of rugby, the game is considered in relation to the social, industrial and religious life of Wales during this period. Also included is a comprehensive list of Welsh international players, international results plus a list of Welshmen involved in British Touring Teams.

775 **The illustrated history of Welsh rugby.**
J. B. G. Thomas. London: Pelham Books, 1980. 256p. illus.
This volume, published on the occasion of the centenary of the Welsh Rugby Union (WRU) in 1981, presents a popular history of the game in Wales during its first 100 years. Two chapters are devoted to the record of the international team between 1880 and 1980, one chapter is a tribute to some of the outstanding players of the period and a further chapter presents anecdotes on some notable characters and amusing incidents surrounding the game.

776 **Rugby Annual for Wales.**
Edited by Arwyn Owen. Cardiff: Welsh Brewers, 1972-. annual.
This publication includes: a review, and the results of the previous rugby season's international matches at senior, youth and school level; details of Welsh club rugby at senior and lower levels; and statistics about past international games and players. It also provides a list of the major club and international fixtures for the following season.

777 **The rugby clubs of Wales.**
David Parry-Jones. London: Stanley Paul, 1989. 176p. illus.
A personal survey of the major rugby union clubs and a selection of the smaller clubs in Wales. The author attempts to outline the history of each club and to describe their major triumphs and provide sketches of the leading heroes. He also attempts to define the distinct atmosphere of each club and ground. Maps and diagrams are included to help the visitor to find his or her way to the grounds.

778 **Taff's acre: a history and celebration of Cardiff Arms Park.**
Edited by David Parry-Jones. London: Willow Books, 1984. 198p. illus.
A collection of short articles by ex-players, authors, rugby administrators and a professional historian which taken together, outline the main developments in the history of one of the most famous rugby grounds in the world. The volume includes personal recollections of the finest games and the most outstanding individual performances seen at the Arms Park. As well as describing some of the famous chapters in the history of Welsh rugby union, the volume also provides detailed

information about the ground itself during the past 100 years and, in particular, the major reconstruction which took place during the 1970s and 1980s.

779 **A touch of glory: 100 years of Welsh rugby.**
Alun Richards.   London: Michael Joseph, 1980. 176p. illus.
The personal reflections of a Welsh novelist on the national game of Wales on the occasion of the Welsh Rugby Union's (WRU) centenary. The book is a spin-off from a film which the author was commissioned to research and script on behalf of BBC Wales. Supported by a wide range of photographs, Richards traces the development of the game in Wales reflecting on how it developed into a national obsession. He also tries to discover the main attributes of the game in Wales. Carwyn James, the ex-British Lions coach, contributed an afterword which offers a penetrating analysis on the relationship between the game and Welsh national consciousness.

780 **Welsh Rugby Union Handbook.**
Cardiff: Welsh Rugby Union, 1965-. annual.
Includes: the names of officers and committee members of the WRU; the WRU's constitution and bye-laws; international results and the names of Welsh international players; a directory of current referees; international and club fixtures for the forthcoming season; a directory of member clubs; and the laws of the game.

Association football

781 **The early development of association football in South Wales, 1890-1906.**
Brian Lile, David Farmer.   *Transactions of the Honourable Society of Cymmrodorion*, (1984), p. 193-215.
An attempt to demonstrate that soccer was as much a Welsh institution as rugby union by the close of the nineteenth century. This paper traces the growing popularity of soccer at local level in South Wales, and outlines the development of the administrative organisation of the game, with particular reference to the South Wales and Monmouthshire Football Association.

782 **Football Association of Wales Annual Report.**
Cardiff: Football Association of Wales, 1913-. annual.
This annual report includes the names of officers and committee members of the Football Association of Wales (FAW) and regional bodies, a directory of clubs, the rules and standing orders of the FAW, retrospective lists of Welsh Cup final results at various levels, international results at all levels and the laws of the game.

783 **Football wizard: the story of Billy Meredith.**
John Harding.   Derby, England: Breedon Books, 1985. 240p. illus.
Billy Meredith was probably association football's first legendary figure. Not only was he a highly skilled and entertaining player, but he was also one of the most colourful personalities in the early history of the professional game. This objective biography

follows his career from leaving the coal mines of his native village in North Wales to his success with both the Manchester clubs and with the Welsh international side. By reading the details of his achievements and his skirmishes with football management at club and international level, it is possible to learn a great deal about the early development of professional soccer in England and Wales.

784   **Swansea City 1912-1982.**
David Farmer.   London: Pelham Books, 1982. 272p. illus.
This official history of one of Wales' premier soccer clubs considers the changing fortunes of the club from its foundation in the early years of the twentieth century to the peak of its achievement to date when the club finished in sixth position in the first division of the English Football League in the 1981-82 season. The appendices to the main text include an analysis of the team's league position at the end of each season since its foundation, a list of all first team players and their career with the 'Swans'.

785   **100 years of Welsh soccer: the official history of the Football Association of Wales.**
Peter Corrigan.   Cardiff: Welsh Brewers, [1976]. 96p. illus.
The official history of the Football Association of Wales, published to mark its centenary in 1976. This illustrated work, written for the general reader, traces the development of soccer at club and international level for those 100 years and includes portraits of leading personalities in the game, as well as graphic accounts of some of the most important and memorable games. An important feature of the publication is the detailed statistics of international appearances at senior, under-twenty-three, amateur and youth levels.

Mountaineering and walking

786   **Best walks in North Wales.**
Richard Sale.   London: Constable, 1988. 293p. illus. map.
A guide book to thirty-six walks in North Wales, of which all but eight are located within the Snowdonia National Park. The other eight walks are located in Anglesey, the Llŷn Peninsula and the Berwyn and Clwydian ranges. The walks have been grouped together by area, or hill range, and include a brief introduction to the historical, geographical and geological features of the area. Individual walks are then classified as easy, intermediate or difficult on the basis of their length and the nature of their respective terrain. For each walk the author provides a route description and sketch map.

787   **A guide book to Offa's Dyke Path.**
Christopher John Wright.   London: Constable, 1986. 2nd. ed. 362p. bibliog. illus.
Offa's Dyke Path is a designated long-distance footpath which is 270km long and was officially opened in July 1971. Unlike numerous other long-distance paths, it follows an archaeological construction rather than a geographical feature. The dyke was built

twelve hundred years ago on the orders of Offa, King of Mercia, to mark the boundary with Wales. This volume provides a detailed guide to the path and is divided into sections recommended as being suitable for a day's walk. In numerous places it is difficult to follow the route and, accordingly, the guide includes route-finding notes, sketch maps and photographs as well as background information about the dyke itself and about the towns and countryside nearby.

788　**A guide to the Pembrokeshire Coast Path.**
Christopher John Wright.　London: Constable, 1986. 391p. illus. bibliog.

The Pembrokeshire Coast Path was the first designated long-distance path in Wales when it was opened in 1970. This guide is written for those who wish to walk the entire length of the path, or selected stretches of it. The author has provided sketch maps and photographs both to aid the walker along the path and to help him or her discover nearby towns of interest which have added to the route. The work also includes introductory chapters on the most interesting features which can be observed by the walker.

789　**The mountain men: an early history of rock climbing in North Wales.**
Alan Hankinson.　London: Heinemann Educational Books, 1977. 202p. bibliog. illus.

An account of the pioneering years of rock climbing in Snowdonia before the outbreak of World War I. The achievements of climbers such as George Mallory, James Merriman, Archer Thomson and Geoffrey Winthrop are described, as are the fraternity of climbers who met regularly at the Pen-y-gwryd and later Pen-y-pass hotels. The author has included descriptions of the climbs which were established in the area during those early years.

790　**The mountains of Wales: a walker's guide to the 600-metre summits.**
Terry Marsh.　London: Hodder & Stoughton, 1985. 256p. illus.

A guide book to over 100 walks in seventeen mountain areas in Wales which, in good weather, do not pose technical difficulties for the walker. The work also includes a list of all Welsh peaks of 600 metres, or more.

791　**North Wales limestone.**
Andy Pollitt.　Climbers' Club, 1987. 223p. (Climbers' Club Guides to Wales, no. 8).

A guide to the rock climbs on carboniferous limestone of varying quality and texture on Craig y Forwyn, Great Orme and Little Orme crags. In addition to the notes on climbing for each route, the work contains an introduction to the development of rock climbing on these crags and a list of the dates and the names of the climber(s) involved in the first recorded ascents of the climbs described in the work. The book also includes helpful diagrams of the various routes.

792 **Ridges of Snowdonia.**
Steve Ashton.   Milnthrope, England: Cicerone Press, 1985. 248p. illus.

A guide aimed at hill walking enthusiasts which presents a selection of the ridge walks to be found in Snowdonia. The information on each walk includes a map, a route description, information about the distance of the walk, the terrain, the main difficulties and associated matters. The walks are grouped into eight areas: Carneddau; Glyders; the Snowdon group; Moelwyns; Nantlle; Rhinogs; Cadair Idris; and the Arans. Also includes is the Snowdonia Traverse which links the fourteen highest peaks in Snowdonia.

793 **Rock climbing in Wales.**
Ron Jones.   London: Constable, 1975. 2nd. rev. ed. 242p. illus

A guide book to 200 rock climbs in Snowdonia and its near environs, personally selected by the author to include a reasonably balanced selection of grades of difficulty. The main text is divided into five climbing centres namely Ogwen Valley, Llanberis Pass, Beddgelert, Dolwyddelan and Holyhead Mountain. For each climb Jones provides practical information including a crag and route description, and route and pitch lengths.

794 **Snowdonia rock climbs.**
Paul Williams.   Sheffield, England: Extreme Books & Designs, 1982. 302p. illus.

A guide to approximately 350 rock climbing routes in North Wales at all levels of difficulty, covering the best known climbs in Snowdonia as well as the cliffs of Tremadog and Gogarth and a small selection of limestone crags on the North Wales coast. Each entry includes a route description, a grading, a photo-diagram of crags and details about the usual descents.

795 **The Welsh peaks.**
W. A. Poucher.   London: Constable, 1987. 9th ed. 426p. illus. maps.

The first edition of this work was published in 1962 and since that time it has established the reputation of being the standard work for walking enthusiasts in Wales. In all, the book contains detailed descriptions to fifty-six mountain routes. The areas covered are Snowdon, Glyders, Carneddau, Moel Siabod, Moel Hebog, Cadair Idris, Harlech Dome, Arennigs, Arans, Plynlimon, the Black Mountains, the Brecon Beacons and Carmarthen Fan.

796 **Welsh winter climbs.**
Malcolm Campbell, Andy Newton.   Milnthorpe, England: Cicerone Press, 1988. 248p. illus.

Winter climbing has experienced an unprecedented boom in popularity during the past decade and therefore this is a timely guide book to over 200 winter climbs in North Wales. As winter conditions in this area are unpredictable, the author rightly advises climbers to study weather patterns closely before setting off, to avoid disappointment. The short route descriptions of the individual climbs are arranged into twelve areas, namely: Carneddau; Glyderau; Llanberis; Snowdon; Nantlle; the Llŷn Peninsula; Moelynion; Rhinog; Cadair Idris; Aran; Dyfi; and Berwyn.

Angling

797 **Angling guide to Wales.**
Edited by Clive Gammon.   Cardiff: Wales Tourist Board, 1974. 96p.
illus. maps.
A practical reference guide to the sea angling, game fishing and coarse fishing facilties available in Wales. In addition to offering information and maps identifying the location and characteristics of the various centres for the different types of fishing, the booklet provides a range of practical hints on such issues as bait, equipment, fishing seasons, licence requirements and boat hire.

798 **The Angling Times book of the Wye.**
Leslie Baverstock.   Newton Abbott, England: David & Charles, 1981.
192p. illus.
A detailed guide to one of the finest fishing rivers in the British Isles written for the angling enthusiast. The work is divided into three sections, i.e., game fishing, coarse fishing and practical advice on where to fish. The section on game fishing deals chiefly with salmon and includes information about past and present fishing policies for the River Wye, the salmon's life cycle and the use of various fishing techniques on the river. The second section, presents information about the supply and fishing of chub, dace, eels and elvers, grayling, perch, pike, roach, shad and other fish found in the Wye. The final section, provides details, regarding, for example the limits of catches, techniques, and the availability of permits, as well as access.

799 **Fly patterns for the rivers and lakes of Wales.**
Moc Morgan.   Llandysul, Wales: Gomer, 1984. 334p. bibliog. illus.
A reference book which considers some 300 fly-patterns used throughout Wales. The entries on patterns have been classified into the following categories: sewin flies; salmon; trout wet fly; lures; nymphs; and graylings. In addition to technical information relating to these patterns, the author has provided brief biological notes and details about the origin of the pattern where the information exists. In an introductory essay, Lynn Hughes traces the origins and background of fly-patterns in Wales. The work also includes coloured plates and black-and-white drawings to illustrate many of the patterns mentioned in the text.

800 **Guide to freshwater fishing in Wales and the Marches.**
Brecon, Wales: Welsh Water Authority, [ca. 1985.] 184p. illus. maps.
A comprehensive guide to the facilities available for salmon and trout fishing in the rivers, lakes and reservoirs of Wales. The guide is divided into eight sections corresponding to the Divisional Areas of the Welsh Water Authority. Within each section there is a brief description on the nature of the fishing, a directory of bailiffs and fishing licence agents and brief entries on each fishing location. The diagrammatic maps which accompany the text offer practical help to locate the various venues and to identify the type of fishing offered.

Miscellaneous sports

801 **Fifty years of racing at Chepstow.**
Pat Lucas. Tenby, Wales: H. G. Walters, 1976. 215p. illus. bibliog.
Chepstow is the only surviving racecourse in South Wales and this book provides a
popular history of the course from its foundation in 1926 up to 1976 to mark its golden
jubilee. Written for the racing enthusiast and the general reader, it recalls some of the
personalities and great races which were held on the course during those fifty years and
it includes a chapter on the Welsh Grand National which was held at Chepstow for the
first time in 1949. The appendix includes a list of the winners of this particular race
from 1949 to 1976, together with the names of the trainer and the jockey.

802 **The history of Glamorgan Cricket Club.**
Andrew Hignell. London: Christopher Helm, 1988. 356p. illus.
bibliog.
Glamorgan County Cricket Club is the only first-class cricket team in Wales. The
publication of this detailed and thoroughly researched history of the club coincided
with its centenary. The account provided of the fortunes of the club during its first one
hundred years both on, and off, the field includes vivid descriptions of outstanding
players and matches together with full score cards. The author has also compiled a
comprehensive statistical record of players' performances throughout the club's history
and these are included in an appendix. Tony Lewis, the current Chairman of the Club
and a former captain of the team, has contributed a short personal essay on the club.

Libraries, Art Galleries, Museums and Archives

803 **Art galleries and exhibition spaces in Wales.**
Nicholas Pearson. Cardiff: Welsh Arts Council, 1981. 232p.
A survey of art galleries and exhibition venues in Wales which was commissioned by the Welsh Arts Council. The aim of the report was to provide a descriptive and analytical study of existing facilities in Wales together with recommendations to the Arts Council as to what could be done to support and develop art galleries and other exhibition facilities in Wales. An appendix provides a directory of galleries and exhibition spaces available in Wales. This is a very useful guide for art and exhibition officers, although a number of new facilities have been established since this survey was undertaken.

804 **Directory of information sources in Wales. Cyfeiriadur ffynonellau gwybodaeth yng Nghymru.**
Edited by Dianne M. Hooper. [Cardiff:] Welsh Development Agency, in association with the Information Services Group (Wales), 1989. 83p.
A directory of libraries and information units found in Wales. In addition to providing information on addresses and phone numbers the entries give details concerning subject coverage, special collections, special services, opening hours and information about access and restrictions of use for all the organisations listed. The publication supersedes *Library resources in Wales* published by the LIbrary Association in 1972 and is an invaluable reference source for those undertaking research in Wales.

805 **Exploring museums: Wales.**
J. Geraint Jenkins. London: HMSO, 1990. 114p. illus. map.
(Exploring Museums Series).
This work written for the general reader is one of a series of eleven regional guides to museums in the British Isles and includes a personal guide to the sixty most worthy museums in Wales selected and presented by the curator of the National Folk Museum in Cardiff. These museums have either been selected for the quality of their collections or because they have interesting or unusual features. In addition to the descriptive

196

guides to these examples the work also includes a gazetteer with brief annotations to other museums found in Wales.

806 **Housing the visual arts in Wales: preliminary appraisal by the Advisory Group appointed by the Secretary of State for Wales.**
Cardiff: Welsh Office. 1986. 133p. illus.
The terms of reference given to the group included examining the various options available for exhibiting the collections of paintings and sculptures at the National Museum of Wales. The group was also asked to make suggestions as to what galleries should be developed in other parts of Wales in order to establish coherent national facilities. This report includes a set of recommendations which need to be examined further.

807 **An introductory survey of 18th century Welsh libraries.**
Eiluned Rees. *Journal of the Welsh Bibliographical Society*, vol. 10, no.
4 (June 1971), p. 197-258.
An introductory essay on the provision and nature of libraries in Wales during the eighteenth century. The growing interest in antiquities and genealogy during the century brought about an upsurge of interest in book-collecting amongst the gentry and this factor, together with the fact that Wales had no natural cultural centre or large educational institution, meant that the finest libraries of the age were in private ownership. The author discusses aspects of these private libraries, such as their methods of acquiring books and their stock and also briefly mentions other types of libraries to be found at the time, such as school and circulating libraries.

808 **Llyfrgell Genedlaethol Cymru adroddiad blynyddol. National Library of Wales Annual Report.**
Aberystwyth, Wales: National Library of Wales, 1909-. annual.
This publication describes the activities of the various departments of the library during the previous year, lists major additions to the different collections, and also includes the financial statement of the library.

809 **Museums and galleries.**
Donald Moore. In: *The arts in Wales 1950-1975*. Edited by Meic Stephens. Cardiff: Welsh Arts Council, 1979, p. 87-141.
A survey of the facilities for collecting and exhibiting the visual arts in art galleries, museums, libraries and arts centres in Wales between 1950 and 1975. The essay also presents a short review of the development of organisations and institutions found in Wales during this period to promote the visual arts.

810 **The making of a national museum.**
Douglas A. Bassett. *Transactions of the Honourable Society of Cymmrodorion*, (1982), p. 153-85; (1983), p. 187-220; (1984), p. 217-316.
A study of the history of the National Museum of Wales from 1907, when it was granted a Royal Charter, to 1982. This series of articles is an extended version of a talk

delivered to the Society of Cymmrodorion in 1982 to mark the seventy-fifth anniversary of the National Museum of Wales. The author traces the concept of establishing a national museum in Wales and then demonstrates the achievements of the museum by examining six components: the planning and construction of the building; the acquisition and management of the collections; the provision of other public services; the appointment and deployment of staff; financial resources; and the methods by which the museum authorities created a truly national institution. This is the only significant contribution to be published so far on the history of the museum.

811 **A national library for Wales: the prologue.**
David Jenkins. *Transactions of the Honourable Society of Cymmrodorion*, (1982), p. 139-52.
A standard history of the National Library of Wales has yet to be published. This article, which was originally delivered to the Society of Cymmrodorion in Bangor in 1982 by the National Librarian of Wales at the time, traces the events which led to the opening of the library in 1909.

812 **The National Library of Wales: a survey of its history, its contents and its activities.**
W. Ll. Davies. Aberystwyth, Wales: National Library of Wales, 1937. 212p. illus.
An outline history written by the first librarian of the National Library of the movement which led to the foundation of the National Library of Wales in 1907 and its history and development during its first twenty-five years. In addition to evaluating the contribution of the major benefactors, Sir John Williams and Sir Herbert Lewis, the volume also describes the activities and the collections of all the departments of the institution.

813 **National Museum of Wales Annual Report. Amgueddfa Genedlaethol Cymru adroddiad blynyddol.**
Cardiff: National Museum of Wales, 1907-. annual.
Reports on the activities of the National Museum, the Welsh Folk Museum, the Welsh Industrial and Maritime Museum and their various departments and outposts. This publication also provides details of donations, acquisitions, exhibitions, financial statements, as well as information on staff and committee members.

814 **The report of a working party on public library services.**
Library and Information Services Council, Wales. Cardiff: Library and Information Services Council (Wales), 1988. 43p
This report is based on a comprehensive survey of current public library practice in Wales and of reports published recently by bodies such as the Department of Education and Science, the Library and Information Services Council and the Library Association on various aspects of public library services. Armed with this information, and a knowledge of the economic and cultural background in which the libraries operate, the working party was able to present a set of recommendations which would enable library authorities in Wales to provide an efficient public library service in the 1990s.

815 **Report on museums in Wales.**
Brian Morris.   London: HMSO, 1981. 50p.
Presents the findings of a study to examine the needs of museums in Wales other than the National Museum of Wales in the light of a recent report on the future of museums. This report contains a survey of museum provision in each Welsh county at the beginning of the 1980s, together with a list of recommendations for the future framework of museums in Wales.

816 **Survey of miners' institute and welfare hall libraries October 1972-February 1973.**
Hywel Francis.   *Llafur*, vol. 1 no. 2 (1973), p. 55-64.
Between the 1890s and the end of the 1930s over 100 miners' institute and welfare hall libraries were established in the South Wales coalfield. The purpose of this survey, conducted in the early 1970s, was triggered by the fact that, with the decline of the coal industry, many of these libraries had been destroyed. There was, therefore, an urgent need to salvage what remained of them and also to assess the influence and quality of these libraries in their heyday. This article describes the state of the remaining libraries by the 1970s, and considers the reasons for their decline and destruction. It also describes the establishment of the South Wales Miners' Library to preserve remaining collections for research purposes.

817 **Trysorfa cenedl: hanes Llyfrgell Genedlaethol Cymru. A nation's treasury: the story of the National Library of Wales.**
Aberystwyth, Wales: National Library of Wales, 1982. 56p. illus.
An illustrated booklet which presents an outline of the history, activities and range of services provided by the National Library of Wales. The booklet was originally produced as a handbook to accompany a special exhibition to celebrate the seventy-fifth anniversary of the library, but it can also serve as a practical introduction to the library and its services. The text is in Welsh and English.

818 **Y Ddolen. Cylchgrawn Cymdeithas Llyfrgelloedd Cymru. Journal of the Welsh Library Association.**
Welsh Library Association, 1970-. three times per year.
A newsletter which covers the public, academic, special and national library scene in Wales. In addition to its coverage of recent developments and events, and the reports of Welsh Library Association business and activities, it occasionally includes short articles or features. Some of the items are in the Welsh language.

Books

Book production, past and present

819 **Byd llyfrau Cymreig. The world of Welsh books.**
[Eiluned Rees] with a foreword by Brynley F. Roberts.   Aberystwyth,
Wales: National Library of Wales, 1989. 24p.

A short bilingual account of printing and publishing in Wales from 1546 (the date of
the first book to be printed in the Welsh language) to the present time which indicates
the significant landmarks in the history of book production. This publication is a
booklet which was designed to accompany a major exhibition of the same title held at
the National Library in 1989. It is illustrated, and has sections on the early days,
ephemera, the nineteenth century, periodicals and newspapers, music books, and the
twentieth century.

820 **Cyhoeddi yn yr iaith Gymraeg. Publishing in the Welsh Language.**
Cardiff: Council for the Welsh language, 1978. 97p.

Provides a wide-ranging review of publishing, and an assessment of the influence on
the Welsh language of the system of publishing, including grant-aid from various
services. Chapters are devoted to commercial publishers, academic publishing, support
from public grants, authors, the reading public, books for children, periodicals for
children, journals and magazines for adults and there is also a summary of conclusions
and recommendations. Appendices list various data and statistics of primary
significance including: books published 1971-76; lists of grants; reading in secondary
schools; and the patterns of borrowing of Welsh-language materials from public
libraries.

821 **A history of printing and printers in Wales to 1810, and of successive and related printers to 1923. Also a history of printing and printers in Monmouthshire to 1923.**
Ifano Jones.   Cardiff: William Lewis (Printers) Ltd., 1925. 367p.

Despite its age, this work remains the only attempt at a comprehensive history of the subject, but it is a study which should be used and quoted with considerable care, since subsequent research in specific areas, or of specific printers and publishers has indicated that dates cited and Jones' interpretation of evidence are prone to error. The study is organized chronologically and by locations and places of significance, and contains numerous appendices.

822 **A history of the Gregynog Press.**
Dorothy A. Harrop.   Pinner, Middlesex, England: Private Libraries Association, 1980. 266p. bibliog.

An illustrated history of an outstanding press which represents a unique venture among major private presses, as it is situated in Wales and produces materials in English and Welsh. It is also acknowledged as being a press which has the highest standards in design, printing and binding. This work is essentially a chronological history, which traces the origins, the ideas, the first productions and the early books of the press. In addition, it offers detailed studies of certain publications and of individuals concerned with the work of the press, and examines the eventual demise of the press. The bibliography and handlists are very important sources of information as are the further readings suggested.

823 **A history of the House of Spurrell, Carmarthen, 1840-1969.**
Richard E. Huws.   Ann Arbor: University Microfilms International, 1985. 2 vols. bibliog.

An extensive consideration of the most outstanding publishing house in the history of the book in Wales in the modern period. The volume places the family in a publishing and geographical context, and examines the genealogy of the family. It then offers studies of two of the primary personalities, William Spurrell and Walter Spurrell, and an analysis of the Spurrell Dictionaries. The work concludes with a discussion of the post-Spurrell era and offers an assessment of the contribution made by the House of Spurrell to the development of the book trade in Wales.

824 **Publishing in minority languages. Cyhoeddi mewn ieithoedd lleiafrifol.**
Proceedings of a conference 29 July–2 August 1985. Edited by D. Hywel E. Roberts.   Aberystwyth, Wales. College of Librarianship Wales, 1986. 107p.

Presents twelve papers delivered at the conference, six of which relate to the situation in Wales and include studies of: publishing for children and young adults in Welsh; academic and scholarly publishing in Welsh; and publishing and the challenge of the newer media in Wales. The other papers relate to minority situations in Catalonia, Iceland, Scotland and Brittany.

825 **Y wasg gyfnodol Gymreig. The Welsh periodical press 1735-1900.**
Aberystwyth, Wales: National Library of Wales, 1987. 41p.
An essay published to accompany a major exhibition mounted at the National Library
of Wales. It reflects the remarkable number of journals published in Wales on a wide
range of subjects and traces their history. This publication is an effective guide to the
history of this important facet of Welsh culture and numerous illustrations augment the
text.

826 **The Welsh book-trade before 1820.**
Eiluned Rees.   Aberystwyth, Wales: National Library of Wales, 1988.
121p. maps.
An extended essay which originally appeared as part of *Libri Walliae: a catalogue of
Welsh books and books printed in Wales, 1546-1820* (Aberystwyth, 1987), and which is
an important study which places the material gathered for the catalogue into the
appropriate context. Following a brief introduction, the work is divided into the
following sections: 1546-1695: manuscript copying, the work of Protestant reformers,
Renaissance scholarship, orthography, patents and privileges and distribution; 1696-
c.1770: Shrewsbury printing, printing in Wales, Welsh printing in London and Oxford,
ancillary book-trade activities in Wales; c.1770-1820: printing-houses, presses and
types, ink, illustration, jobbing printing, advertising, bookselling and catalogues, the
London book-trade and Wales, other English towns, the publishing process, societies,
typography, private presses and the books. Appendices include some ornaments used
by printers of Welsh books, and a list of printers in Wales before 1820.

Book trade

827 **The book trade in Wales. Market research and general survey
commissioned by the Welsh Arts Council, the Welsh Books Council and
the Welsh Joint Education Committee September 1986–November 1987.**
Aberystwyth, Wales: Market research working party, 1988. 288p.
A report of a study carried out by the Department of Welsh Studies at the College of
Librarianship Wales, Aberystwyth. It represents the first market research exercise
undertaken of reading, book buying and readers in Wales. The report commences with
a brief historical overview of Welsh publishing and the contemporary support system,
then it enumerates the results of the market research. Subsequent chapters analyse
authorship and authors, publishing and publishers, marketing, market research of
bookshop customers, a survey of books in schools in Wales, the public libraries and the
book trade in Wales, and it also offers a large number of recommendations for future
action and development.

828 **Llais Llyfrau. Book news from Wales.**
Aberystwyth, Wales: Welsh Books Council, 1964-. quarterly.
The journal of the book-trade in Wales. It contains articles and news, reviews, and
quarterly listings of books published in Welsh, as well as books about Wales, and
books in English, as distributed by the Welsh Books Centre at Aberystwyth. The

journal is bilingual, the Welsh language material bears the title *Llais Llyfrau* and the English-language material bears the title *Book news from Wales*. Originally published as the magazine of the local Welsh Book societies, it now fulfills all the functions of a book-trade journal.

829 **The Welsh Books Council. Y Cyngor Llyfrau Cymraeg. Annual report.**
1966-. annual.

A primary source of information about both the book trade in Wales and publishing for adults and children in Wales in Welsh and English. The Council is based at Aberystwyth as is the Welsh Books Centre, the marketing and wholesaling arm of the Council.

Mass Media

General

830 **The mass media in Wales.**
Ian Hume.   In: *The Welsh and their country*. Edited by Ian Hume, W.
T. R. Pryce. Llandysul: Gomer Press in association with the Open
University, 1986, p. 324-47.
A study which centres on the rôle of the Welsh mass media of the 1980s in presenting
to their audiences images of Wales and the world. It deals with the historical
perspective, the printed work, Welsh-language newspapers and British dailies, the
broadcast media and to conclude, makes recommendations for research and
investigative work. Appended are useful supplementary materials inlcuding, tables of
viewing figures, newspaper circulation, news broadcasting and hours of service in
English and Welsh.

831 **More words and pictures in the air.**
David Skilton.   In: *The new Wales*. Edited by David Cole. Cardiff:
University of Wales Press, 1990, p. 179-92.
Considers the development of the mass media in recent decades in Wales, and assesses
the issues and controversies. Attention is paid to readership, employment, viewing
figures, franchises, and journalism, in both the English and Welsh-language media.

Newspapers and periodicals

832 **The Bulletin of the Board of Celtic Studies. Bwletin y Bwrdd Gwybodau Celtaidd.**
Cardiff: University of Wales Press on behalf of the Board of Celtic Studies of the University of Wales, 1923-. annual.
This is the major Welsh scholarly journal concerning the Celtic languages and studies. Its contents are divided into three sections: language and literature; history and law; and archaeology and art.

833 **Planet. The Welsh Internationalist.**
Aberystwyth, Wales: 1970-. bi-monthly.
A journal of current affairs, politics, literature and social and cultural issues, with reviews, short notices and shorter items. It began as a bi-monthly publication in 1970, and started publishing irregular double issues in 1974; it became a regular bi-monthly again in 1975 and remained as such until it ceased publication after the January 1980 number (49/50). The publication re-emerged in 1985 (number 51), again as a bi-monthly, stating that '. . . at least Welsh people are turning to each other and talking to each other more than before, and *Planet* hopes to be part of that process. *Planet* is a cultural magazine with an understanding of culture broad enough to encompass this dialectic . . . *Planet* takes the whole of Wales, geographically and linguistically as its subject and hopes to project its various communities to each other and to the outside world. . .'

834 **Transactions of the Honourable Society of Cymmrodorion. Trafodion Anrhydeddus Gymdeithas y Cymmrodorion.**
London: The Society, 1873-. annual.
A major scholarly publication which includes studies in literature, language, geography, history, law, sociology, education, the arts, politics, economics and industry, as well as occasional studies in science, with reviews, notices, obituaries and notes. All contributions normally relate to Wales, or Welsh affairs.

835 **Wales on Sunday.**
1989-. Sundays.
This is a relative newcomer from the Thomson Group of newspapers. Produced in Cardiff, it has a circulation of approximately 50,000. It includes a Welsh-language insert *Acen*, and a separate major sports section. Its editorial policies are independent but very similar to those of its sister paper, the *Western Mail.*

836 **Western Mail: The National Newspaper of Wales.**
1869-. daily.
Published in Cardiff, this is a newspaper in the ownership of the Thomson Group of newspapers. It has a circulation of approximately 78,000 predominantly in South, south-west and mid-Wales, and wins frequent industry prizes and awards in regional newspaper categories. Politically independent, it occasionally publishes articles, or features, in the Welsh language. This is the predominant printed medium in Wales for news, current affairs, features and sport.

Radio and television

837 Annual Report and Accounts.
HTV Group. 1968-. annual.

The report and financial statement of the company which has, since 1968, held the independent television contract for Wales and the west of England, working from two centres, Cardiff and Bristol. It is a major supplier of Welsh-language programmes, along with BBC Wales and the independent producers, for S4C, the Welsh-language Fourth Channel in Wales.

838 Annual Report and Accounts.
Welsh Fourth Channel Authority. 1981-. annual.

A bilingual document which provides a detailed account of S4C, the Welsh Fourth Channel, including: a programme report and a rationale for the composition of the schedule; audience figures, with viewing and listening patterns in Welsh and for Wales as a whole; the programme guide *Sbec*; training activities; publishing ventures; special features such as animation and co-productions with overseas producers; as well as a detailed financial statement of income, expenditure, enterprises and notes to the statements.

839 BBC Annual Report and Accounts.
London: British Broadcasting Corporation. 1927-. annual.

This publication always contains numerous sections on Wales, including a report of the work of the Broadcasting Council for Wales which, for a while, issued its own separate report.

840 The committee on the future of broadcasting 1974: memorandum from the Broadcasting Council for Wales.
[Cardiff]: Broadcasting Council for Wales, 1975. 59p.

A significant document in the history of broadcasting in Wales. It outlines the physical and linguistic problems that beset broadcasting, and lists the aims of broadcasting in Wales as well as describing contemporary services. In addition, it speculates as to the future of radio and television, with particular reference to the proposed fourth network, its structure and adminstrative arrangements. The work has seven important appendices: extracts from evidence previously submitted to enquires into broadcasting (such as the Crawford Committee in 1973) on radio and television in Wales; information on technical issues relating to Wales; details concerning staffing structures within BBC Wales; data on education output; and a memorandum to the Minister of Posts and Telecommunications in 1973 regarding the important issues in Welsh broadcasting; and two papers outlining possible future scenarios in radio and television.

841 The fourth channel in Wales: a statement by HTV Wales.
Cardiff: HTV Wales, [n.d.]. 19p.

This was a significant statement from the company holding the Independent Television franchise for Wales and the west of England when the Welsh fourth channel service was established in Wales in 1982.

842 **Report of the working party on the Welsh Television fourth channel project. Adroddiad y Gweithgor ar y cynllun Pedwaredd Sianel i Gymru.**
London: HMSO, 1978. 99p.

A bilingual report (pps. 1-48 are in English), of the Working Party of the Home Office to consider 'how progress might be made with the project for a fourth television channel in Wales . . . so that, once money is available, an immediate start could be made with it: and to make recommendations'. Sections of the report offer observations on: the background to, and issues arising from broadcasting in Wales; the rôle of the media in the maintenance of Welsh language and culture; the prospects for more Welsh programmes on the existing channels; programmes on the Welsh-language service; policy options available for the fourth channel in Wales; and engineering aspects, with a summary and conclusions.

843 **S4C and the grassroots? A review of past and future research on the mass media in the Welsh language.**
Sara Delamont. *Contemporary Wales*, vol 1, (1987), p. 91-106.

A study which 'is a review of research already conducted, and an agenda of priorities for future investigations, on the relations between the mass media and the Welsh language'. The central focus is S4C, the Welsh-language television channel, but other media are also discussed. It considers completed research and offers an agenda for future research.

844 **Study group on broadcasting and the press: report on television in Wales.**
[Cardiff]: Welsh Council of Labour, 1972. 44p.

This work was published as a contribution to Labour Party discussion in Wales in order to help prepare policies for the party. It examines constraints on television in Wales in the areas of programming in English, in Welsh and for children, as well as in technical areas, and in reception. In addition, it considers the future structure and public control of television broadcasting in Wales, its financing, and presents a summary of recommendations. The report has useful appendices analysing types of programmes, offering selected statistics, details of minority-language broadcasting in other countries and other aspects.

845 **The television industry in Wales.**
Philip Cooke, Carmel Gahan. [Cardiff]: Regional industrial research, Igam Ogam research, 1988. 86p.

A report which was carried out in 1987 and 1988, of a research study funded by the Fourth Channel Authority in Wales, BBC Wales, and the Welsh Development Agency, into 'the current situation and future prospects of the television industry in Wales'. The scheme had four goals: to provide a cross-sectional profile of the industry; to identify areas for development; to formulate a strategy to promote discussion within the industry on the future pattern of development; and to collate base information on the participants in the industry, their suppliers and their needs. It offers a summary of findings and recommendations, among which is the need for more programmes emanating from Wales for English-language audiences in Wales, an issue of current and growing concern.

846 **Television in Wales – the new industry. 1982-87 teledu yng Nghymru – y diwydiant newydd.**
Cardiff: S4C, [1987]. 36p.

An overview of the first five years of activity of the Fourth Channel in Wales, with a description of output, schedules, technical advances, and various kinds of (and individual) programmes. It also includes a consideration of the historical background and an assessment of future developments.

847 **The voice of a nation? A concise account of the BBC in Wales 1923-1973.**
Rowland Lucas. Llandysul: Gomer Press, 1981. 233p.

The starting point of this historical study is 1923 when a Welsh region of the BBC was created following a period of pressure to establish more Welsh-language programmes and a clearer Welsh identity. The coming of television in 1952 is also documented as is the formal establishment of BBC Wales television in 1964. The work is based on the author's own recollection of events – he was employed in the information office of the BBC in Cardiff for some twenty-seven years – newspaper reports, and BBC documents and archives and photographs.

848 **Wales on the wireless: a broadcasting anthology.**
Edited by Patrick Hannan. Llandysul, Wales: Gomer, in association with BBC Cymru Wales, 1988. 200p.

An anthology of items from the archives of the BBC in Wales since 1934 which reflects the nature of broadcasting in English in Wales and the work of some of its most famous broadcasters. The introduction is an interesting essay on journalism and broadcasting in Wales and by the Welsh.

Directories

849 Alternative Wales.
Jon Preston, Jane Preston.   Llandeilo, Wales: Orkid Books, 1982. 161p.

A directory reflecting the work of Alternative Wales Information i.e., 'an information centre for those people involved with community and radical movements to exchange ideas, news . views and plans'. It has sections on crafts, ecology, energy, food, gays, husbandry, law, sex, the home, therapy, transport, women as well as 'liberation politics' and 'cheap highs'. A work which caused a degree of sensation when it was issued, it now appears a little dated.

850 British directories: a bibliography and guide to directories published in England and Wales (1850-1950) and Scotland (1773-1950).
Gareth Shaw, Allison Tipper.   London: Leicester University Press, 1988. 440p.

This is the first national guide to British directories published before 1950. It offers introductory essays tracing the origins and development of directories, explains their forms and variety, and indicates their varying contents. Chapter five is devoted to Wales and Welsh counties (pre-1974 local authority borders) and is a particularly useful list, though by no means comprehensive and many local town guides are not recorded.

851 Business directory for Dyfed.
Carmarthen, Wales: Dyfed County Council Economic Development Officer, 1988. 206p.

An irregular publication offering a list of agencies, bodies and organisations concerned with industrial and business development together with a classified and alphabetical list of businesses.

Directories

852 **Business Directory of Gwent.**
Cwmbran, Wales: Gwent County Council County Planning Committee and Industrial Development Sub-Committee, 1982-. annual.
The information about local business is given in two sequences, classified and alphabetical.

853 **The county of Clwyd, Wales, industrial directory.**
Mold, Wales: Clwyd County Council Economic Development Unit, 1975-. irregular.
A directory of manufacturing and service sector activity throughout the county. Information is listed in a classified sequence and an alphabetic sequence, with symbols used to denote the size of the enterprise in terms of the number of employees. Occasional supplements are also issued.

854 **Development Board for Rural Wales. Bwrdd Datblygu Cymru Wledig. Cyfarwyddiadur diwydiannol. Industrial directory.**
Newtown, Wales: The Development Board for Rural Wales, 1979-. irregular.
This publication essentially presents an index of firms, their products and requirements, operating within the Board's area.

855 **Guide to the national and provincial directories of England and Wales, excluding London, published before 1856.**
Jane E. Norton. London: Offices of the Royal Historical Society. 241p.
The work lists thirteen items for Wales (p. 222-25) including local directories. They are listed chronologically by date of first publication.

856 **Guide to Welsh Businesses.**
Cardiff: Western Mail and Echo, 1982-. annual.
This guide seems to have ceased publication in 1986 but its previous numbers retain a certain historical usefulness. It contains a classified sequence of businesses by activity or product, a contacts guide, telephone numbers of significant offices and agencies, and short studies of sectors and trends.

857 **Gwynedd industrial directory.**
Caernarfon, Wales: Gwynedd County Council Economic Development Office, 1990. 99p.
The fifth in an occasional series listing the details of industrial and commercial enterprises in north-west Wales, organisations and institutions providing development support, the names and addresses of development agencies, local authorities, training and enterprise organisations and transport facilities. This publication is representative of the directories issued by local authorities as part of their economic and business development initiatives.

858   An index of Welsh associations, movements, bodies, committees and institutions. Mynegai i gymdeithasau, mudiadau, sefydliadau, pwyllgorau a chyrff Cymraeg a Chymreig.
[Aberystwyth], Wales: Welsh Library Association, 1984. 98p. (Welsh Library Association Index Series).

A directory of more than 500 associations, movements, bodies, committees and institutions, with contact names and addresses, listed in alphabetical order by title with a detailed index indicating spheres of activity, or responsibility.

859   Jordan's regional directories of key business prospects: Wales.
Bristol, England: Jordan and Sons, 1989. 150p.

A directory which includes: an overview of Wales and its economy; tables concerning the performance of 500 companies in Wales; a list of those companies in descending order of turnover, with addresses, business activity and directors; a list of a further 160 companies of the smaller variety; and a final section which cites additional sources of information for the business community.

860   Mid Glamorgan Industrial Directory.
Cardiff: Mid Glamorgan County Council Economic Development and Employment Committee, 1978-. annual.

The information is provided in classified and alphabetical sequences, and there is also a useful list of contacts, addresses, and assisted area development details.

861   South Glamorgan Business Directory.
Cardiff: South Glamorgan County Council Economic Development Office, 1980-. annual.

This work offers: a list of services given by the Council to commerce and industry; an alphabetic business index; a products, processes and services index; and a list of contacts and addresses. Clients are invited to join the County's Business Directory Database which is the basis of this work.

862   Wales (North and South). Trades' directories.
Edinburgh: Trades' Directories, 1972.

This is the most recent, if rather dated, edition, which retains a certain usefulness in a historical perspective. The business and trades are listed by location, Cardiff and Swansea being two major centres, and then by counties (pre-1974 local government reorganization boundaries) by product and activity.

863   Wales Business Directory.
Solihull, England: The Kemps Group (Printers and Publishers), on behalf of the Federation of Welsh Chambers of Commerce and the Welsh Development Agency.
1987-. annual.

This is the primary business directory for Wales. It contains brief preliminary sections, followed by an alphabetical list of companies, an index to classifications, a classified section, and other materials in appended lists. The work is quadri-lingual, English, French, German and Arabic.

Directories

864 Wales Council for Voluntary Action. Cyngor Gweithredu Gwirfoddol Cymru. Directory of voluntary organisations.
Caerffili, Wales: WCVA, 1984.

A directory for each of the counties of Wales based on the data gathered during a national survey of locally based voluntary action in Wales, conducted by the Council between July and August 1983. More than 19,000 groups were identified throughout Wales and the names and addresses of each one is provided in the appropriate county volume. Each list is further divided into two sections, those which responded to the survey and those which failed to do so. Details regarding the aims, objectives and activities of those groups which responded to the survey (which are listed in the first section of each volume) can be obtained from the Wales Council for Voluntary Action on request. This is the most comprehensive directory of its kind produced for Wales.

865 Welsh Chambers of Commerce Directory. Llawlyfr Siambr Fasnach Cymru.
Sheldon (Birmingham), England: Kemps Group, on behalf of the Federation of Welsh Chambers of Commerce, 1978-. annual.

A wide-ranging directory listing members in an alphabetical sequence and in a classified sequence by product or activity. It also has short introductory essays on incentives for industry, road and communications, a section for each of the Welsh counties, and on the Development Board for Rural Wales. In addition, it provides a conference facilities and hotel guide, and details about tourist attractions and information centres.

866 Welsh Development Agency Industrial Directory.
Cardiff: Welsh Development Agency. 1976-. irregular.

This directory contains information about tenants of WDA factories and firms which occupy premises provided by the agency or land on WDA estates. The directory is divided into three parts: a list of businesses in classified order according to their products and services; a list by county with a brief description of business activity; and one comprehensive alphabetic sequence.

867 West Glamorgan Business Directory.
Swansea: West Glamorgan County Council. 1976-. irregular.

A directory for a local authority area in South Wales which is typical of many *ad hoc* publications in this field. It contains information on manufacturing businesses and businesses providing services directly to industry. They are listed in a classified sequence according to industrial and service activities, and a further alphabetical sequence of companies by name.

Bibliographies

868 **Bibliotheca Celtica: a register of publications relating to Wales and the Celtic peoples and languages.**
Aberystwyth, Wales: National Library of Wales, 1910-. irregular.
The most comprehensive bibliography of books, pamphlets, and periodical articles written in the Welsh language, or pertaining to Wales and the Welsh people and their activities. The work is based on new additions to the collection of printed materials housed in the National Library of Wales and each volume is prepared by members of staff at the library. Since its inception eighty years ago, there have been several changes to its arrangement and coverage. Currently, the items are classified by the Library of Congress Classification Scheme. The most recent volume covers items published during the period 1976 to 1980.

869 **Books of Welsh interest.**
Compiled by Sally Roberts Jones. Aberystwyth, Wales: Welsh Books Council, 1977. 236p.
An annotated bibliography of over 900 books and pamphlets in the English language about Wales and the Welsh people which were in print at the end of August 1976, together with a supplement of similar books published between September 1976 and March 1977. The first section, lists books which are arranged under broad subject headings such as sport, architecture and politics and local government, whilst the second section deals entirely with literature.

870 **Cylchgronau Cymreig a'u lleoliad. A union list of Welsh periodicals.**
Aberystwyth, Wales: National Library of Wales, 1976. 215p.
A catalogue of current and defunct periodicals in the Welsh language, or published in Wales, housed in the National Library of Wales, together with the holdings of the main public and academic libraries in the country. This publication is a useful bibliographical source for students and scholars wishing to trace an issue, or a volume, of a Welsh journal.

213

871 **Ffynonellau gwybodaeth am Gymru a'r iaith Gymraeg. Information sources relating to Wales and the Welsh language.**
Gwilym Huws.   Aberystwyth, Wales: Welsh Library Association, 1984. 19p.
A select list of 250 basic sources of information about Wales and the Welsh language published up to December 1983. The items are arranged into two main sections: section one, consists of bibliographies, indexes and catalogues; and section two, standard reference books. The bibliography includes material in the Welsh and English languages.

872 **Libri Walliae: a catalogue of Welsh books and books printed in Wales 1546-1820.**
Eiluned Rees.   Aberystwyth, Wales: National Library of Wales, 1987. 2 vols.
A comprehensive bibliography of 5,656 printed books produced in the Welsh language or printed in Wales between 1546 and 1820. Items are arranged alphabetically by author/title and the work also includes title, name and chronological indexes together with a detailed analysis of the people and places involved in the book trade, and a scholarly essay by the editor on the Welsh book trade before 1820. This is an indispensable volume for scholars and others interested in the early history of the book trade in Wales.

873 **A reader's guide to Wales: a selected bibliography.**
Edited by Meic Stephens.   London: National Book League, 1973. 109p.
A selective bibliography compiled by the staff at the National Library of Wales containing approximately 1,700 items relating to most aspects of life in Wales. This work is particularly useful for non-Welsh speakers who wish to investigate the life and culture of Wales.

874 **Subject index to Welsh periodicals.**
Aberystwyth, Wales: National Library of Wales, 1978-. irregular.
An index to articles in the Welsh language, or relating to Wales, which have been published in a selection of·Welsh and English periodicals published in Wales. Certain categories of material such as editorials, news items, poems and readers' correspondence are excluded. The first volume in this new series covers the period between 1968 and 1970 and the most recent issue covers the years 1981 to 1984.

875 **Traethodau ymchwil Cymraeg a Chymreig a dderbyniwyd gan brifysgolion Prydeinig. Americanaidd ac Almaenaidd, 1887-1971. Welsh language and Welsh dissertations accepted by British, American and German universities, 1887-1971.**
Compiled by Alun Eirug Davies.   Cardiff: University of Wales Press, 1973. 205p.
A list of 1,636 dissertations, accepted for higher degrees by British, Irish, American, German and Austrian universities between 1887 and 1971, which dealt with Wales, the Welsh people and their endeavours, or were written in the Welsh language. The items

are arranged into thirty-seven subject categories covering most areas of human activity. Supplements to the list have been published as follows in *Studia Celtica*: Vol. 10/11, (1975/6); Vol. 12/13. (1977/8); Vol. 14/15, (1979/80); Vol. 16/17, (1981/2); Vol. 18/19, (1983/4); and Vol. 20/21, (1985/6).

876 **Wales.**

Compiled by Richard H. Lewis. Library Association Public Libraries Group, 1980. 24p. (Readers' Guide, no. 23).

A concise, annotated bibliography of books and pamphlets on various aspects of Wales and the Welsh people considered appropriate for the interested layman. Most of the items included were published after March 1977 and have been arranged into broad subject categories.

Indexes

There follow three separate indexes: authors (personal and corporate); titles; and subjects. Title entries are italicized and refer either to the main titles, or to other works cited in the annotations. The numbers refer to bibliographic entries, not to pages. Individual index entries are arranged in alphabetical sequence.

Index of Authors

A

Aberystwyth Policy Group 603
Adams, Sam 629-30, 667
Adamson, David 366
Aitchison, J.W. 265
Alcock, Leslie 165, 169
Allchin, A. M. 286
Allen, P. M. 21
Andrews, J. A. 405, 415
Anthony, Ilid E. 769
Ap Gwilym, Dafydd 644
Archer, Brian 66
Archer, Michael Scott 522
Arnot, R. Page 565-66
Ashby, A. W. 472
Ashton, Elwyn T. 237
Ashton, Steve 792
Atkinson, Michael 446
Austin, David 128
Automobile Association 75, 86, 91
Avent, Richard 144
Awbery, G.M. 272

B

Baber, Colin 446
Baggs, Teresa 422
Baker, Colin 419, 613, 618
Ball, Martin J. 242, 258
Ballard, Paul H. 422
Balsom, Denis 367, 376, 378, 380
Barber, Chris 80-81, 131
Barber, W. T. 78

Bartrum, Peter Clement 207-08
Bassett, Douglas A. 18-19, 23, 52, 810,
Bassett, Michael. G. 22-23
Bassett, T. M. 305, 595
Bates, Denis E.B. 24
Baverstock, Leslie 798
Beach, Russell 74
Beazley, Elizabeth 87, 93
Beddoe, Deirdre 234
Bell, David 669
Bell, H. Idris 634
Bell, P. M. H. 290
Bennett, Carol 231
Benson, John 454
Betts, Clive 244
Binns, Richard 765
Bogdanor, Vernon 391
Bollom, Chris 330
Booth, John 48
Borrow, George 60
Bowen, David Q. 27
Bowen, E. G. 46, 302
Bowen, Robin Huw 707
Bowles Research 432
Bragg, Melvyn 719
Brereton, J.M. 210
Brierley, Peter 320
British Broadcasting Corporation 839
Broadcasting Council for Wales 840
Bromwich, Rachel 644, 647
Brooks, Rowland 475
Brown, E. H. 30
Brown, John 123
Bunch, Martin 367

C

Cadw. Welsh Historic Monuments 141
Caine, C.V. 577
Cambrian Archaeological Association 121
Cambrian Ornithological Society 114
Campbell-Jones, Susan 550
Campbell, Malcolm 796
Carter, Harold 40, 43-44, 49, 245, 265, 405
Casserley, H. C. 534
Centre for Alternative Technology 572
Chadwick, Nora K. 166, 174
Challinor, John 24
Charles, B.G. 278
Charles-Edwards, T.M. 412, 416
Chatfield, June E. 100, 119
Christiansen, Rex 524-26
Church in Wales 331
Clancy, Joseph P. 641, 648, 655
Clayton, G. 505
Cloke, Paul J. 502, 523
Clwyd County Council 853
Cole, David 9, 65, 321, 323, 475, 582, 587, 627, 704, 734, 831
Colyer, Richard J. 473, 482, 517
Combs, Thomas Olivitt 379
Coombes, G.J. 677
Coombes, Katherine 677

217

H

Hall, Irene M. 338
Hallett, Graham 544
Hamilton-Edwards, Gerald 206
Hammond, Reginald J. W. 76, 89-90
Hankinson, Alan 789
Hannah, Patrick 848
Harding, John 783
Harper, Peter S. 213
Harris, C. C. 323, 344
Harris, Hywel 686
Harris, Mary Corbett 754
Harrison, S.G. 110
Harrop, Dorothy A. 822
Hartmann, Edward George 224
Hartnup, R. 31
Haslam, Richard 744
Heaton, P. M. 546, 551
Hebbert, Antonia 765
Hechter, Michael 377
Henderson, H. John R. 483
Henken, Elissa R 304
Henshaw, L.G. 415
Herbert, Trevor 170, 184, 186, 195, 200, 202
Hignell, Andrew 802
Hilling, John Bryan 730-2, 735, 743
HMI (Wales) 602, 623
Hoffman, David 357
Hogenkamp, Bert 717
Holding, David 514
Holland, Peter Crossley 708
Hooper, Dianne M. 804
Hopkins, Deian 370
Houlder, Christopher 142
Howell, Peter 87, 93
Howells, M.F. 20
Howells, Roscoe 479
Howe, G. Melvyn 35
HTV Group 837
HTV Wales 841
Hubbard, Edward 733
Hughes, Glyn Tegai 311
Hughes, Gwilym Rees 591, 595, 629-30, 643, 645
Hughes, Harold 742
Hughes, Marian Beech 239

Hughes, T. Jones 501
Hume, Ian 328, 830
Humphreys, Graham 420, 459
Huws, Gwilym 871
Huws, Richard E. 823
Hyde, H. A. 110-11
Hywel, John 700

I

Institute of Welsh Affairs 217, 436
Ireson, Richard 444

J

Jackson, Audrey A. 21
Jackson, Kenneth 249
James, Arnold J. 371, 373
James, Dan L. 274
James, Hywel 600
James, Mari 393
Jarman, A.O.H. 640, 643, 645
Jenkins, Dafydd 410-11
Jenkins, David 470, 501
Jenkins, David 811
Jenkins, David Fraser 685
Jenkins, Geraint H. 181, 196, 295, 370, 755
Jenkins, Gwyn 157
Jenkins, J. Geraint 453, 494, 512, 539, 543, 681, 805
Jenkins, Randal 668
Jenkins, R.T. 204
Jenkins, T. N. 474, 480
John, Arthur H. 445, 448
John, W. D. 677
Johnson, Peter 533
Jones, Alun R. 654
Jones, Anthony 749
Jones, A. Neville 579
Jones, A.E. 679
Jones, A.E. (Cynan) 728
Jones, Beti 361
Jones, Bobi see Jones, R.M.
Jones, Brynmor 658
Jones, Dafydd Glyn 263

Jones, David J. V. 197, 558
Jones, David Lewis 156
Jones, Don Dale 668
Jones, Emrys 501
Jones, Gareth Elwyn 170, 186, 195, 200, 202, 607
Jones, Glyn 628, 660
Jones, Gwyn 637, 646
Jones, G. R. H. 468
Jones, Ieuan Gwynedd 161, 191-92, 300-01
Jones, Ifano 821
Jones, John Llewelyn 33
Jones, J. Barry 387, 390, 395, 397, 400, 402
Jones, J. Goronwy 372
Jones, J. Graham 153, 363, 392
Jones, J. Gwynfor 179
Jones, Mary Eirwen 680
Jones, Peter Ellis 604
Jones, Peter Hope 104
Jones, Philip Henry 150
Jones, Richard 467
Jones, Ron 793
Jones, R. Brinley 1, 4, 45, 255, 291, 327, 423,451, 585, 587, 590, 631, 687, 702
Jones, R. Emrys 532
Jones, R. Gerallt 626, 652-53,
Jones, R. Merfyn 562
Jones, R.M. 633
Jones, Sally Roberts 869
Jones, Thomas 646
Jones, T. Gwynn 758
Jones, T.I. Jeffreys 188
Jones, T.J. Rhys 275
Jones, W. Dyfri 476, 481
Jones, W.R. 617
Joseph, Leslie 679

K

Kay, Heather 5
Keating, Michael 387
Keineg, Katell 348
Kellas, James G. 399
Kenyon, John R. 144
Khleif, Bud B. 252
Kinney, Phyllis 694

219

Index of Titles

225

230

Index of Subjects

A

Aberdaron 501
Aberporth 501
Abraham, William
  (Mabon) 560
Acid Rain 571
Administrative Devolution
  387-88, 390, 394-95,
  397-98, 400, 402-03
Agrarian Discontent
  197-98
Agriculture 9, 11, 474-87
  Economics 424, 431,
  438-39
  History 470-73,
  Labour History 563
  Periodicals 485
  Statistics 468, 486
  Transport 512
Air Transport 511, 536,
  541
Alternative Society 849
Alternative Technology
  572
Amman Valley 4
Ancient Monuments
  121-24, 127-28
  Inventories 130-42,
  145-47
  Maps and atlases 54
Anglesey
  Archaeological Sites 139
  Education 606
  Unemployment 345
Angling 797-800
Anglo-Welsh Literature 1,
  9, 13, 624-25, 627-31,
  669, 672
  Anthologies 626, 657,
  667-68
  Bibliographies 658
  History 656-57, 662, 666
  Periodicals 663, 665
  Poetry 657, 659, 661,
  664-65, 668
  20th century 659-61,
  664-65, 663, 666, 668
Ap Gwilym, Dafydd 644,
  648

Architecture 9, 669, 730,
  734, 747
  Cardiff 732
  Chapels 731, 749
  Conservation 740
  Domestic 179, 187,
  737-40, 742, 750-52
  Ecclesiastical 306, 741
  History 731-33, 735-46,
  748-52
  South Wales Valleys 732
  Towns 75
Archaeology 121-29, 165,
  169, 173
  Anglesey 139
  Breconshire 136
  Carmarthenshire 139
  Caernarvonshire 140
  Clwyd 141
  Denbighshire 139
  Flintshire 139
  Glamorganshire 137-38,
  141
  Gwent 141
  Gwynedd 141
  Industrial 148-49
  Inventories 130-142
  Medieval 132, 138,
  143-47
  Meirionethshire 139
  Montgomeryshire 139
  Pembrokeshire 139
  Periodicals 121, 125, 832
  Powys 139, 141
  Roman 136
Archives 203-06
Art Galleries 669, 803, 809
Arts 1, 9, 13, 669-72
Association Football
  781-85
Atlases and maps 48-49,
  53-54, 74, 76, 83
  Antique 48
  Bibliographies 52, 54
  Estate 50
  Historical 151
  Mid Wales 84
  North Wales 88
  Transport History 545
  Welsh-speakers 273

Australia
  Welsh Immigrants 225,
  234
Aviation 541

B

Banking 418-19, 445
Baptist Church 305
Bardsey Island 104
Betws-y-Coed
  Geology 20
Bevan, Aneurin 358
Bible
  Welsh Translation
  313-14
Bibliographies 868-75
  Anglo-Welsh Literature
  658
  Classical Music 705
  Coal Industry 454
  Directories 850
  Dissertations 874
  Education 616
  Environmental Issues
  577, 579
  Folk Dancing 699
  Geology 18-19
  History 150, 156
  Hymns 287
  Jones, Ieuan Gwynedd
  196
  Labour History 555
  Medicine 356
  Periodicals 870
  Politics 359
  Socioeconomics 422
  Traditional Music 695,
  713
  Welsh Language 238-39,
  242, 276
  Welsh Literature 636,
  647
  Williams, Glanmor 161
Bilingual Education
  613-15, 617-23
Biographies 204
  Bevan, Aneurin 358
  Burton, Richard 719

246

Map of Wales

This map shows the more important towns and other features.

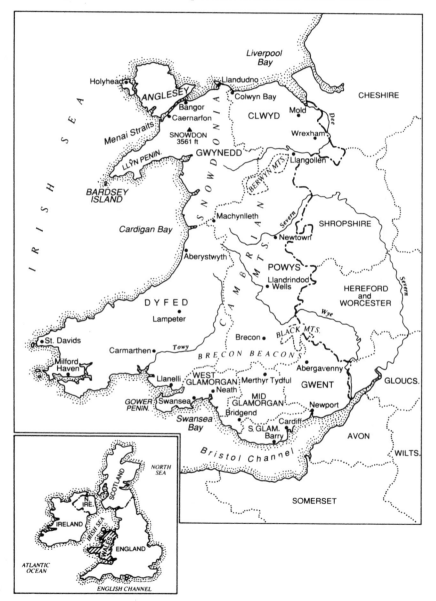